IC-REFA,

D1199518

The United States in World War I

The War/Peace Bibliography Series

RICHARD DEAN BURNS, EDITOR

This Series has been developed in cooperation with the Center for the Study of Armament and Disarmament, California State University, Los Angeles.

#1 *Songs of Protest, War & Peace*
A Bibliography & Discography
R. SERGE DENISOFF

#2 *Warfare in Primitive Societies*
A Bibliography
WILLIAM TULIO DIVALE

#3 *The Vietnam Conflict*
Its Geographical Dimensions, Political
Traumas & Military Developments
MILTON LEITENBERG & RICHARD DEAN BURNS

#4 *Modern Revolutions and Revolutionists*
A Bibliography
ROBERT BLACKEY

#5 *The Arab-Israeli Conflict*
A Historical, Political, Social
& Military Bibliography
RONALD M. DEVORE

#6 *Arms Control & Disarmament*
A Bibliography
RICHARD DEAN BURNS

#7 *The United States in World War I*
A Selected Bibliography
RONALD SCHAFFER

The United States in World War I
A Selected Bibliography

Ronald Schaffer

Clio Books

Santa Barbara, California
Oxford, England

Library of Congress Cataloging in Publication Data

Schaffer, Ronald.
    The United States in World War I.

    (The War/peace bibliography series ; no. 7)
    Includes index.
    1.   European War, 1914—1918—United States—
Bibliography.   I.   Title.
Z6207.E8S3   [D570]   016.940373   78-18456
ISBN 0-87436-274-1

American Bibliographical Center—Clio Press
Riviera Campus, 2040 A.P.S., Box 4397
Santa Barbara, California 93103

Clio Press, Ltd.
Woodside House, Hinksey Hill
Oxford, OX1 5BE, England

Manufactured in the United States of America

Contents

Foreword / xiii

Acknowledgments / xv

Brief Chronology of U.S. Involvement
in World War I / xvii

Introduction / xxi

Notes on Use as a Research Tool / xxiii

I / GENERAL REFERENCES / 1

A / Bibliographies / 1
B / Guides and Indexes / 3
C / Catalogs / 3
D / Atlases / 3

II / THE EUROPEAN WAR / 5

A / General Accounts / 5
B / Origins / 6

III / THE UNITED STATES AND
WORLD WAR I—GENERAL / 7

A / Overviews / 7
B / Biographical Works / 8
C / Memoirs / 10
D / Letters and Diaries / 10

IV / AMERICAN INTERVENTION   / 13

A / Historiography   / 13
B / Documents   / 13
C / Collections   / 13
D / Biographies, Diaries, Letters, Memoirs   / 14
E / Background Studies   / 14
F / Overviews   / 16
G / Specific Studies   / 17

V / MILITARY ACTIVITY
(INCLUDING AIR AND NAVAL)   / 21

A / Documents   / 21
B / Historiography   / 21
C / Background Studies   / 21
D / Overviews   / 21
E / Guides to Battlefields   / 22
F / Pictorials and Cartoons   / 22
G / Accounts By or About Participants   / 23
   Biographical Works   / 23
   Collective Biography   / 25
   Memoirs and Personal Narratives   / 25
   Letters and Diaries   / 32
H / Land Operations (Army and Marine Corps)   / 35
   General   / 35
   Specific Accounts   / 37
I / Naval Operations   / 39
   General   / 39
   Specific Accounts   / 40
J / Air Operations   / 42
   General   / 42
   Specific Accounts   / 44
K / Enemy Operations   / 45
   Land   / 45
   Naval   / 45
L / Strategy, Command, and Administration   / 45
   United States   / 45
   Joint United States — Allies   / 47

M / Siberian Expedition / 48
    General / 48
    U.S. Military Operations / 49

N / U.S. Occupation of Germany / 50
O / Civil-Military Relations / 50
P / Prisoners of War, U.S. and Enemy / 50
Q / U.S. Military Personnel / 51
    General / 51
    Prebelligerency Preparedness Movement / 51
    Recruitment and Conscription / 52
    Training / 54
    Reserves and National Guard / 55
    Recreation and Morale of Servicemen / 56
    Education (in Service) of Military Personnel / 57
    Military Justice / 57
    Military Police / 57
    Military Journalism / 57
    Language of U.S. Troops / 58
    Military Medicine / 58

R / Logistics / 61
S / Technology and Weapons / 63
T / Doctrine — Strategic and Tactical / 65
U / Intelligence-related Activities / 65
    U.S. Military and Naval Intelligence / 65
    Enemy Espionage and U.S. Counterespionage / 66
    Psychological Warfare / 67

V / U.S. Troops and Other Nationals / 67
    Americans with Allied Units / 67
    European Views of U.S. Forces / 69
    U.S. Servicemen View the Allies / 69

W / American Auxiliaries / 70
    General / 70
    American Ambulance Volunteers / 72

X / Military Statistics / 74

VI / UNIT HISTORIES / 75

A / Army Ground Forces / 75
    General Classification / 75
    Ambulance Companies / 75

Ammunition Trains   / 76
Artillery Park   / 76
Armies   / 76
Balloon Section   / 77
Base Hospitals   / 77
Cavalry   / 78
Coast Artillery   / 78
Corps   / 79
Engineers (General)   / 79
Engineer Units   / 80
Evacuation Hospitals   / 84
Field Artillery   / 84
Field Hospitals   / 91
Field Signal Battalions   / 91
Gas Regiments   / 91
General Hospitals   / 92
Infantry Brigades   / 92
Infantry Divisions   / 92
Infantry Regiments   / 98
Machine Gun Battalions   / 108
Military Motor Corps   / 110
Military Police   / 110
Pioneer Infantry   / 110
Supply Units   / 111
Telegraph Battalions   / 111
Trench Artillery   / 111

B / Air Units   / 111
General   / 111
Lafayette Escadrille and Lafayette Flying Corps
   (103d Aero Squadron)   / 113

C / Naval Units   / 115
D / Marine Corps Units   / 115

VII / THE WAR AND AMERICAN SOCIETY   / 117

A / General Works   / 117
B / Comparison Studies (The War and Other Societies) / 117
C / Collections   / 118
D / State and Local Studies   / 118
General   / 118
Alphabetically by State, County, and City   / 118

E / Economic Mobilization / 127
   General / 127
   Background Studies / 129
   Biographical Studies and Memoirs / 129
   Prewar Preparations / 130
   English Models for the United States (See also VII,
      B/Comparison Studies [The War and Other Societies]) / 131
   Mobilization Agencies: The War Industries Board and Others / 131
   Military Procurement / 133
   Business-Government Relations in Economic Mobilization / 133
   The System of Business Self-Regulation / 134
   War Finance / 135
   Price Regulation / 137
   War Profits / 138
   International Trade / 138
   Transportation / 139
   Energy / 141
   Agricultural Products and Processing / 141
   Statistics / 143

F / Regulation of Public Attitudes / 143
   General / 143
   Biographies and Memoirs / 144
   Federal Information Programs / 144
   Federal Government and Civil Liberties / 147
   State and Local Regulation of Public Opinion (See also VII,
      D/State and Local Studies) / 148
   The Civil Liberties Movement / 149

G / Pacifism and Antimilitarism / 149

H / Ethnic Groups and Nativism in Wartime / 151

I / The War and American Workers / 153
   General / 153
   The Federal Government and Organized Labor / 154
   Socialism and Radicalism / 156

J / The War and American Race Relations / 158
   General / 158
   Black Servicemen (See also unit histories) / 161

K / American Women in the War / 162

L / The War and Social Reform / 164
   General / 164
   Relief and Welfare Programs / 164

Government Regulation of Sex (See also V,
  Q/U.S. Military Personnel, Recreation and
  Morale of Servicemen; Military Medicine)   / 165
Public Housing Programs   / 167
Prohibition   / 167

M/ Effects of the War on Manners and Morals   / 168
N/ The War and Sports and Recreation   / 168
O/ The War and Religion   / 168
P / Journalism in World War I   / 170
Q/ The War and the Visual Arts   / 170
Works about the Visual Arts in Wartime   / 170
Works by American Artists   / 171

R / The War and Literature   / 171
Works about Wartime Writers   / 171
War Prose   / 172
War Poetry and Song Lyrics   / 174
War Humor   / 176

S / Education in Wartime   / 176
T / War and American Intellectuals   / 179
General   / 179
The Historical Profession in the War   / 181

U/ Science in Wartime America (See also V, S/Technology
  and Weapons)   / 181
V/ Civilian Medicine and Public Health   / 184
W/Domestic Politics   / 185

VIII / PEACEMAKING   / 187

A / Wartime U.S. Diplomacy   / 187
B / The Peace Settlement   / 188
C / The League of Nations   / 191
D/ U.S. Rejection of the Treaty of Versailles   / 192

IX / SURVIVALS AND PRECEDENTS   / 195

A / General Effects of the War on America   / 195
B / Demobilization   / 195
C / Veterans   / 196
General   / 196
Rehabilitation   / 196

D / Reconstruction   / 197

E / The Red Scare   / 197

F / Economic Consequences: Theory and Practice   / 198

G / Disillusion and Isolationism   / 200

H / Precedents for the Hoover and Roosevelt Administrations / 200

Author Index   / 201

About the War/Peace Bibliography Series

With this bibliographical series, the Center for the Study of Armament and Disarmament, California State University, Los Angeles, seeks to promote a wider understanding of martial violence and the alternatives to its employment. The Center, which was formed by concerned faculty and students in 1962– 63, has as its primary objective the stimulation of intelligent discussion of war/peace issues. More precisely, the Center has undertaken two essential functions: (1) to collect and catalogue materials bearing on war/peace issues; and (2) to aid faculty, students, and the public in their individual and collective probing of the historical, political, economic, philosophical, technical, and psychological facets of these fundamental problems.

This bibliographical series is, obviously, one tool with which we may more effectively approach our task. Each issue in this series is intended to provide a comprehensive "working," rather than definitive, bibliography on a relatively narrow theme within the spectrum of war/peace studies. While we hope this series will prove to be a useful tool, we also solicit your comments regarding its format, contents, and topics.

RICHARD DEAN BURNS
SERIES EDITOR

Acknowledgments

Several people assisted in the preparation of this book, including librarians at California State University, Northridge, University of California, Los Angeles, University of Southern California, and the Los Angeles Public Library. Kevin Weir checked several hundred entries for accuracy. Rosario Martinez and Bobette Cloninger helped prepare the index of names. Joyce Leu typed parts of the text. I wish to thank especially the editor of this series, Richard D. Burns, for his encouragement and advice, Nancy Meadows of the CSUN history department, who typed the bibliographic entries, and Paulette Wamego of Clio Books, who performed the particularly demanding tasks required to prepare a work of this kind. For any errors I am, of course, entirely responsible.

Brief Chronology of U.S. Involvement in World War I

1914   (August)   Outbreak of World War I. President Wilson proclaims U.S. neutrality

(September)   U.S. bankers complete negotiations for half-billion dollar loan to France and Britain

1915   (February)   Germany announces sink-on-sight policy for enemy merchant ships around British Isles

(May)   U-boat sinks British liner *Lusitania* killing Americans. U.S. sends Germany first of series of notes demanding end to unrestricted submarine warfare

(September)   German ambassador pledges Germany wil not sink liners without warning

1916   (January– April)   U.S. government tries to arrange negotiated peace

(March)   U-boat torpedoes British channel steamer *Sussex* injuring Americans

(April– May)   U.S. demands Germans immediately cease current submarine warfare methods. Germany agrees, providing U.S. compels Allies to respect International Law

(June)   National Defense Act provides for expansion of U.S. armed forces, makes provisions for industrial preparedness

(October)   Council of National Defense formed of six Cabinet members. Its civilian Advisory Board develops plans for mobilizing home front

(November)   Wilson re-elected with slogan "He kept us out of war"

1917   (February)   Germany resumes unrestricted submarine warfare. U.S. breaks diplomatic relations

(March)   Wilson administration orders U.S. merchant ships armed. U.S. vessels sunk

(April 2)   Wilson asks Congress for Declaration of War

(April 6)   President signs resolution declaring war on Germany

(April)   Committee on Public Information established. Liberty Loan Act authorizes public borrowing to help finance war

(May)   Selective Service Act provides for registration and conscription

(June)   Espionage Act passes — aimed at suppressing disloyal and treasonable activities

American Alliance for Labor and Democracy formed; a left-liberal front organization for the Committee on Public Information

Draft registration

First A.E.F. troops arrive in France

(July)   War Industries Board established

Secretary of War draws first draft numbers

Vigilantes deport members of the antiwar Industrial Workers of the World and other strikers from Bisbee, Arizona

(August)   Lever Act authorizes President to regulate production and distribution of food and fuel

Fuel Administration established

IWW organizer Frank Little lynched in Montana

(September)   Federal agents raid IWW offices throughout the West

(October)   War Revenue Act authorized graduated income tax, imposes excess profits

Military and Naval Insurance Act provides welfare benefits for servicemen and dependents

Secretary of War Baker calls for an "invisible armor" to protect the morals and health of soldiers about to go to France

(December)   Prohibition Amendment passes Congress, partly as a war measure

Declaration of War against Austria-Hungary

U.S. Railroad Administration created to manage and coordinate most of U.S. railway system

(December–January 1918)   Senate Committee on Military Affairs (Chamberlain Committee) investigates near-breakdown of war mobilization

1918   (January)   Wilson issues statement of peace objectives, the Fourteen Points

House of Representatives passes woman suffrage amendment

(March)   War Industries Board strengthened. Bernard Baruch placed at its head

Germans begin spring offensive

(April)　War Finance Corporation established

War Labor Board created as court of last resort in labor disputes

(May)　Wilson signs Overman Act, which greatly extends his wartime domestic powers

Sedition Act extends government authority to attack opponents of war

War Labor Policies Board created to regulate flow of workers

(June)　American units help French stem German advance at Château-Thierry. U.S. soldiers and marines recapture Belleau Wood

(July)　W. E. B. Du Bois urges fellow blacks to close ranks with whites fighting Germany

(September)　American Protective League, government sponsored vigilante group, launches "slacker" roundup in New York City

U.S. forces reduce St. Mihiel salient

American soldiers join Allied intervention in Russian Revolution

(September–November 11)　As part of a general Allied attack, over a million Americans take part in Meuse-Argonne offensive

(November 11)　Armistice signed

(November 21)　War Prohibition Act bans future sales of beer and wine

1919　(January)　Peace negotiations begin at Paris. President Wilson heads U.S. delegation

(June)　Germans sign Treaty of Versailles with attached covenant for a League of Nations

(June–September)　Race riots in American cities

(October)　Volstead prohibition act passes over President's veto

(November)　U.S. Senate rejects Treaty of Versailles

Federal government begins roundup and deportation of radical aliens

1920　(January–March)　Wilson and U.S. Senate fail to compromise on Senate's treaty reservations. Senate again refuses to ratify peace treaty

1921　(July)　Congress terminates war with Germany and Austria-Hungary by joint resolution

Introduction

Because of its great scope and far-reaching significance, World War I generated a large body of literature. It was a transforming event in world history, sweeping away ten million persons and reshaping the lives of countless survivors. Its material costs, estimated at over a third of a trillion dollars, devastated world economies and contributed to the Great Depression of the 1930s. The war produced drastic changes in political boundaries and altered international power relationships and the structures of social class. It helped bring about the Soviet, Fascist, and National Socialist revolutions and contributed to the origins of a second world conflict. Although its lasting effects were more conspicuous in Europe than in the United States, which participated officially for less than nineteen months, World War I was a major factor in the evolution of modern America.

The war affected the international relations of the United States by accelerating existing tendencies, and it also heralded changes manifested years after the fighting stopped. It advanced the rise of American military power that had begun with the reconstruction of the United States fleet in the 1880s. Strengthening the Anglo-American entente which first developed during the nineteenth century, it drew the United States into a regional alliance system similar to that which emerged under American leadership during World War II. It helped bring about America's primacy in international commerce and financial affairs and foreshadowed the time, a quarter century later, when the United States would exercise military and economic hegemony over half the globe.

The war strengthened internal efforts to homogenize an ethnically diverse population and reinforced prewar arrangements between certain labor, business, and government officials to soften class differences and avert social revolution. As a belated culmination of the prewar reform movement, it gave rise to a war-welfare state in which the federal government bestowed publicly financed benefits on those in society whose cooperation it needed to wage mass war. This system, which tended to provide the largest rewards

to groups with the greatest power, anticipated the so-called broker state of
the New Deal years and afterward. When the Wilson administration
managed public attitudes through propaganda, control of media, and coercion of dissenters, its efforts resembled those of later administrations,
particularly in the Cold War years. These connections between wartime
events and past and future developments are reflected in sections of the
bibliography on backgrounds, survivals, and precedents.

The works included here reveal innumerable contradictions in America's World War I experience. National leaders announced that the war was
being fought to make governments more responsive to peoples, an idea that
made sense if the people of each nation had reliable information on which
to base judgments. Yet the United States government developed an ap-
paratus for keeping information it disapproved from the American people,
swamping them meanwhile with propaganda. Exhorting Americans to wage
war for world democracy, it abridged the civil liberties of one of the world's
most democratic nations. The wartime president, while running for office a
few years earlier, had warned about the danger of allowing close ties
between business and government regulators. During 1917 and 1918 he
presided over an economic mobilization system in which businessmen,
acting on behalf of the government, were the leading agents in regulating
the national economy. On one level, the war was fought for ideals like
freedom and lasting peace. On another, it was a never-ending process of
bargaining: between government purchasers and war contractors, between
labor and management, between the military services and government
mobilization agencies, among the military services themselves, between
American leaders who wanted a separate expeditionary force and Allied
governments and generals who wanted to integrate Americans piecemeal
into their own battered lines. In a world conflict ostensibly waged for largely
altruistic reasons, grinding political conflicts never ceased. Interest groups
like suffragists and steel manufacturers, union leaders and advocates of
prohibition tried to use the war as an argument for securing their particular
objectives while the federal government tried to manage interest groups
with rewards and punishments, cajoling and coercing them into supporting
its policies. Why and how these contradictions and conflicts occurred can
be learned from the sources described here.

This bibliography is designed to assist the study of war in its broadest
sense, as a cultural phenomenon affecting all aspects of human affairs. From
the immense quantity of publications dealing with World War I, we have
selected approximately twenty-nine hundred English-language sources dealing with the war experience of the American people. We have also
provided citations for certain works that describe the history of other
belligerents. These give perspective to the American experience and clarify
what happened to the United States.

The publications listed vary widely in form and content. They include biographies, novels, narrative histories, diaries, letters, extensive monographs and brief analyses of particular events, joke books, photograph collections, lists of persons who fought — in short, any kind of published book, article, or government document containing evidence that may be useful to investigators. The topics include, among other things, how the war began, how the United States became a belligerent, how it mobilized its material resources and public sentiment while shifting from neutral to belligerent, how it fought against the Central Powers and negotiated with the Allies and the part it played in the peace settlement. Works listed here also consider the war's effects on American institutions and on the lives of the American people.

Many of the sources in this bibliography which deal with American military activities will serve a variety of users. They provide specialists and military history buffs information about large- and small-scale actions in which members of the American armed forces participated. They are a guide for veterans and their descendants who wish information about particular units and persons. But they are also organized to assist laymen, students, and scholars to reconstruct part of the American past. For example, an investigator writing his family history may know that a relative served in one of the listed units during the war. From sources that describe the unit he can discover what members of the unit experienced and then infer the effects of those experiences directly on his relative and indirectly on other family members. The bibliography can also help scholars answer certain questions about shifting attitudes of Americans. For instance, the reaction of American men of military age to the women's movement in 1917–1918 (which was reaching a peak of activity at that time) can be investigated by sampling the hundreds of diaries, unit histories, military memoirs, and fictional works listed here in which men state or imply feelings about women. The sections of this book that categorize military matters may well prove as useful to social historians as to specialists in military affairs.

This guide should be of help to persons examining any significant element of America's participation in World War I. It is hoped that it will impart to users a sense of the richness and complexity of what Woodrow Wilson called "the most terrible and disastrous of all wars."

Notes on Use as a Research Tool

Reflecting the multifaceted nature of a great war, this bibliography is divided into nine sections, some essentially military, others social and economic or concerned with issues of international relations. The final section lists works that describe the war's long-term consequences and the precedents it generated for American society. Between these major elements there are numerous overlaps. Since duplicate entries have been used sparingly, the reader who cannot find what he is looking for in a particular section should consult the table of contents, the index, and the notes that follow on the nine divisions of the bibliography. Almost all the publications cited are readily available to scholars by interlibrary loan. Rare works are included only when they are essential to understanding the war's impact on the development of American society.

I/General References

To assist students and scholars who need to go beyond this selective bibliography, we have provided a section of general references. Within that category there is one particularly important work: the *Subject Catalog of the World War I Collection* of the New York Public Library (34). While much has been written about World War I since the catalog's publication in 1961, anyone who wants to dig deeply into the history of the war—for any belligerent—will wish to use the NYPL collection, with its rare works not found in the Library of Congress or major university libraries.

II/The European War

Works listed here provide an introduction to the literature on the World War of 1914–1918. Most of the items cited in the first subsection, General Accounts, are essentially military histories, but there are two brief but notable exceptions: Albrecht-Carrié's extended essay (39) and the collection edited by Roth (49). These works, which look at the war from several angles, perceive it as a major turning point in the history of Western societies.

The subsection on origins reflects a complex, persistent controversy which is itself a causal element in modern history. Beliefs about how the war began and about who bore the main responsibility influenced the behavior of Europeans and Americans from 1914 onward. American propaganda stressed German war guilt, which Germany was forced to acknowledge in the Treaty of Versailles. The reluctance of many Americans to join in a second world war was based partly on the view of historical revisionists that Germany had not been chiefly responsible for starting World War I. And long after World War II, German scholars, incited by the works of Fritz Fischer, were still arguing over the intentions of German leaders in 1914 when an international incident grew into general war. Anthologies by Koch (60) and Lee (62) and others introduce readers to these controversies.

III/The United States and World War I—General

The publications listed in this section discuss a number of phenomena that were occurring in America during its involvement in the Great War. We have included biographical studies, autobiographical writings, and letters and diaries concerning persons whose wartime activities extend beyond any single area, such as diplomacy or military operations. Inevitably, writings about Woodrow Wilson predominate in this section, including Arthur Link's magisterial biography. Neither Link's nor any other biography of Wilson can be called definitive, however, since interpretation of the President's actions have continued to shift, even in Link's own writings. The elusiveness of some of Wilson's motives makes him one of the most fascinating leaders of the wartime great powers.

IV / American Intervention

Why did the United States enter World War I? Should it have joined in the war on the side of the Allies? These questions, heatedly debated when the nation stood on the brink of conflict, have continued as subjects of historical inquiry. As the works listed here testify, the arguments are not settled and students of history, re-weighing the evidence, can form conclusions that vary greatly from those of highly regarded scholars of the past.

To help readers who wish to attempt fresh appraisals or simply to understand the context of America's decision for war there is a subsection called Background Studies. Here we have listed two kinds of works: interpretive volumes by such persons as George Kennan (167), William A. Williams (177), and Robert E. Osgood (173) that establish long-term frameworks within which the decisions of 1914 to 1917 may be viewed; and specific studies, not directly connected to U.S. involvement in World War I, that provide clues to what American leaders were aiming for in the months preceding intervention. Thus Rayford Logan's *Haiti and the Dominican Republic* (170), seemingly remote from the subject of this bibliography, is included because it documents a conflict between real and purported foreign policy objectives. Logan shows that when the United States invaded Haiti, Wilson and his advisors, Bryan and Lansing, were concerned about the national security of the United States and particularly about the threat posed by Germans to sea routes near the Panama Canal. Meanwhile, they spoke as if they were defending the right of Haitians to self-government although Lansing certainly and Wilson probably considered the black Haitians incapable of self-government. If the Wilson administration offered altruistic reasons, like the need for local self-determination, for a Caribbean policy governed by United States self-interest, there may have been a similar gap between reasons and rationales in the administration's European policy. If that is the case, theories of Woodrow Wilson's idealistic, missionary motivation should be re-examined and the views of such writers as Edward Buehrig become more credible.

The reasons and rationales for American intervention affected the way the United States fought the war and how Americans felt about the conflict after it ended. Lacking a dramatic single act of enemy aggression, like the Japanese assault on Pearl Harbor in 1941, the Wilson administration had to lead a nation that, initially, at least, was far from united behind the war.

Real disunity and official fears of the effect of dissent in an all-out war, impelled the federal government to take steps (described by works listed in VII, F) aimed at coaxing or forcing all Americans to line up behind the war effort. Failure to secure the official war aims that had motivated many Americans helped provoke the postwar disillusion that writings in section IX, G exemplify and describe.

V/Military Activities and VI/Unit Histories

These sections list works concerned with United States military (including air and naval) participation in the war. Where possible, publications that focus on a particular military unit appear with the unit histories. William Brown's *The Adventures of an American Doughboy* (1440) for instance, which could logically appear in V, G, Accounts By or About Participants, has been located with the histories of the Ninth Infantry Regiment in VI. This arrangement is intended to help researchers comprehend the impact of the war on groups of people who shared similar experiences and on individual servicemen who belonged to specific military units.

We have included substantial numbers of war diaries, narratives, and letters, even though some of these sources are rare items (usually found in the New York Public Library). It was felt that materials which show the war as a personal experience, viewed from the battleground or hospital ward, are so valuable for re-creating the effects of World War I that they should be listed even if some readers may find them hard to get hold of. Since artists, poets, and prose fiction writers also depicted the impact of the war on society and individuals, users of this section may wish to investigate references in subsections of VII, The War and the Visual Arts, and The War and Literature.

A large part of section V is devoted to military personnel—not only the recruitment, conscription, and training of officers and men, but their recreation, their education while in the service, the newspapers they read, their diseases, wounds, and medical care, and the language they used. Again, the object is to enable users to read history on the level of particular human beings, seeing as much as possible of what it was like to be part of the American armed forces or the civilian auxiliaries during the Great War. For an overview of the life of American troops, see especially, Fred Baldwin's dissertation, "The American Enlisted Man in World War I" (728). The U.S. government tried to regulate the sexual behavior of its military personnel during the war. Since this attempt was part of the early twentieth century reform movement, works that discuss it are found chiefly in the subsection of VII, The War and Social Reform.

Edward Coffman's *The War to End All Wars* (257) will introduce the reader to the major controversies that arose from U.S. military activity in the Great War. Here, we wish to mention two particularly significant disputes. The first was the heatedly debated question of whether the United States should integrate its armed forces with those of the Allies or form its own expeditionary army. The second was whether the United States should join the Allies in sending troops to intervene in Russia after the Bolshevik Revolution. Together, these controversies show that the war was far more complex than just a struggle between the United States and Associated Powers on the one hand and the Central Powers on the other and that it in fact involved serious conflict within the Western Alliance even before the peace settlement and between the Western powers and the revolutionary leaders struggling for ascendancy in the Soviet Union.

VII/The War and American Society

The impact of World War I was felt throughout the United States. This was a consequence of the scale of the conflict. With huge armies engaging one another, it was necessary to mobilize, as thoroughly as possible, the nations that supported them. For America, mobilization meant, among other things, the imposition of centralized control over what had been an essentially market economy. This turned out to be a very difficult experience with many false starts performed under great pressure of time (since no one knew in the early months of belligerency when or even whether American aid would prevent an Allied defeat). At one point in the winter of 1917–1918, the economic war effort nearly collapsed. Then, gradually, under guidance of war managers mostly recruited from business organizations, the nation rechanneled its production and distribution systems.

The economic rechanneling process and the recruitment and conscription of young men entailed a centralized management of public opinion; to make Americans do what the government thought was best for the war effort government officials considered it necessary to educate them, to strengthen their motivation to fight or do war work and to coerce the dissenters. Motivation was coordinated by the Committee on Public Information. The coercing agencies included Congress, which outlawed various forms of behavior it thought harmful to the war effort, the Post Office Department, which banned suspect materials from the mail, and the Justice Department, which launched thousands of prosecutions against suspected opponents of war. These agencies were assisted by state organizations and by groups of private citizens. Those subject to coercion included German-Americans, pacifists, conscientious objectors, and socialists, as well as people whom the war made it easier for their enemies to assail.

Although elements of the American labor movement (see section I) were harassed during these months, organized labor as a whole adapted well to the war situation. While federal and state agencies prosecuted radical workers, used troops to end strikes, and devastated the militant, antiwar Industrial Workers of the World, prowar unions increased their membership. Under government pressure, job conditions improved and for certain types of workers, whose skills were desperately needed, wages rose spectacularly. Prowar unions benefited from advantages they held at the beginning of mobilization: their initial organization; the skills of their members; and

the fact that the government thought it would be helpful to have conserva-
tive prowar union leaders like Samuel Gompers spearhead the propaganda
battle against labor radicals.

Woman suffragists, whose activities are described in subsection
K, American Women in the War, were also in a good position to gain from
war conditions. Before 1917 they had developed political machines that
paralleled those of the regular political parties, and with some control over
votes from states where women already had the ballot, they wielded
significant political power. Once the United States was actually in the
conflict, they were able to point to services women performed as nurses, war
workers, farmers, conservers of scarce commodities, and morale-builders for
the armed forces and to ask for the vote as a reward for patriotic service.
Add to this the tactics of one of their organizations, the Woman's Party,
which persistently badgered the Wilson administration for failing to demand
voting rights for women during a war to save the world for democracy, and
the wartime progress of the federal suffrage amendment is easily understood.

Black Americans, on the other hand, had little political power at the
start of hostilities and were only beginning to organize national pressure
groups. They went into the war, as blacks had entered previous wars,
hoping that their service would be rewarded; but, as usual, their hopes
proved weakly founded. Inside the United States there were race riots as
blacks and whites, thrown together in cities like East St. Louis, competed
for jobs. Blacks were discriminated against in the armed forces, generally
assigned to manual tasks regardless of their qualifications, and, in France,
confined to segregated areas lest they mingle with friendly civilians. During
the postwar years their positive accomplishments in battle went largely
ignored and their military deficiencies were publicized, though as an
examination of works listed in subsection J will show, recent scholars have
attempted to appraise them fairly.

We have listed works about blacks in section VII, under two headings,
one of which concerns the training, treatment, and performance of black
troops. Researchers should also refer to section VI, for the histories of black
units, particularly the 365th, 369th, 370th, 371st, and 372d Infantry
Regiments and the 92d and 93d Divisions.

It is also necessary to go beyond a single section if one wishes to sample
the literature on the American reform movement during World War I.
Subsection L notes books and articles about four significant elements of that
movement: the attempt to have the federal government place a floor of
minimum welfare standards under certain vulnerable elements of the population (a precursor of today's massive welfare system); the campaign to
provide war workers not just with decent housing but in some cases with
beautiful housing; and two crusades each of which was intended simulta-
neously to preserve the morals, health, and efficiency of Americans—the
campaign to immunize American servicemen against "illicit" sex and the
attempt to control alcohol consumption. Readers who seek further informa-

tion about the reform movement may wish to examine subsection I for bibliography of attempts to benefit American workers; K for connections between woman suffrage and other elements of progressivism; T for the works of progressive theorists in wartime; W for American reform politics, and the general biographical section, III, B. Since so much of the reform movement involved economic issues like the regulation of business combinations, most of VII, E is also relevant.

Finally, readers will note the sizable numbers of listings in the subsections on the war and education (S and part of T) and the war and science (U). This was one of the periods, like World War II and the Cold War years, when strong ties developed between the federal government and many of the nation's educational, scientific, and technological leaders.

VIII / Peacemaking

If one is to understand the major diplomatic developments of the post-Armistice period, such as the hammering out of a peace settlement and the U.S. Senate's rejection of the Versailles Treaty, one needs to be aware of the wartime and even prewar context of those events. While this section lists several works about the international relations of the United States (1918– 1920), one should also refer to several earlier parts of this bibliography—specifically to the studies of pre-1917 American diplomacy in section IV; to the works about American military cooperation and conflict with the Allies in V, L; to the articles and books in V, M which describe American reactions to the Russian Revolution, an event that contributed substantially to the behavior of participants at the peace negotiations; and to the biographical and autobiographical works in section III. Background information for the struggle over ratification of the Versailles Treaty in the United States Senate can be found in the biographies and memoirs of participants, in works about wartime suppression and control of ethnic minorities (section VII, H), and particularly in studies of the political controversies that erupted during American belligerency (VII, W) when, as Seward Livermore makes clear, politics was never adjourned.

IX / Survivals and Precedents

Aside from the diplomatic consequences discussed in works listed above, World War I had substantial postwar effects on American society. The next great crisis, the Depression of the 1930s, led the United States government to restore, with appropriate modifications, some of the rhetoric and managerial techniques and even a few of the agencies developed for World War I. Yet some of the war's effects, on the values, for instance, and on the economic system of the Americans, were apparent throughout the 1920s. Perhaps the best understanding of how the war survived in people's consciousnesses can be developed from the memoirs and postwar narratives of participants (in III, C; IV, D; V, G) and from the postwar writings of novelists and poets (in VII, R).

I/General References

A/Bibliographies

1   Almond, Nina, and Ralph H. Lutz. *An Introduction to a Bibliography of the Paris Peace Conference.* Stanford: Stanford University Press, 1935.

2   Bayliss, Gwyn. *Bibliographical Guide to the Two World Wars: An Annotated Survey of English-Language Reference Materials.* London: Bowker, 1977.

3   Beaver, Daniel R. "World War I and the Peacetime Army, 1917–1941." In *A Guide to the Sources of United States Military History,* edited by Robin Higham. Hamden, Connecticut: Archon Books, 1975.

4   Brown, Mabel W. *Neuropsychiatry and the War. A Bibliography with Abstracts.* New York: National Committee for Mental Hygiene, War Work Committee, 1918.

5   Casari, Robert B. "A Bibliography of Federal World War I Aviation Agencies and Their Records, 1917–1921." *American Aviation Historical Society Journal* 10 (Spring 1965): 62–63.

6   [Commission Internationale pour l'Enseignement de l'Histoire.] *The Two World Wars: Selective Bibliography.* Oxford: Pergamon, 1964.

6a   Dollen, Charles. *Bibliography of the United States Marine Corps.* New York: Scarecrow Press, 1963.

7   Dornbusch, Charles E., comp. *Histories of American Army Units: World Wars I and II and Korean Conflict, with Some Earlier Histories.* Washington, D.C.: Department of the Army, Office of the Adjutant General, Special Services Division, Library and Service Club Branch, 1956.

8   ———. *Unit Histories of the United States Air Forces Including Privately Printed Personal Narratives.* Hampton Bays, New York: Hampton Books, 1958.

9   Falls, Cyril B. *War Books: A Critical Guide.* London: Davies, 1930.

10 *Foreign Affairs Bibliography: A Selected and Annotated List of Books on International Relations, 1919– 1972.* [Publisher varies.]

11 Genthe, Charles V. *American War Narratives, 1917– 1918: A Study and Bibliography.* New York: David Lewis, 1969.

12 Hilliard, Jack B. *An Annotated Bibliography of the United States Marine Corps in the First World War.* Washington, D.C.: Headquarters U.S. Marine Corps, Historical Branch, G– 3 Division, 1967.

13 Link, Arthur S., and William M. Leary, comps. *The Progressive Era and the Great War, 1896– 1920.* New York: Appleton-Century-Crofts, 1969.

13a Moran, John B. *Creating a Legend: The Complete Record of Writing about the United States Marine Corps.* Chicago: Moran, Andrews, 1973.

14 Nims, Marion R. *Woman in the War: A Bibliography.* Washington, D.C.: G.P.O., 1918.

15 Pappas, George S. *United States Army Unit Histories.* Carlisle Barracks, Pennsylvania: U.S. Army Military History Research Collection, 1971.

16 Richardson, Ernest C. *The Bibliography of the War and the Reconstruction of Bibliographical Methods.* Chicago: Bibliographical Society of America, 1920.

17 Ross, Frank A., and Louise V. Kennedy. *A Bibliography of Negro Migration.* New York: Columbia University Press, 1935.

18 Slonaker, John. *The U.S. Army and the Negro.* Carlisle Barracks, Pennsylvania, 1971.

19 Smith, Myron J. *The American Navy, 1865– 1918: A Bibliography.* Metuchen, New Jersey: Scarecrow, 1974.

19a ——. *World War I in the Air: A Bibliography and Chronology.* Metuchen, New Jersey: Scarecrow, 1977.

20 Social Science Research Council. Committee on Public Administration. *Civil-Military Relations: Bibliographical Notes of Administrative Problems of Civilian Mobilization.* Edited by Pendleton Herring. Chicago: Public Administration Service, 1940.

21 Turnbull, Laura S. *Woodrow Wilson: A Selected Bibliography of His Published Writings, Addresses, and Public Papers.* Princeton: Princeton University Press, 1948.

22 U.S. Library of Congress. Division of Bibliography. *The United States at War: Organizations and Literature.* Washington, D.C.: Library of Congress, 1917.

23 War Camp Community Service. *Community Service in Periodical Literature.* New York: War Camp Community Service, 1920.

24 *Writings on American History, 1902–1961.* [Publisher varies.]

25 *Writings on American History: A Subject Bibliography of Articles 1962–.* Millwood, New York: Kraus-Thomson, 1974–.

B/Guides and Indexes

26 *Air University Library Index to Military Periodicals.* Maxwell Air Force Base, Alabama: Air University Library, 1949–. [Quarterly.]

27 *America: History and Life: A Guide to Periodical Literature.* Santa Barbara: ABC–Clio, 1963–.

28 Leland, Waldo G., and Newton D. Mereness, comps. *Introduction to the American Official Sources for the Economic and Social History of the World War.* New Haven: Yale University Press, 1926.

29 *The New York Times Index.* New York: The New York Times. 1851–1858, 1860, 1863–1905, 1913–.

30 *Readers Guide to Periodical Literature.* New York: H. W. Wilson, 1905–.

31 *Social Sciences and Humanities Index.* New York: H. W. Wilson, 1913–. [Quarterly.]

32 U.S. National Archives. *Handbook of Federal World War Agencies and Their Records, 1917–1921.* Washington, D.C.: G.P.O., 1943.

C/Catalogs

33 Adams, Ephraim D. *The Hoover War Collection at Stanford University, California.* Stanford: Stanford University Press, 1921.

34 New York Public Library. *Subject Catalog of the World War I Collection.* 4 vols. Boston: C. K. Hall, 1961.

35 U.S. Army, A.E.F. General Staff, G–2. Library. *Catalogue of Books and Pamphlets in the Library, General Staff, G–2 (1917–1920).* Paris: American Expeditionary Forces, General Headquarters, 1918.

D/Atlases

36 Banks, Arthur. *A Military Atlas of the First World War.* New York: Taplinger, 1975.

37 Gilbert, Martin. *The First World War Atlas.* New York: Macmillan, 1971.

38 U.S. Military Academy. Department of Military Art and Engineering. *The West Point Atlas of American Wars, 1689–1953.* Edited by Vincent J. Esposito et al. 2 vols. New York: Praeger, 1959.

II/The European War

A/General Accounts

39 Albrecht-Carrié, René. *The Meaning of the First World War*. Englewood Cliffs, New Jersey: Prentice-Hall, 1965.

40 Baldwin, Hanson W. *World War I: An Outline History*. New York: Harper & Row, 1962.

41 Churchill, Winston L. S. *The World Crisis*. 4 vols. in 5. New York: Scribner's, 1923–1929.

42 Falls, Cyril B. *The Great War*. New York: Putnam's, 1959.

43 Halsey, Francis W., ed. *Literary Digest History of the World War, Compiled from Original and Contemporary Sources: American, British, French, German, and Others*. 10 vols. New York: Funk & Wagnalls, 1919–1920.

44 Howland, Charles R. *A Military History of the World War*. 2 vols. Fort Leavenworth, Kansas: General Service Schools, 1923.

45 Liddell Hart, B. H. *History of the First World War*. London: Cassell, 1970.

46 ———. *The Real War: 1914–1918*. Boston: Little, Brown, 1930.

47 Marshall, S. L. A., ed. *The American Heritage History of World War I*. New York: American Heritage Publishing Co., 1964.

48 Mayer, S. L., comp. *History of World War I*. London: Octopus Books, 1974.

49 Roth, Jack J., ed. *World War I: A Turning Point in Modern History*. New York: Knopf, 1967.

50 Simonds, Frank H. *History of the World War*. 5 vols. New York: Doubleday, Page, 1917–1920.

51 Taylor, A. J. P. *The First World War: An Illustrated History*. London: Hamilton, 1964.

B/Origins

52   Albertini, Luigi. *The Origins of the War of 1914.* Translated and edited by Isabella M. Massey. 3 vols. New York: Oxford University Press, 1952–1957.

53   Barnes, Harry Elmer. *The Genesis of the World War: An Introduction to the Problem of War Guilt.* New York: Knopf, 1926.

54   Cooper, John M., Jr., ed. *Causes and Consequences of World War I.* New York: Quadrangle Books, 1972.

55   Fay, Sidney B. *The Origins of the World War.* 2 vols. New York: Macmillan, 1930.

56   Fischer, Fritz. *Germany's Aims in the First World War.* New York: Norton, 1967.

57   ——. *World Power or Decline: The Controversy Over Germany's Aims in the First World War.* New York: Norton, 1974.

58   Fleming, Denna F. *The Origins and Legacies of World War I.* Garden City, New York: Doubleday, 1968.

59   Hale, Frederick A. "Fritz Fischer and the Historiography of World War I." *History Teacher* 9 (Feb. 1976): 258–79.

60   Koch, H. W., ed. *The Origins of The First World War: Great Power Rivalry and German War Aims.* London: Macmillan, 1972.

61   Lafore, Laurence. *The Long Fuse: An Interpretation of the Origins of World War I.* Philadelphia: Lippincott, 1965.

62   Lee, Dwight E., ed. *The Outbreak of the First World War: Who or What Was Responsible?* Lexington, Massachusetts: Heath, 1970.

63   Remak, Joachim. *The Origins of World War I, 1871–1914.* New York: Holt, Rinehart & Winston, 1967.

64   Renouvin, Pierre. *The Immediate Origins of the War (28 June–4 August 1914).* Translated by Theodore C. Hume. New York: Fertig, 1969.

65   Schmitt, Bernadotte E. *The Coming of the War, 1914.* New York: Fertig, 1966.

66   Tuchman, Barbara W. *The Guns of August.* New York: Macmillan, 1962.

67   Van Alstyne, Richard W. "World War I and Its Aftermath." *Current History* 35 (Oct. 1958): 193–98.

III/The United States and World War I—General

A/Overviews

68 Abbot, Willis J. *The United States in the Great War.* New York: Leslie-Judge, 1919.

69 Daniels, Josephus. *The Wilson Era.* 2 vols. Chapel Hill: University of North Carolina Press, 1944, 1946.

70 DeWeerd, Harvey A. *President Wilson Fights His War: World War I and the American Intervention.* New York: Macmillan, 1968.

71 Dos Passos, John R. *Mr. Wilson's War.* Garden City, New York: Doubleday, 1962.

72 Fredericks, Pierce G. *The Great Adventure: America in the First World War.* New York: Dutton, 1960.

73 Graham, Otis L., Jr. *The Great Campaigns: Reform and War in America, 1900–1928.* Englewood Cliffs, New Jersey: Prentice-Hall, 1971.

74 Leuchtenburg, William E. *The Perils of Prosperity, 1914–1932.* Chicago: University of Chicago Press, 1958.

75 Link, Arthur S., ed. *The Impact of World War I.* New York: Harper & Row, 1969.

76 Lloyd, Nelson. *How We Went to War.* New York: Scribner's, 1922.

77 McMaster, John B. *The United States in the World War.* New York: Appleton, 1918.

78 Moore, Samuel T. *America and the World War.* New York: Greenberg, 1937.

79 Nida, William L. *Story of the World War for Young People.* Oak Park, Illinois: Hale Book Co., 1917.

80 Paxson, Frederic L. *American Democracy and the World War.* 3 vols. Vols. 1, 2. Boston: Houghton Mifflin, 1936, 1939; Vol. 3. Berkeley: University of California Press, 1948.

81 Slosson, Preston W. *The Great Crusade and After: 1914–1928.* New York: Macmillan, 1930.

82 Smith, Daniel M. *The Great Departure: The United States and World War I, 1914–1920.* New York: Wiley, 1965.

83 Werstein, Irving. *Over Here and Over There: The Era of the First World War.* New York: Norton, 1968.

84 Young, Ernest W. *The Wilson Administration and the Great War.* Boston: Richard G. Badger, 1922.

B/Biographical Works (Alphabetically by Subject)

85 Beaver, Daniel R. *Newton D. Baker and the American War Effort, 1917–1919.* Lincoln: University of Nebraska Press, 1967.

86 Cramer, Clarence H. *Newton D. Baker: A Biography.* Cleveland: World, 1961.

87 Keppel, Frederick B. "Newton D. Baker." *Foreign Affairs* 16 (Apr. 1938): 503–14.

88 Palmer, Frederick. *Newton D. Baker: America at War.* 2 vols. New York: Dodd, Mead, 1931.

89 Thompson, J. A. "An Imperialist and the First World War: The Case of Albert J. Beveridge." *Journal of American Studies* 5 (Aug. 1971): 133–50.

90 Levine, Lawrence W. *Defender of the Faith: William Jennings Bryan; The Last Decade, 1915–1925.* New York: Oxford University Press, 1965.

91 Dodd, William E. "Josephus Daniels." *Public* 21 (June 22, 1918): 791–94; (June 29, 1918): 822–25.

92 Morrison, Joseph L. *Josephus Daniels: The Small-d Democrat.* Chapel Hill: University of North Carolina Press, 1966.

93 Freidel, Frank. *Franklin D. Roosevelt.* Vol. 1: *The Apprenticeship.* Boston: Little, Brown, 1952.

94 Ness, Gary. "William Howard Taft and the Great War." *Cincinnati Historical Society Bulletin* 34 (Spring 1976): 7–24.

95 Blum, John M. *Joe Tumulty and the Wilson Era.* Boston: Houghton Mifflin, 1951.

96   Baker, Ray S., ed. *Woodrow Wilson: Life and Letters.* 8 vols. Garden City, New York: Doubleday, Page, 1927– 1939.

97   Bell, Herbert C. F. *Woodrow Wilson and the People.* Reprint. Hamden, Connecticut: Archon Books, 1968.

98   Blum, John M. *Woodrow Wilson and the Politics of Morality.* Boston: Little, Brown, 1956.

99   Folliard, Edward T. "When the Cheering Stopped: The Last Years of Woodrow Wilson." *Historic Preservation* 16 (July– Sept. 1964): 87– 91.

100   Freud, Sigmund, and William C. Bullitt. *Thomas Woodrow Wilson, Twenty-eighth President of the United States: A Psychological Study.* Boston: Houghton Mifflin, 1967.

101   Garraty, John A. *Woodrow Wilson: A Great Life in Brief.* New York: Knopf, 1965.

102   George, Alexander L., and Juliette L. George. *Woodrow Wilson and Colonel House: A Personality Study.* New York: John Day, 1956.

103   Grayson, Cary T. *Woodrow Wilson: An Intimate Memoir.* New York: Holt, Rinehart & Winston, 1960.

104   Hoover, Herbert C. *The Ordeal of Woodrow Wilson.* New York: McGraw-Hill, 1958.

105   Link, Arthur S. *Wilson: The Road to the White House.* Princeton: Princeton University Press, 1947.

106   ——. *Wilson: The New Freedom.* Princeton: Princeton University Press, 1956.

107   ——. *Wilson: The Struggle for Neutrality, 1914– 1915.* Princeton: Princeton University Press, 1960.

108   ——. *Wilson: Confusions and Crises, 1915– 1916.* Princeton: Princeton University Press, 1964.

109   ——. *Wilson: Campaigns for Progressivism and Peace, 1916– 1917.* Princeton: Princeton University Press, 1965.

110   ——. *Wilson the Diplomatist: A Look at His Major Foreign Policies.* Baltimore: Johns Hopkins Press, 1957.

111   ——. *Woodrow Wilson and the Progressive Era, 1910– 1917.* New York: Harper & Row, 1954.

112   ——, et al. *Wilson's Diplomacy: An International Symposium.* Cambridge, Massachussetts: Schenkman, 1973.

113 Palmer, John M. *Washington, Lincoln, Wilson: Three War Statesmen.* Garden City, New York: Doubleday, Doran, 1930.

114 Randall, James G. "Lincoln's Task and Wilson's." *South Atlantic Quarterly* 29 (Oct. 1930): 349–68.

115 Smith, Gene. *When the Cheering Stopped: The Last Years of Woodrow Wilson.* New York: Morrow, 1964.

116 Tumulty, Joseph P. *Woodrow Wilson as I Know Him.* Garden City, New York: Doubleday, Page, 1921.

117 Viereck, George S. *The Strangest Friendship in History: Woodrow Wilson and Colonel House.* New York: Liveright, 1932.

118 Walworth, Arthur C. *Woodrow Wilson.* 2 vols. Rev. ed. Boston: Houghton Mifflin, 1965.

119 Watson, Richard L., Jr. "Woodrow Wilson and His Interpreters, 1947–1957." *Mississippi Valley Historical Review* 44 (Sept. 1957): 207–36.

120 Weinstein, Edwin A. "Denial of Presidential Disability: A Case Study of Woodrow Wilson." *Psychiatry* 30 (Nov. 1967): 376–91.

121 ——. "Woodrow Wilson's Neurological Illness." *Journal of American History* 57 (Sept. 1970): 324–51.

C/Memoirs

122 Hoover, Herbert C. *An American Epic.* 4 vols. Chicago: Regnery, 1959–1964.

123 ——. *The Memoirs of Herbert Hoover: Years of Adventure, 1874–1920.* New York: Macmillan, 1951.

124 Houston, D. F. *Eight Years with Wilson's Cabinet: 1913–1920, with a Personal Estimate of the President.* 2 vols. Garden City, New York: Doubleday, Page, 1926.

125 Lansing, Robert. *War Memoirs of Robert Lansing, Secretary of State.* Indianapolis: Bobbs-Merrill, 1935.

126 McAdoo, William G. *Crowded Years: The Reminiscences of William G. McAdoo.* Boston: Houghton Mifflin, 1931.

127 Stimson, Henry L., and McGeorge Bundy. *On Active Service in Peace and War.* New York: Harper, 1948.

D/Letters and Diaries (Alphabetically by author)

128 Daniels, Josephus. *The Cabinet Diaries of Josephus Daniels, 1913–*

1921. Edited by E. David Cronon. Lincoln: University of Nebraska Press, 1963.

129 Hoover, Herbert C. *The Hoover-Wilson Wartime Correspondence, September 24, 1914 to November 11, 1918.* Edited by Francis W. O'Brien. Ames: Iowa State University Press, 1974.

130 House, Edward M. *The Intimate Papers of Colonel House Arranged as a Narrative by Charles Seymour.* 4 vols. Boston: Houghton Mifflin, 1926–1928.

131 Lane, Franklin K. *The Letters of Franklin K. Lane: Personal and Political.* Edited by Anna W. Lane and Louise H. Wall. Boston: Houghton Mifflin, 1922.

132 Grenville, John A. S., ed. "The United States Decision for War 1917: Excerpts from the Manuscript Diary of Robert Lansing." *Renaissance and Modern Studies* 4 (1960): 59–81. [Lansing.]

IV/American Intervention

A/Historiography

133 Cohen, Warren I. *American Revisionists: Lessons of Intervention in World War I.* Chicago: University of Chicago Press, 1967.

134 Leopold, Richard W. "The Problem of American Intervention in 1917: An Historical Retrospect." *World Politics* 2 (Apr. 1950): 404–25.

135 May, Ernest R. *American Intervention: 1917 and 1941.* Washington, D.C.: Service Center for Teachers of History, 1960.

136 Smith, Daniel M. "National Interest and American Intervention, 1917: An Historiographical Appraisal." *Journal of American History* 52 (June 1965): 5–24.

137 Trotter, Agnes A. "The Development of Merchants of Death Theory of American Intervention in the First World War, 1914–1937." Ph.D. dissertation, Duke University, 1966.

B/Documents

138 U.S. Department of State. *Papers Relating to the Foreign Relations of the United States, 1914–1918: Supplement, The World War.* 9 vols. Washington, D.C.: G.P.O., 1928–1933.

C/Collections

139 Bass, Herbert J., ed. *America's Entry into World War I: Submarines, Sentiment or Security.* New York: Holt, Rinehart & Winston, 1964.

140 Buehrig, Edward H., ed. *Wilson's Foreign Policy in Perspective.* Bloomington: Indiana University Press, 1957.

141 Cohen, Warren I., ed. *Intervention, 1917: Why America Fought.* Englewood Cliffs, New Jersey: Heath, 1966.

D/Biographies, Diaries, Letters, Memoirs

142 Bernstorff, Johann A. H. A. graf von. *My Three Years in America.* New York: Scribner's, 1920.

143 Coletta, Paola E. *William Jennings Bryan.* Vol. 2: *Progressive Politician and Moral Statesman, 1909–1915.* Lincoln: University of Nebraska Press, 1969.

144 Curti, Merle. *Bryan and World Peace.* Reprint. New York: Octagon Books, 1969.

145 Gerard, James W. *Face to Face with Kaiserism.* New York: Doran, 1918.

146 ———. *My Four Years in Germany.* New York: Doran, 1917.

147 Gregory, Ross. *Walter Hines Page: Ambassador to the Court of St. James.* Lexington: University Press of Kentucky, 1970.

148 Hendrick, Burton J. *The Life and Letters of Walter Hines Page.* 3 vols. Garden City, New York: Doubleday, Page, 1923–1926.

149 Norris, George W. *Fighting Liberal: The Autobiography of George W. Norris.* New York: Macmillan, 1945.

150 Smith, Daniel M. *Robert Lansing and American Neutrality, 1914–1917.* Berkeley: University of California Press, 1958.

151 Wilkins, Robert P. "Tory Isolationist: Porter J. McCumber and World War I, 1914–1917." *North Dakota History* 34 (Summer 1967): 192–207.

152 Whitlock, Brand. *Belgium: A Personal Narrative.* 2 vols. New York: Appleton, 1919.

E/Background Studies

153 Adler, Selig. "Bryan and Wilsonian Caribbean Penetration." *Hispanic-American Historical Review* 20 (May 1940): 198–226.

154 Allen, Howard W. "Republican Reformers and Foreign Policy, 1913–1917." *Mid-America* 44 (Oct. 1962): 222–29.

155 Baker, George W. "Robert Lansing and the Purchase of the Danish West Indies." *Social Studies* 57 (Feb. 1966): 64–71.

156 Bell, Sidney. *Righteous Conquest: Woodrow Wilson and the Evolution of the New Diplomacy.* Port Washington, New York: Kennikat, 1972.

157   Cooper, John M., Jr. *The Vanity of Power: American Isolationism and the First World War, 1914–1917.* Westport, Connecticut: Greenwood, 1969.

158   Curry, Roy W. *Woodrow Wilson and Far Eastern Policy, 1913–1921.* New York: Bookman Associates, 1957.

159   Davis, Forrest. *The Atlantic System: The Story of Anglo-American Control of the Seas.* New York: Reynal & Hitchcock, 1941.

160   Diamond, William. *The Economic Thought of Woodrow Wilson.* Baltimore: Johns Hopkins Press, 1943.

161   Earle, Edward M. "A Half-Century of American Foreign Policy: Our Stake in Europe, 1898–1918." *Political Science Quarterly* 64 (June 1949): 168–88.

162   Epstein, Fritz T. "Germany and the United States: Basic Patterns of Conflict and Understanding." In *Issues and Conflicts: Studies in Twentieth Century American Diplomacy,* edited by George L. Anderson. Lawrence: University of Kansas Press, 1959.

163   Fifield, Russell H. *Woodrow Wilson and the Far East: The Diplomacy of the Shantung Question.* 1952. Reprint. Hamden, Connecticut: Archon Books, 1965.

164   Greene, Fred. "The Military View of American National Policy, 1904–1940." *American Historical Review* 66 (Jan. 1961): 354–77.

165   Grenville, John A. S., and George B. Young. *Politics, Strategy, and American Diplomacy: Studies in Foreign Policy, 1873–1917.* New Haven: Yale University Press, 1966.

166   Haley, P. Edward. *Revolution and Intervention: The Diplomacy of Taft and Wilson with Mexico, 1910–1917.* Cambridge: M.I.T. Press, 1970.

167   Kennan, George F. *American Diplomacy, 1900–1950.* New York: New American Library, 1952.

168   Li, T'ien-i. *Woodrow Wilson's China Policy, 1913–1917.* Kansas City, Missouri: University of Kansas City Press, 1952.

169   Lippmann, Walter. *United States Foreign Policy: Shield of the Republic.* Boston: Little, Brown, 1943.

170   Logan, Rayford W. *Haiti and the Dominican Republic.* New York: Oxford University Press, 1968.

171   Munro, Dana G. *Intervention and Dollar Diplomacy in the Caribbean, 1900–1921.* Princeton: Princeton University Press, 1964.

172 Notter, Harley. *The Origins of the Foreign Policy of Woodrow Wilson.* Baltimore: Johns Hopkins Press, 1937.

173 Osgood, Robert E. *Ideals and Self-Interest in America's Foreign Relations.* Chicago: University of Chicago Press, 1953.

174 Smith, Daniel M. "Robert Lansing and the Formulation of American Neutrality Policies, 1914– 1915." *Mississippi Valley Historical Review* 43 (June 1956): 59– 81.

175 Trask, David F. "Woodrow Wilson and the Reconciliation of Force and Diplomacy." *Naval War College Review* 27 (Jan.– Feb. 1975): 23– 31.

176 Vagts, Alfred. "Hopes and Fears of an American-German War, 1870– 1915." *Political Science Quarterly* 54 (Dec. 1939): 514– 35; 55 (Mar. 1940): 53– 76.

177 Williams, William A. *The Tragedy of American Diplomacy.* New York: Dell, 1962.

F/Overviews

178 Buehrig, Edward H. "Wilson's Neutrality Re-Examined." *World Politics* 3 (Oct. 1950): 1– 19.

179 ———. *Woodrow Wilson and the Balance of Power.* Bloomington: Indiana University Press, 1955.

179a Coogan, John W. "The End of Neutrality: The United States, Britain, and Neutral Rights, 1899– 1915." Ph.D. dissertation, Yale University, 1976.

180 Devlin, Patrick. *Too Proud to Fight: Woodrow Wilson's Neutrality.* New York: Oxford University Press, 1975.

181 Fleming, Denna F. "Our Entry into the World War in 1917: The Revised Version." *Journal of Politics* 2 (Feb. 1940): 75– 86.

182 Frothingham, Thomas G. "The Entrance of the United States into the First World War." *U.S. Naval Institute Proceedings* 53 (Apr. 1927): 399– 402.

183 Grattan, C. Hartley. *Why We Fought.* New York: Vanguard, 1929.

184 Gregory, Ross. *The Origins of American Intervention in the First World War.* New York: Norton, 1971.

185 May, Ernest R. *The World War and American Isolation, 1914– 1917.* Cambridge: Harvard University Press, 1959.

186 Millis, Walter. *The Road to War: America 1914– 1917.* Boston: Houghton Mifflin, 1935.

187   Schmitt, Bernadotte E. "American Neutrality." *Journal of Modern History* 8 (June 1936): 200–211.

188   Seymour, Charles. *American Neutrality, 1914–1917: Essays on the Causes of American Intervention in the World War.* New Haven: Yale University Press, 1935.

189   Tansill, Charles C. *America Goes to War.* Boston: Little, Brown, 1938.

G/Specific Studies

190   Bailey, Thomas A. "German Documents Relating to the *Lusitania.*" *Journal of Modern History* 8 (Sept. 1936): 320–37.

191   ——. *The Policy of the United States Towards the Neutrals, 1917–1918.* Gloucester, Massachusetts: Peter Smith, 1966.

192   ——. "The Sinking of the *Lusitania.*" *American Historical Review* 41 (Oct. 1935): 54–73.

193   ——. "The United States and the Blacklist during the Great War." *Journal of Modern History* 6 (Mar. 1934): 14–35.

194   ——, and Paul B. Ryan. *The Lusitania Disaster: An Episode in Modern Warfare and Diplomacy.* New York: Free Press, 1975.

195   Billington, Monroe. "The Gore Resolution of 1916." *Mid-America* 47 (Apr. 1965): 89–98.

196   Birdsall, Paul. "Neutrality and Economic Pressures, 1914–1917." *Science and Society* 3 (Spring 1939): 217–28.

197   Birnbaum, Karl E. *Peace Moves and U-Boat Warfare: A Study of Imperial Germany's Policy toward the United States, April 18, 1916–January 9, 1917.* Stockholm: Almquist & Wiksell, 1958.

198   Bonadio, Felice A. "The Failure of German Propaganda in the United States, 1914–1917." *Mid-America* 41 (Jan. 1959): 40–57.

199   Borchard, Edwin. "Neutrality Claims Against Great Britain." *American Journal of International Law* 21 (Oct. 1927): 764–68.

200   Bridges, Lamar W. "Zimmerman Telegram: Reaction of Southern, Southwestern Newspapers." *Journalism Quarterly* 46 (Spring 1969): 81–86.

201   Buchanan, A. Russell. "Theodore Roosevelt and American Neutrality, 1914–1917." *American Historical Review* 43 (July 1938): 775–90.

202   Burdick, Charles B. "A House on Navidad Street: The Celebrated Zimmerman Note on the Texas Border." *Arizona and the West* 8 (Spring 1966): 19–34.

203 Child, Clifton J. "German-American Attempts to Prevent the Exportation of Munitions of War, 1914– 1915." *Mississippi Valley Historical Review* 25 (Dec. 1938): 351– 68.

204 Clapp, Edwin J. *Economic Aspects of the War: Neutral Rights, Belligerent Claims, and American Commerce in the Years 1914–1915.* New Haven: Yale University Press, 1915.

205 Cooper, John M., Jr. "Progressivism and American Foreign Policy: A Reconsideration." *Mid-America* 51 (Oct. 1969): 260– 77.

206 Crighton, John C. "The Wilhemina: An Adventure in the Assertion and Exercise of American Trading Rights during the World War." *American Journal of International Law* 34 (Jan. 1940): 74– 88.

207 Davis, Gerald H. "The 'Ancona' Affair: A Case of Preventive Diplomacy." *Journal of Modern History* 38 (Sept. 1966): 267– 77.

208 ——. "The 'Petrolite' Incident: A World War I Case Study on the Limitations of Warfare." *Historian* 29 (Feb. 1967): 238– 48.

209 Dignan, Don K. "The Hindu Conspiracy in Anglo-American Relations during World War I." *Pacific Historical Review* 40 (Feb. 1971): 57– 76.

210 Dupuy, Richard E. *Five Days to War: April 2– 6, 1917.* Harrisburg, Pennsylvania: Stackpole, 1967.

211 Erskine, Hazel. "The Polls: Is War a Mistake?" *Public Opinion Quarterly* 34 (Spring 1970): 134– 50.

212 Esslinger, Dean R. "American, German and Irish Attitudes toward Neutrality, 1914– 1917: A Study of Catholic Minorities." *Catholic Historical Review* 53 (July 1967): 194– 216.

213 Foster, H. Schuyler, Jr. "How America Became Belligerent: A Quantitative Study of War News 1914– 1917." *American Journal of Sociology* 40 (Jan. 1935): 464– 75.

214 Fry, M. G. "The Imperial War Cabinet, the United States, and the Freedom of the Seas." *Royal United Service Institution Journal* 110 (Nov. 1965): 353– 62.

215 Fuller, Joseph V. "The Genesis of the Munitions Traffic." *Journal of Modern History* 6 (Sept. 1934): 280– 93.

216 Gregory, Ross. "A New Look at the Case of the *Dacia.*" *Journal of American History* 55 (Sept. 1968): 292– 96.

217 Hirst, David. "German Propaganda in the United States, 1914– 1917." Ph.D. dissertation, Northwestern University, 1962.

218 Hoehling, Adolph A., and Mary Hoehling. *The Last Voyage of the Lusitania.* London: Longmans, Green, 1957.

219 Kernek, Sterling J. "The British Government's Reaction to President Wilson's 'Peace' Note of December 1916." *Historical Journal* 13:4 (1970): 721– 66.

220 Kihl, Mary R. "A Failure of Ambassadorial Diplomacy." *Journal of American History* 57 (Dec. 1970): 636– 53.

221 Link, Arthur S. "The Cotton Crisis, the South, and Anglo-American Diplomacy, 1914– 1915." In *Studies in Southern History in Memory of Albert Ray Newsom, 1894– 1951 . . .* , edited by Joseph Sitterson. Chapel Hill: University of North Carolina Press, 1957.

222 Lowitt, Richard. "The Armed-Ship Bill Controversy: A Legislative View." *Mid-America* 46 (Jan. 1964): 38– 47.

223 Lundeberg, Philip K. "The German Naval Critique of the U-Boat Campaign, 1915– 1918." *Military Affairs* 27 (Fall 1963): 105– 18.

224 McDiarmid, Alice M. [Morrissey]. *The American Defense of Neutral Rights, 1914– 1917.* Cambridge: Harvard University Press, 1939.

225 McDonald, Timothy G. "The Gore-McLemore Resolution: Democratic Revolt against Wilson's Submarine Policy." *Historian* 26 (Nov. 1963): 50– 74.

226 ——. "Southern Democratic Congressmen and the First World War, August 1914– April 1917: The Public Record of Their Support for or Opposition to Wilson's Policies." Ph.D. dissertation, University of Washington, 1962.

227 Patterson, David S. "Woodrow Wilson and the Mediation Movement, 1914– 1917." *Historian* 33 (Aug. 1971): 535– 56.

228 Peterson, Horace C. *Propaganda for War: The Campaign against American Neutrality, 1914– 1917.* Norman: University of Oklahoma Press, 1939.

229 Rappaport, Armin. *The British Press and Wilsonian Neutrality.* Stanford: Stanford University Press, 1951.

230 Ripley, G. Peter. "Intervention and Reaction: Florida Newspapers and United States Entry into World War I." *Florida Historical Quarterly* 49. (Jan. 1971): 255– 66.

231 Ryan, Paul B. "The Great Lusitania Whitewash." *American Neptune* 35 (Jan. 1975): 36– 52.

232 Ryley, Thomas W. *A Little Group of Willful Men: A Study of Congressional-Presidential Authority.* Port Washington, New York: Kennikat, 1975.

233 Siney, Marion C. *The Allied Blockade of Germany, 1914– 1916.* Ann Arbor: University of Michigan Press, 1957.

234 ———. "British Negotiations with American Meat Packers, 1915–1917: A Study of Belligerent Trade Controls." *Journal of Modern History* 23 (Dec. 1951): 343–53.

235 Smith, Gaddis. *Britain's Clandestine Submarines, 1914–1915.* New Haven: Yale University Press, 1964.

236 ———. "The Clandestine Submarines of 1914–1915: An Essay in the History of the North American Triangle." *Canadian Historical Association Annual Report* (1963): 194–203.

237 Spencer, Samuel R., Jr. *Decision for War, 1917: The Laconia Sinking and the Zimmerman Telegram as Key Factors in the Public Reaction against Germany.* Rindge, New Hampshire: Smith, 1953.

238 Squires, J. D. *British Propaganda at Home and in the United States from 1914–1917.* Cambridge: Harvard University Press, 1935.

239 Sutton, Walter A. "Bryan, La Follette, Norris: Three Mid-Western Politicians." *Journal of the West* 8 (Oct. 1969): 613–30.

240 ———. "Progressive Republican Senators and the Submarine Crisis, 1915–1916." *Mid-America* 47 (Apr. 1965): 75–88.

241 Syrett, Harold C. "The Business Press and American Neutrality, 1914–1917." *Mississippi Valley Historical Review* 32 (Sept. 1945): 215–30.

242 Tuchman, Barbara W. *The Zimmerman Telegram.* New York: Viking, 1958.

243 U.S. Congress. Senate. Special Committee to Investigate the Munitions Industry. Hearings: *Munitions Industry,* 73d–74th Cong., 1934–1937.

244 ———. *Munitions Industry: Reports . . . ,* 74th Cong., 1st Sess., 1935–36.

245 Van Alstyne, Richard W. "The Policy of the United States Regarding the Declaration of London at the Outbreak of the Great War." *Journal of Modern History* 7 (Dec. 1935): 435–47.

246 ———. "Private American Loans to the Allies, 1914–1916." *Pacific Historical Review* 2 (June 1933): 180–93.

247 Viereck, George S. *Spreading Germs of Hate.* New York: Liveright, 1930.

248 Woodward, David R. "Great Britain and President Wilson's Efforts to End World War I in 1916." *Maryland Historian* 1 (Spring 1970): 45–58.

V/Military Activity (Including Air and Naval)

A/Documents

249 Horne, Charles F., ed. *Source Records of the Great War.* 7 vols. Indianapolis: American Legion, 1930.

250 U.S. War Department. *The Official Record of the United States' Part in the Great War.* Washington, D.C.: G.P.O., 1923.

B/Historiography

251 Smythe, Donald. "The Battle of the Books: Pershing versus March (versus Harbord)." *Army* 22 (Sept. 1972): 30–32.

252 ———. "Literary Salvos: James C. Harbord and the Pershing-March Controversy." *Mid-America* 57 (July 1975): 173–83.

C/Background Studies

253 Brooks, Edward H. "The National Defense Policy of the Wilson Administration, 1913–1917." Ph.D. dissertation, Stanford University, 1950.

254 Jenkins, Innis L. "Josephus Daniels and the Navy Department, 1913–1916: A Study in Military Administration." Ph.D. dissertation, University of Maryland, 1960.

255 Sprout, Harold, and Margaret Sprout. *The Rise of American Naval Power 1776–1918.* Princeton: Princeton University Press, 1946.

256 ———. *Toward a New Order of Sea Power: American Naval Policy and the World Scene, 1918–1922.* Princeton: Princeton University Press, 1943.

D/Overviews

257 Coffman, Edward M. *The War to End All Wars: The American Military Experience in World War I.* New York: Oxford University Press, 1968.

258 Fredericks, Pierce G. *The Great Adventure: America in the First World War.* New York: Dutton, 1960.

259 Frothingham, Thomas G. *The American Reinforcement in the World War.* Garden City, New York: Doubleday, Page, 1927.

259a Leonard, Thomas C. *Above the Battle: War-making in America from Appomattox to Versaille.* New York: Oxford University Press, 1978.

E/Guides to Battlefields

260 American Battle Monuments Commission. *American Armies and Battlefields in Europe: A History, Guide, and Reference Book.* Washington, D.C.: G.P.O., 1938.

261 *The Americans in the Great War.* 3 vols. Clermont-Ferrand: Michelin & cie., 1920.

262 Moss, James A., and Harry S. Howland. *America in Battle: With Guide to the American Battlefields in France and Belgium.* Menasha, Wisconsin: Banta, 1920.

F/Pictorials and Cartoons

263 Antrim, Ray P. *Where the Marines Fought in France.* Chicago: Park & Antrim, 1919.

264 Daniels, Josephus. *Our Navy at War.* Washington, D.C.: Pictorial Bureau, 1922.

265 Duncan-Clark, Samuel J. *History's Greatest War: A Pictorial Narrative.* Chicago: Geographical Publishing Co., 1920.

266 Freidel, Frank B. *Over There: The Story of America's First Great Overseas Crusade.* New York: Bramhall House, 1964.

267 Hecht, George J., ed. *The War in Cartoons.* New York: Garland, 1971.

268 Mackey, Frank J., and Marcus W. Jernegan, eds. *Forward-March! The Photographic Record of America in the World War and the Post-War Social Upheaval.* Chicago: Disabled American Veterans of the World War, Department of Rehabilitation, 1934.

269 Moore, William E., and James C. Russell. *U.S. Official Pictures of the World War: Showing America's Participation.* Washington, D.C.: Pictorial Bureau, 1920.

270 Moss, James A., and William H. Waldron. *What Sammy's Doing: Being a Pictorial Sketch of the Soldier's Life.* Menasha, Wisconsin: Banta, 1917.

271 Raemaekers, Louis. *America in the War.* New York: Century, 1918. [Cartoons.]

272 Randall, Roy O., and John S. Baxter, eds. *A Photographic History: Why America Won the War.* Chicago: Union Books, 1922.

273 Russell, James C., and William E. Moore. *The United States Navy in the World War: Official Pictures Selected from the Files of the Navy Department, the War Department and the United States Marine Corps: With Supplemental Photographs from Unofficial Sources.* Washington, D.C.: Pictorial Bureau, 1921.

274 Stallings, Laurence. *The First World War.* New York: Simon & Schuster, 1933.

275 Wallgren, Abian A. *The A.E.F. in Cartoon.* Philadelphia: Sowers, 1933.

276 "When the Marines Went to France, 1917– 1918." *U.S. Naval Institute Proceedings* 93 (Nov. 1967): 86– 100.

277 Wise, James E., Jr. "U-Boats Off Our Coasts." *U.S. Naval Institute Proceedings* 91 (Oct. 1965): 84– 101.

G/Accounts By or About Participants

Biographical Works (Alphabetically by Subject)

278 Howe, Mark A. De Wolfe. *Oliver Ames, Jr., 1895– 1918.* Boston, 1922.

279 Hayes, Ralph A. *Secretary Baker at the Front.* New York: Century, 1918.

280 Palmer, Frederick. *Bliss, Peacemaker: The Life and Letters of General Tasker Howard Bliss.* New York: Dodd, Mead, 1934.

281 Millett, Allan R. *The General: Robert L. Bullard and Officership in the United States Army, 1881– 1925.* Westport, Connecticut: Greenwood, 1975.

282 Thomas, Lowell. *Old Gimlet Eye: The Adventures of Smedley D. Butler.* New York: Farrar & Rinehart, 1933.

283 Lockmiller, David A. *Enoch H. Crowder: Soldier, Lawyer and Statesman.* Columbia: University of Missouri Press, 1955.

284 Price, Theodore H. "Josephus Daniels: The Man Who has Democratized the Navy." *Outlook* 118 (Mar. 27, 1918): 484– 86.

285 Rouzer, E. McClure. *The Last Drive and Death of Major G. H. H. Emory.* Baltimore: Sun Printing, 1922.

286 Pearson, LeRoy. "Major General William G. Haan." *Michigan History* 9 (Jan. 1925): 3– 16.

287 Hudson, James J. "Captain Field E. Kindley: Arkansas Air Ace of the First World War." *Arkansas Historical Quarterly* 18 (Summer 1959): 3– 31.

288 Hall, Norman S. *The Balloon Buster: Frank Luke of Arizona.* Garden City, New York: Doubleday, Doran, 1928.

289 James, D. Clayton. *The Years of MacArthur.* Vol. 1: *1880– 1941.* Boston: Houghton Mifflin, 1970.

290 Coffman, Edward M. *The Hilt of the Sword: The Career of Peyton C. March.* Madison: University of Wisconsin Press, 1966.

291 Pogue, Forrest C. *George C. Marshall.* Vol. 1: *Education of a General, 1880– 1939.* New York: Viking, 1963.

292 Miner, Margaret M. *Asher Miner: Citizen and Soldier.* Cambridge: Harvard University Press, 1929.

293 Hurley, Alfred F. *Billy Mitchell: Crusader for Air Power.* Bloomington: Indiana University Press, 1975.

294 Lahm, Frank P. "A Commentary on Mitchell's Memoirs of World War I." *Airpower Historian* 9 (July 1962): 189– 91.

295 Levine, Isaac Don. *Mitchell: Pioneer of Air Power.* Rev. ed. New York: Duell, Sloan & Pearce, 1958.

296 Andrews, Avery D. *My Friend and Classmate John J. Pershing.* Harrisburg, Pennsylvania: Military Service Publishing, 1939.

297 Coffman, Edward M. "John J. Pershing, General of the Armies." *U.S. Army Military History Research Collection: Essays in Some Dimensions of Military History* 4 (Feb. 1976): 48– 61.

298 Goldhurst, Richard. *Pipe Clay and Drill.* New York: Reader's Digest Press, 1977. [John J. Pershing.]

299 O'Connor, Richard. *Black Jack Pershing.* Garden City, New York: Doubleday, 1961.

300 Palmer, Frederick. *John J. Pershing, General of the Armies: A Biography.* Harrisburg, Pennsylvania: Military Service Publishing, 1948.

301 Smythe, Donald. "Pershing and General J. Franklin Bell, 1917– 1918." *Mid-America* 54 (Jan. 1972): 34– 51.

302 ———. "You Dear Old Jack Pershing." *American History Illustrated* 7 (Oct. 1972): 18– 24.

303 Vandiver, Frank G. *Black Jack: The Life and Times of John J. Pershing.* 2 vols. College Station: Texas A & M University Press, 1977.

304 Allard, Dean C. "Admiral William S. Sims and United States Naval Policy in World War I." *American Neptune* 35 (Apr. 1975): 97– 110.

305 Baldridge, Harry A. "Sims the Iconoclast." *U.S. Naval Institute Proceedings* 63 (Feb. 1937): 183– 90.

306 Morison, Elting E. *Admiral Sims and the Modern American Navy.* Boston: Houghton Mifflin, 1942.

307 Kahana, Yoram. "Captain Harry: The Cussing Doughboy of Battery D." *Mankind* 5 (Feb. 1977): 37– 41. [Harry Truman.]

308 Ruhl, Robert K. "Corporal Williams' War." *Airman* 18 (Nov. 1974): 14– 19. [Waller S. Williams.]

309 Thomas, Lowell. *[Samuel] Woodfill of the Regulars: A True Story of Adventure from the Arctic to the Argonne.* Garden City, New York: Doubleday, Doran, 1929.

310 Skeyhill, Thomas. *Sergeant York: Last of the Long Hunters.* Philadelphia: John C. Winston, 1930.

Collective Biography

311 Bullard, Robert L. *Fighting Generals.* Ann Arbor: J. W. Edwards, 1944.

312 Miller, Warren H. *The Boys of 1917: Famous American Heroes of the World War.* Boston: Page, 1939.

313 Smith, Chellis V. *Americans All: Nine Heroes Who in the World War Showed that Americanism is Above Race, Creed or Condition.* Boston: Lothrop, Lee & Shepard, 1925.

314 [Ticknor, Caroline], ed. *New England Aviators, 1914– 1918: Their Portraits and Their Records.* 2 vols. Boston: Houghton Mifflin, 1919– 1920.

315 Toliver, R. F., and T. J. Constable. *Fighter Aces.* New York: Macmillan, 1965.

316 Whitehouse, Arch. *Heroes of the Sunlit Sky.* New York: Doubleday, 1967. [Air Aces.]

Memoirs and Personal Narratives

317 Aldrich, Mildred. *The Peak of the Load* . . . . Boston: Small, Maynard, 1918.

318 Allen, Hervey. *Toward the Flame.* New York: Doran, 1926.

319   *Americans Defending Democracy: Our Soldiers' Own Stories.* New York: World's War Stories, 1919.

320   Archibald, Norman. *Heaven High, Hell Deep, 1917–1918.* New York: Boni, 1935.

321   Arnold, Henry H. *Global Mission.* New York: Harper, 1949.

322   Barkley, John L. *No Hard Feelings.* New York: Cosmopolitan Book Corp., 1930.

323   Benson, Samuel C. *"Back from Hell."* Chicago: McClurg, 1918.

324   Berlin, Ira, ed. "A Wisconsinite in World War I: Reminiscences of Edmund Arpin, Jr." *Wisconsin Magazine of History* 51 (Autumn 1967): 3–25; (Winter 1967–1968): 124–38; (Spring 1968): 218–37.

325   Bernheim, Bertram M. *"Passed as Censored."* Philadelphia: Lippincott, 1918.

326   Bingham, Hiram. *An Explorer in the Air Service.* New Haven: Yale University Press, 1920.

327   Blackford, Charles M. *Torpedoboat Sailor.* Annapolis: U.S. Naval Institute, 1968.

328   Buck, Beaumont B. *Memories of Peace and War.* San Antonio: Naylor, 1935.

329   Bullard, Robert L. *Personalities and Reminiscences of the War.* Garden City, New York: Doubleday, Page, 1925.

330   Burdick, Joel W. *Lorraine: 1918.* New Haven: Yale University Press, 1919.

331   Carter, William A. *The Tale of a Devil Dog by William A. Carter, One of Them.* Washington, D.C.: Canteen Press, 1920.

332   Christian, Royal A. *Roy's Trip to the Battlefields of Europe.* Chambersburg, Pennsylvania: Kerr, 1918.

333   Churchill, Winston L. S. *A Traveller in War-Time.* New York: Macmillan, 1918.

334   Clover, Greayer. *A Stop at Suzanne's and Lower Flights.* New York: Doran, 1919.

335   Cobb, Irvin S. *The Glory of the Coming.* New York: Doran, 1918.

336   Codman, Charles R. *Contact.* Boston: Little, Brown, 1937.

337 Conner, Virginia. *What Father Forbad.* Philadelphia: Dorrance, 1951.

338 Cook, George C. "One in 2,000,000." *Quartermaster Review* 18:3 (1938): 18–22, 71–72.

339 Corning, Walter D. *The Yanks Crusade: A Book of Reminiscences.* Chicago, 1927.

340 Craighill, Edley. *The Musketeers.* Lynchburg, Virginia: J. P. Bell Co., 1931.

341 cummings, e.e. *The Enormous Room.* New York: Boni & Liveright, 1922.

342 Curtiss, Elmer H. *Going and Coming as a Doughboy.* Palo Alto, California: Press of F. A. Stuart, 1920.

343 Cutchins, John A. *An Amateur Diplomat in the World War.* Richmond, Virginia: American Legion, Commanders Committee, 1938.

344 Dawes, Charles G. *A Journal of the Great War.* 2 vols. Boston: Houghton Mifflin, 1921.

345 Dorr, Rheta C. *A Soldier's Mother in France.* Indianapolis: Bobbs-Merrill, 1918.

346 DuPuy, Charles M. *A Machine Gunner's Notes: France 1918.* Pittsburgh: Reed & Witting, 1920.

347 [Edwards, Richard A.] "World War I: Experiences of Stephen Loch Edwards." *Register of the Kentucky Historical Society* 67 (July 1969): 211–20.

348 Empey, Arthur G. *"Over the Top," by an American Soldier Who Went. . . .* New York: Putnam's, 1917.

349 [Fuller, Ruth W.] *Silver Lining: The Experience of a War Bride.* Boston: Houghton Mifflin, 1918.

350 [Grider, John M.] *Marse John Goes to War.* Memphis, Tennessee: Davis Printing, 1933.

351 Hall, Bert. *"En l'air!" (In the Air!): Three Years On and Above Three Fronts.* New York: New Library, 1918.

352 Halsey, William F., and Joseph Bryan III. *Admiral Halsey's Story.* New York: Whittlesey House, 1947.

353 Hamilton, Craig, ed. *Echoes from Over There, by the Men of the Army and Marine Corps Who Fought in France.* New York: Soldiers Publishing, 1919.

354   Haslett, Elmer. *Luck on the Wing: Thirteen Stories of a Sky Spy.* New York: Dutton, 1920.

355   Herring, Ray De W. *Trifling with War.* Boston: Meador, 1934.

356   Holden, Frank. *War Memories.* Athens, Georgia: Athens Book Co., 1922.

357   Holmes, Robert D. *A Yankee in the Trenches.* Boston: Little, Brown, 1918.

358   Hubbard, Samuel T. *Memoirs of a Staff Officer, 1917–1919.* Bronxville, New York, 1959.

359   Hungerford, Edward. *With the Doughboy in France: A Few Chapters of an American Effort.* New York: Macmillan, 1920.

360   Husband, Joseph. *A Year in the Navy.* Boston: Houghton Mifflin, 1919.

361   Irwin, William H. *A Reporter at Armageddon. . . .* New York: Appleton, 1918.

362   Jenks, Chester W. *Our First Ten Thousand.* Boston: Four Seas, 1919.

363   Johnson, Wesley R. "War Experiences of a University Student as a Doughboy." *University of North Dakota Quarterly Journal* 10 (Oct. 1919): 93–120.

364   [Johnston, Edward S., et al.] *Americans vs. Germans: The First A.E.F. in Action.* Washington, D.C.: Infantry Journal, 1942.

365   Kendall, Harry. *A New York Actor on the Western Front.* Boston: Christopher Publishing House, 1932.

366   Knapp, Shepherd. *On the Edge of the Storm: The Story of a Year in France.* Worcester, Massachusetts: Commonwealth Press, 1921.

367   Knight, Clayton. *Pilot's Luck.* Philadelphia: David McKay, 1929.

368   Kurtz, Leonard P. *Beyond No Man's Land.* Buffalo: Foster T. Stewart, 1937.

369   Lejeune, John A. *The Reminiscences of a Marine.* Philadelphia: Dorrance, 1930.

370   Levell, Robert O. *"War on the Ocean": A Sailor's Souvenir.* Newcastle, Indiana, 1937.

371   Liggett, Hunter. *A.E.F.: Ten Years Ago in France.* New York: Dodd, Mead, 1928.

372 ——. *Commanding an American Army: Recollections of the World War*. Boston: Houghton Mifflin, 1925.

373 Lukens, Edward C. *A Blue Ridge Memoir*. Baltimore: Sun Printing, 1922.

374 MacArthur, Douglas. *Reminiscences*. New York: McGraw-Hill, 1964.

375 McCarthy, Timothy F. *"A Year at Camp Gordon": United States Army Cantonment No. 123*. Wilkes-Barre, Pennsylvania: Caxton Press, 1920.

376 March, Peyton C. *The Nation at War*. Garden City, New York: Doubleday, Doran, 1932.

377 Marshall, George C. *Memoirs of My Service in the World War, 1917–1918*. Boston: Houghton Mifflin, 1976.

378 Matthews, William, and Dixon Wector. *Our Soldiers Speak, 1775–1918*. Boston: Little, Brown, 1943.

379 Meredith Ellis. "Edward R. Kingsland: A Son of Columbia." *Colorado Magazine* 29 (1952) 131–37.

380 Minturn, Joseph A. *The American Spirit*. Indianapolis: Globe Publishing, 1921.

381 Mitchell, William. *Memoirs of World War I. "From Start to Finish of Our Greatest War."* Reprint. Westport, Connecticut: Greenwood, 1975.

382 Murnane, Mark R. *Ground Swells: Of Sailors, Ships and Shellac*. New York: Exposition, 1949.

383 New York Life Insurance Company. *NYLIC War Stories*. New York, 1920.

384 Palmer, Frederick. *My Year of the Great War*. New York: Burt, 1918.

385 ——. *With My Own Eyes: A Personal Story of Battle Years*. Indianapolis: Bobbs-Merrill, 1933.

386 Peixotto, Ernest C. *The American Front*. New York: Scribner's, 1919.

387 Pershing, John J. *My Experiences in the World War*. 2 vols. New York: Stokes, 1931.

388 Peterson, Wilbur. *I Went to War*. Marshall, Minnesota: Messenger Press, 1938.

389 Pickell, James R. *Twenty-four Days on a Troopship*. Chicago: Rosenbaum Review, 1919.

390   Riggs, Arthur S. *With Three Armies on and behind the Western Front.* Indianapolis: Bobbs-Merrill, 1918.

391   Roberts, E. M. *A Fighting Flier: An American above the Lines in France.* New York: Harper, 1918.

392   Rodman, Hugh. *Yarns of a Kentucky Admiral.* Indianapolis: Bobbs-Merrill, 1928.

393   Roosevelt, Theodore, Jr. *Average Americans.* New York: Putnam's, 1919.

394   Rounds, Ona M. *Buck Privates on Parnassus.* Boston: Meador, 1933.

395   Scott, Hugh L. *Some Memoirs of a Soldier.* New York: Century, 1928.

396   Sharp, John E. *From Funston to Germany via the "Sherman" Route.* Tulsa, Oklahoma: General Refining, Co., 1919 (?).

397   Smith, Joseph S. *Over There and Back in Three Uniforms.* New York: Dutton, 1918.

398   Snow, William J. *Signposts of Experience: World War Memoirs.* Washington, D.C.: U.S. Field Artillery Association, 1941.

399   Speakman, Harold. *From a Soldier's Heart.* New York: Abingdon, 1919.

400   Springs, Elliott W. *Above the Bright Blue Sky.* Garden City, New York: Doubleday, Doran, 1928.

401   ———. "War Birds: Diary of an Unknown Aviator." *Aerospace Historian* 13 (Autumn 1966): 97–104; 14 (Spring 1967): 37–41; (Autumn 1967): 151–62; (Winter 1967): 219–25; 15 (Summer 1968): 34–51.

402   Stamas, Christ K. *The Road to St. Mihiel.* New York: Comet Press, 1957.

403   Sterne, Elaine, ed. *Over the Seas for Uncle Sam.* New York: Britton, 1918.

404   Stevenson, William Y. *At the Front in a Flivver.* Boston: Houghton Mifflin, 1917.

405   Stone, Ernest. *Battery B: Thru the Fires of France.* Los Angeles: Wayside Press, 1919.

406   Stringfellow, John S. *Hell! No! This and That: A Narrative of the Great War.* Boston: Meador, 1936.

407   Tarbot, Jerry. *Jerry Tarbot: The Living Unknown Soldier.* New York: Tyler, 1928.

408   Therese, Josephine. *With Old Glory in Berlin: The Story of an American in Berlin: The Story of an American Girl's Life and Trials in Germany and Her Escape from the Huns.* Boston: Page, 1918.

409   Thomason, John W., Jr. *Fix Bayonets!* New York: Scribner's, 1926.

410   Thompson, Terry B. *Take Her Down: A Submarine Portrait.* New York: Sheridan House, 1937.

411   Tippett, Edwin J., Jr. *Who Won the War? . . .* Toledo, Ohio: Toledo Typesetting & Printing, 1920.

412   Trounce, Harry D. *Fighting the Boche Underground.* New York: Scribner's, 1918.

413   Trueblood, Edward A. *Observations of an American Soldier during His Service with the A.E.F. in France, in the Flash Ranging Service.* Sacramento, California: News Publishing, 1919.

414   "Two Pike County Hoosiers in World War I." *Indiana Magazine of History* 38 (Sept. 1942): 269–306.

415   Van Dyke, Henry. *Fighting for Peace.* New York: Scribner's, 1917.

416   Vogel, Virgil J., ed. "An Iowa Doughboy's View of World War I." *Annals of Iowa,* 3d ser. 39 (Fall 1968): 424–35.

417   Waldo, Fullerton L. *America at the Front.* New York: Dutton, 1918.

418   Warren, Maude L. *The White Flame of France.* Boston: Small, Maynard, 1918.

419   Watson, Samuel N. *Those Paris Years: With the World at the Crossroads.* New York: Revell, 1936.

420   Werner, Morris R. *"Orderly!"* New York: Cape & Smith, 1930.

421   Wheeler, William J. "Reminiscences of World War Convoy Work." *U.S. Naval Institute Proceedings* 55 (May 1929): 385–92.

422   Wilder, Fred C. *War Experiences of F. C. Wilder.* Belchertown, Massachusetts: F. C. Wilder, 1926.

423   Williams, Ashby. *Experiences of the Great War: Artois, St. Mihiel, Meuse-Argonne.* Roanoke, Virginia: Stone Printing, 1919.

424   Winant, Cornelius. *A Soldier's Manuscript.* Boston: Merrymount, 1929.

425   Wise, Frederic M., and Meigs O. Frost. *A Marine Tells It to You.* New York: Sears, 1929.

426   Wolfe, Samuel H. *In Service.* Washington, D.C. (?), 1922.

427   Wollman, Solomon. *Diary of Solomon Wollman, September 15, 1917 to July 4, 1918.* Hartford, Connecticut: Case, Lockwood & Brainard, [1919(?)].

428   Wood, Eric F. *The Notebook of an Intelligence Officer.* New York: Century, 1917.

429   Zimmerman, Leander M. *Echoes From the Distant Battlefield.* Boston: Badger, 1920.

430   Zody, Harry. *Over Here and Over There.* New York: Abingdon, 1918.

Letters and Diaries

431   Baker, Horace L. *Argonne Days: Experiences of a World War Private on the Meuse-Argonne Front, Compiled From His Diary.* Aberdeen, Mississippi: Printed by the Aberdeen Weekly, 1927.

432   Bellamy, David. "A Marine at the Front." *American History Illustrated* 5 (Feb. 1917): 30–42.

433   Campbell, Peyton R. *The Diary-Letters of Sergeant Peyton Randolph Campbell.* Buffalo: Pratt & Lambert, 1919.

434   Churchill, Mary. *You Who Can Help: Paris Letters of an American Army Officer's Wife, August 1916–January 1918.* Boston: Small, Maynard, 1918.

435   Clark, Coleman T., and Salter S. Clark, Jr., [eds.] *Soldier Letters.* New York: Middleditch, 1919.

436   Cowing, Kemper F., comp. *"Dear Folks at Home . . .": The Glorious Story of the United States Marines in France as Told by Their Letters from the Battlefield.* Boston: Houghton Mifflin, 1919.

437   Crosley, Harry G. *War Letters.* Paris: Black Sun Press, 1932.

438   Crowe, James R. *Pat Crowe Aviator. . . .* Edited by W. B. Chase. New York: N. L. Brown, 1919.

439   Davis, Arthur K., ed. *Virginia War Letters, Diaries and Editorials.* Richmond: Virginia War History Commission, 1925.

440   Dearing, Vinton A. *My Galahad of the Trenches: Being a Collection of Intimate Letters of Lieutenant Vinton A. Dearing.* New York: Revell, 1918.

441   Edwards, Frederick T. *Fort Sheridan to Montfaucon: The War Letters of Frederick Trevenen Edwards. . . .* De Land (?), Florida, 1954.

442   Elliott, Paul B., ed. *On The Field of Honor: A Collection of War Letters and Reminiscences of Three Harvard Undergraduates Who Gave Their Lives in the Great Cause.* Boston: Merrymount, 1920.

443   Ely, Dinsmore. *Dinsmore Ely: One Who Served.* Chicago: McClurg, 1919. [Diary edited by Dr. James O. Ely.]

444   Evans, Frank E. *Daddy Pat of the Marines: Being His Letters from France to His Son Townie.* New York: Stokes, 1919.

445   Ford, Torrey. *Cheer-up Letters: From a Private with Pershing.* New York: E. J. Clode, 1918.

446   Gow, Kenneth. *Letters of a Soldier.* New York: Covert, 1920.

447   Greene, Warwick. *Letters of Warwick Greene, 1915–1928.* Edited by Richard W. Hale. Reprint. Freeport, New York: Books for Libraries Press, 1971.

448   [Grider, John M.] *War Birds: The Diary of an Unknown Aviator.* Edited by Elliott White Springs. New York: Doran, 1926.

449   Gulberg, Martin G. *A War Diary.* Chicago: Drake Press, 1927.

450   [Guttersen, Granville.] *Granville: Tales and Tail Spins from a Flyer's Diary.* New York: Abingdon, 1919.

451   Harbord, James G. *Leaves from a War Diary.* New York: Dodd, Mead, 1925.

452   [Hoffman, Harry A.] "War Diary of Harry A. Hoffman, 1918–1919." *Rhode Island Jewish History Notes* 6 (Nov. 1973): 327–59.

453   Jelke, Ferdinand F. *Letters from a Liaison Officer.* Chicago: Press of G. F. McKiernan, 1919.

454   Judy, William L. *A Soldier's Diary: A Day-to-Day Record in the World War.* Chicago: Judy Publishing, 1931.

455   Kautz, John I. *Trucking to the Trenches: Letters from France, June–November 1917.* Boston: Houghton Mifflin, 1918.

456   Kimmel, Martin L. "To Be a Soldier: 1917 Diary." *Oregon Historical Quarterly* 75 (Sept. 1974): 241–69.

457   [Lahm, Frank P.] *The World War I Diary of Colonel Frank P. Lahm, Air Service, A.E.F.* Edited by Albert F. Simpson. Maxwell Air Force Base, Alabama: Air University, 1970.

458   Leach, William J. *Poems and War Letters.* Peoria, Illinois: Manual Arts Press, 1922.

459 Lee, Benjamin. *A Record Gathered from Letters, Note-books, and Narratives of Friends, by His Mother Mary Justice Chase.* Boston: Cornhill, 1920.

460 Lindner, Clarence R. *Private Lindner's Letters: Censored and Uncensored.* San Francisco, 1939.

461 MacLeish, Kenneth. *Kenneth: A Collection of Letters.* . . . Chicago, 1919.

462 Mann, Floris P. *History of Telfair County from 1812–1949.* Macon, Georgia: J. W. Burke, 1949. ["Letters from 'Over There': World War I," by Telfair County (Georgia) men in Europe, pp. 163–204.]

463 Millard, Shirley. *I Saw them Die: Diary and Recollections of Shirley Millard.* Edited by Adele Comandini. New York: Harcourt, Brace, 1936.

464 Mills, Quincy Sharpe. *One Who Gave His Life: War Letters of Quincy Sharpe Mills.* New York: Putnam's, 1923.

465 Minder, Charles F. *This Man's War: The Day-by-Day Record of an American Private on the Western Front.* New York: Pevensey, 1931.

466 Moseley, George C. *Extracts from the Letters of George Clark Moseley during the Period of the Great War.* Chicago, 1923.

467 O'Brian, Alice Lord. *No Glory: Letters from France, 1917–1919.* Buffalo: Printed by Airport Publishers, 1936.

468 [O'Brien, Howard V.] *Wine, Women and War: A Diary of Disillusionment.* New York: Sears, 1926.

469 *Oregon Boys in the War.* Edited by Mrs. Frank Wilmot. Portland, Oregon: Glass & Prudhomme, 1918.

470 Poague, Walter S. *Diary and Letters of a Marine Aviator.* Chicago (?), 1919 (?).

471 Rendinell, Joseph E., and George Pattullo. *One Man's War: The Diary of a Leatherneck.* New York: Sears, 1928.

472 Richards, John F. *War Diaries and Letters of John Francisco Richards II, 1917–1918.* Compiled . . . by George B. Richards. Kansas City, Missouri: Lechtman Printing Co., 1925.

473 Roosevelt, Quentin. *Quentin Roosevelt: A Sketch with Letters.* Edited by Kermit Roosevelt. New York: Scribner's, 1921.

474 "Sergeant Jones Goes to War: Extracts from a U.S. Artilleryman's Diary, 1918." *Army Quarterly* 23 (Oct. 1973): 61–71. [Theodore K. Jones.]

475 Shainwald, Richard H. *Letters and Notes from France, June 30, 1917–November 6, 1918.* San Francisco: Abbott, 1919.

476 "Somewhere in France: Letters of a Wisconsin Boy in the A.E.F., 1918." Edited by Paul A. Hass. *Wisconsin Magazine of History* 49 (Autumn 1965): 29–40.

477 Walcott, Stuart. *Above the French Lines: Letters of Stuart Walcott, American Aviator: July 4, 1917 to December 8, 1917.* Princeton: Princeton University Press, 1918.

478 Wheeler, Curtis. *Letters from an American Soldier to His Father.* Indianapolis: Bobbs-Merrill, 1918.

479 Wilson, Ellis E. "A Duffle Bag Diary of an American Red Cross Worker in France." *Annals of Iowa,* 3d ser. 22 (July 1939): 64–76; (Oct. 1939): 128–70; (Jan. 1940): 201–47.

480 Wright, Jack M. *A Poet of the Air: Letters of Jack Morris Wright . . . April 1917–January 1918.* Boston: Houghton Mifflin, 1918.

481 York, Alvin C. *Sergeant York: His Own Life Story and War Diary.* Edited by Thomas Skeyhill. Garden City, New York: Doubleday, Doran, 1928.

H/Land Operations (Army and Marine Corps)

General

482 Broun, Heywood. *The A.E.F.: With General Pershing and the American Forces.* New York: Appleton, 1918.

483 ———. *Our Army at the Front.* New York: Scribner's, 1922.

484 Buell, Charles T. *The Great War and the Americans on the Field of Battle. . . .* Newark, Ohio: C. T. Buell, 1924.

485 Bullard, Robert L., and Earl Reeves. *American Soldiers Also Fought.* New York: Longmans, Green, 1936.

486 De Castlebled, Maurice. *History of the A.E.F. . . .* New York: Bookcraft, 1937.

487 Greene, Francis V. *Our First Year in the Great War.* New York: Putnam's 1918.

488 Harbord, James G. *America in the World War.* Boston: Houghton Mifflin, 1933.

489 ———. *The American Army in France, 1917–1919.* Boston: Little, Brown, 1936.

490 ———. *The American Expeditionary Forces: Its Organization and Accomplishments.* Evanston, Illinois: Evanston Publishing Co., 1929.

491 Hoehling, Adloph A. *The Fierce Lambs.* Boston: Little, Brown, 1960.

492 [McClellan, Edwin N.] *The United States Marine Corps in the World War.* Washington, D.C.: G.P.O., 1920.

493 McCormick, Robert R. *The Army of 1918.* New York: Harcourt, Brace & Howe, 1920.

494 Michael, W. H. "Pleasure and Pain of 1918." *U.S. Naval Institute Proceedings* 60 (Dec. 1934): 1705– 12.

495 Mudd, Thomas B. R. *The Yanks Were There: A Chronological and Documentary Review of World War I.* New York: Vantage, 1958.

496 *The Official Record of the United States' Part in the Great War . . . Prepared Under the Instructions of the Secretary of War. . . .* N.p., 1923 (?).

497 Page, Arthur W. *Our 110 Days Fighting.* Garden City, New York: Doubleday, 1920.

498 Palmer, Frederick. *America in France.* New York: Dodd, Mead, 1918.

499 [Pershing, John J.] *Final Report of General John J. Pershing: Commander-in-Chief, American Expeditionary Forces.* Washington, D.C.: G.P.O., 1919.

500 Pitt, Barrie. *1918: The Last Act.* New York: Norton, 1962.

501 Shulimson, Jack. "The First to Fight: Marine Corps Expansion, 1914– 1918." *Prologue* 8 (Spring 1976): 5– 16.

502 Skillman, Willis R. *The A.E.F.: Who They Were, What They Did, How They Did It.* Philadelphia: Jacobs, 1920.

503 Stallings, Laurence. *The Doughboys: The Story of the A.E.F., 1917– 1918.* New York: Harper & Row, 1963.

504 ———. "The War to End War." *American Heritage* 10 (Oct. 1959): 4– 17, 84– 85.

505 Thomas, Shipley. *The History of the A.E.F.* New York: Doran, 1920.

506 Thomason, John W., Jr. "The Marine Brigade." *U.S. Naval Institute Proceedings* 54 (Nov. 1928): 963– 68.

507 U.S. Department of the Army. Office of Military History. *The United States Army in the World War: 1917– 1919.* 17 vols. Washington, D.C.: G.P.O., 1948– .

508 Van Every, Dale. *The A.E.F. in Battle.* New York: Appleton, 1928.

509 Waldo, Fullerton L. *America at the Front.* New York: Dutton, 1918.

510 Willoughby, Charles A. *The Economic and Military Participation of the United States in the World War.* Fort Leavenworth, Kansas: Command and General Staff School Press, 1931.

Specific Accounts

511 Asprey, Robert B. *At Belleau Wood.* New York: Putnam's, 1965.

512 Babcock, Conrad S. "The Australian-American Tank Action at Hamel, July 4, 1918." *Infantry Journal* 20 (Apr. 1922): 394–400.

513 Barnett, B. J. "Valley of the One-Legged Heinie." *Leatherneck* 26 (Apr. 1943): 22–24, 45–57. [Recollections of Belleau Wood.]

514 Brewster, D. L. S. "An Analysis of the Crossing of the Meuse River." *Marine Corps Gazette* 25 (Mar. 1941): 22–23, 51–52.

515 Catlin, Albertus W., and Walter A. Dyer. *"With the Help of God and a Few Marines."* Garden City, New York: Doubleday, 1919. [Château-Thierry and Belleau Wood.]

516 Colby, Elbridge. "The Taking of Montfaucon." *Infantry Journal* 47 (Mar.– Apr. 1940): 128–40.

517 Evarts, Jeremiah M. *Cantigny: A Corner of the War.* New York: Scribner's, 1938.

518 Farrell, Thomas F. "Memories of the Battle of Soissons." *Military Engineer* 15 (July 1923): 327–33.

519 Fleming, Thomas J. "Two Argonnes." *American Heritage* 19 (Oct. 1968): 44–48, 88–94.

520 Gibbons, Floyd P. *And They Thought We Wouldn't Fight.* New York: Doran, 1918. [Especially Belleau Wood.]

521 Harbord, James G. "A Month in Belleau Wood in 1918." *Leatherneck* 11 (June 1928): 10–12, 54.

522 Hopkins, Johns. "A Point of View in the Thirteenth Infantry." *Field Artillery Journal* 13 (Sept. 1923): 383–89. [2d battle of the Marne.]

523 Johnson, Robert L. ". . . and Belleau Wood." *Marine Corps Gazette* 39 (June 1955): 18–23.

524 Johnson, Thomas M. *Without Censor: New Light on our Greatest World War Battles.* Indianapolis: Bobbs-Merrill, 1928. [St. Mihiel and Meuse-Argonne.]

525 Johnston, E. S. "The Day Before Cantigny." *Coast Artillery Journal* 79 (Sept.– Oct. 1936): 347–57.

526   Kaufman, Thomas. "General Harbord and the Marines." *Marine Corps Gazette* 57 (June 1973): 53– 54. [Belleau Wood.]

527   Krulewitch, M. L. "Belleau Wood." *Marine Corps Gazette* 55 (Nov. 1971): 18– 22.

528   McClellan, Edwin N. "The Aisne-Marne Offensive." *Marine Corps Gazette* 6 (Mar. 1921): 66– 84; (June 1921): 188– 227.

529   ———. "The Battle of Mont Blanc Ridge." *Marine Corps Gazette* 7 (Mar. 1922): 1– 21; (June 1922): 206– 11; (Sept. 1922): 287– 88.

530   ———. "Capture of Hill 142, Battle of Belleau Wood, and Capture of Bouresches." *Marine Corps Gazette* 5 (Sept.– Dec. 1920): 277– 313, 371– 405.

531   ———. "Operations of the Fourth Brigade of Marines in the Aisne Defensive." *Marine Corps Gazette* 5 (June 1920): 182– 214.

532   McLaughlin, Patrick D. "Doughboy Diplomats— The U.S. Army in Italy, 1917– 1919." *Army* 21 (Jan. 1971): 30– 37.

533   MacVeagh, Ewen C., and Lee D. Brown. *The Yankee in the British Zone*. New York: Putnam's, 1920.

534   Maddox, Robert J. "The Meuse-Argonne Offensive." *American History Illustrated* 10 (June 1975): 22– 35.

535   Mowry, William J. "The Greatest Day." *Marine Corps Gazette* 47 (July 1963): 32– 36. [Before Belleau Wood.]

536   Palmer, Frederick. *Our Greatest Battle*. New York: Dodd, Mead, 1919. [Meuse-Argonne.]

537   Pugh, Irving E., and William F. Thayer. *Forgotten Fights of the A.E.F.* Boston: Roxburgh Publishing Co., 1921.

538   Rarey, G. H. "American Light Tank Brigade at St. Mihiel." *Infantry Journal* 32 (Mar. 1928): 279– 87.

539   ———. "American Tank Units in the Forêt d'Argonne Attack." *Infantry Journal* 32 (Apr. 1928): 389– 95.

540   Shaw, Oliver. "The Battle of St. Mihiel, September 12– 14, 1918." *Field Artillery Journal* 15 (Sept. 1925): 448– 56.

541   Sherrill, Stephen H. "The Experiences of the First American Troop of Cavalry to Get into Action in the World War." *Cavalry Journal* 32 (Apr. 1923): 153– 59.

542   Silverthorn, M. H. "A Brigade of Marines." *Marine Corps Gazette* 55 (Nov. 1971): 23– 26. [Belleau Wood.]

543   Smythe, Donald. "A.E.F. Snafu at Sedan." *Prologue* 5 (Fall 1973): 134–49.

544   Stallings, Laurence. "Bloody Belleau Wood." *American Heritage* 14 (June 1963): 65–80.

545   Suskind, Richard. *The Battle of Belleau Wood: The Marines Stand Fast.* New York: Macmillan, 1969.

546   ———. *Do You Want to Live Forever!* New York: Bantam, 1964. [Belleau Wood.]

547   Switzer, J. S., Jr. "The Champagne-Marne Offensive." *Infantry Journal* 19 (Dec. 1921): 653–58.

548   Terraine, John. "The March Offensive, 1918." *History Today* 18 (Mar. 1968): 147–55; (Apr. 1968): 234–43.

549   U.S. Infantry School. Fort Benning, Georgia. *Infantry in Battle.* Washington, D.C.: Infantry Journal, 1939. [Small Unit Actions.]

550   U.S. War Department. *Battle Participation of Organizations of the American Expeditionary Forces in France, Belgium and Italy.* Washington, D.C.: G.P.O., 1920.

551   Weinert, Richard P. "The Second Battle of the Marne." *American History Illustrated* 1 (May 1966): 4–11, 54–58.

552   Wise, Jennings C. *The Turn of the Tide: American Operations at Cantigny, Château-Thierry and the Second Battle of the Marne.* New York: Holt, 1920.

I/Naval Operations

General

553   Abbot, Willis J. *Blue Jackets of 1918: Being the Story of the Work of the American Navy in the World War.* New York: Dodd, Mead, 1921.

554   Daniels, Josephus. "The United States Navy in the World War." *North Carolina Historical Review* 4 (Jan. 1927): 115–26.

555   Frothingham, Thomas G. *The Naval History of the World War.* 3 vols. Cambridge: Harvard University Press, 1924–1926.

556   Hoehling, Adolph A. *The Great War at Sea: A History of Naval Action, 1914–1918.* New York: Thomas Y. Crowell, 1965.

557   Jenkins, John W. *Our Navy's Part in the Great War.* New York: Eggers, 1919.

558 Leighton, John L. *Simsadus: London; The American Navy in Europe.* New York: Holt, 1920.

559 Murdock, Lawrence B. *They Also Served.* New York: Carlton Press, 1967.

560 Perry, Lawrence. *Our Navy in the War.* New York: Scribner's, 1918.

561 ———. "They're in the Navy Now: Yachting Has Gone to War in Earnest." *Country Life* 32 (July 1917): 19–32.

562 Roosevelt, Franklin D. "War Activities of the United States Navy." *Current History* 8 (Apr. 1918): 19–21.

563 Sims, William S., and Burton J. Hendrick. *The Victory at Sea.* Garden City, New York: Doubleday, Page, 1920.

Specific Accounts

564 Alden, Carroll S. "American Submarine Operations in the War." *U.S. Naval Institute Proceedings* 46 (June 1920): 811–50; (July 1920): 1013–48.

565 Alden, John D. *Flush Decks and Four Pipes.* Annapolis: U.S. Naval Institute, 1965.

566 ———. "The Yacht that Was a Destroyer." *U.S. Naval Institute Proceedings* 93 (Dec. 1967): 156–59.

567 Bane, Suda L., and Ralph H. Lutz, eds. *The Blockade of Germany after the Armistice, 1918–1919.* Stanford: Stanford University Press, 1922.

568 Bartimeus [pseud.] (Ricci, Lewis A. da C.) "Admiral Sims and His Fleet." *Living Age* 297 (June 8, 1918): 577–83.

569 Battey, George M., Jr. *70,000 Miles on a Submarine Destroyer: Or the Reid Boat in the World War.* Atlanta: Webb & Vary, 1919.

570 Belknap, Reginald R. *The Yankee Mining Squadron or Laying the North Sea Barrage.* Annapolis: U.S. Naval Institute, 1920.

571 Breckel, H. F. "The Suicide Flotilla." *U.S. Naval Institute Proceedings* 47 (June 1921): 661–70.

572 Buranelli, Prosper. *Maggie of the Suicide Fleet: As Written from the Log of Raymond D. Borden, Lieutenant USNR.* New York: Doubleday, Doran, 1930.

573 Carney, Robert B. "The Capture of the U-58." *U.S. Naval Institute Proceedings* 60 (Oct. 1934): 1401–04.

574 Chatterton, Edward K. *Danger Zone: The Story of the Queenstown Command.* Boston: Little, Brown, 1934.

575 Connolly, James B. *The U-Boat Hunters.* New York: Scribner's, 1918.

576 Cope, Harley F. "U.S. Submarines in the War Zone." *U.S. Naval Institute Proceedings* 56 (Aug. 1930): 711– 16.

577 Cowie, J. S. *Mines, Minelayers, and Minelaying.* New York: Oxford University Press, 1949.

578 French, William F. "Fishing for German Mines." *Illustrated World* 30 (Sept. 1918): 33– 38.

579 Guichard, Louis. *The Naval Blockade, 1914– 1918.* New York: Appleton, 1930.

580 Husband, Joseph. *On the Coast of France: The Story of the United States Naval Forces in French Waters.* Chicago: McClurg, 1919.

581 Jackson, Orton P., and Frank E. Evans. "Our Undersea Fighters." *St. Nicholas Magazine* 44 (May 1917): 628– 32.

582 Kauffman, Reginald W. *Our Navy at Work: The Yankee Fleet in French Waters.* Indianapolis: Bobbs-Merrill, 1918.

583 McClary, Eula. "Somewhere on the Atlantic." *Good Housekeeping* 66 (Jan. 1918): 45– 46, 109– 11. [The work of American destroyers explained for the housekeeper.]

584 Millholland, Ray. *The Splinter Fleet of the Otranto Barrage.* Indianapolis: Bobbs-Merrill, 1936.

585 Paine, Ralph D. *The Corsair in the War Zone.* Boston: Houghton Mifflin, 1920.

586 ——. *The Fighting Fleets: Five Months of Active Service with the American Destroyers and Their Allies in the War Zone.* Boston: Houghton Mifflin, 1918.

587 ——. *Ships across the Sea: Stories of the American Navy in the Great War.* Boston: Houghton Mifflin, 1920.

588 Raquet, Edward C. "United States Submarine Chasers at Gibralter, November 1918." *U.S. Naval Institute Proceedings* 62 (Dec. 1936): 1703– 11.

589 Rodman, Henry. "Deeds of the American Battle Squadron." *Current History* 9 (Feb. 1919): 254– 57.

590   Rose, Harold W. *Brittany Patrol: The Story of the Suicide Fleet.* New York: Norton, 1937.

591   Rucher, Colby G. "The Loss of the *Ticonderoga.*" *U.S. Naval Institute Proceedings* 65 (Feb. 1939): 185–90.

592   [Sheahan, Henry B.] *Full Speed Ahead: Tales from the Log of a Correspondent with Our Navy,* by Henry B. Beston, pseud. Garden City, New York: Doubleday, Page, 1919.

593   Shepherd, W. G. "Chasing the Periscope." *Everybody's* 39 (Oct. 1918): 26–32.

594   Sims, William S. "How We Nearly Lost the War." *World's Work* 53 (Mar. 1927): 474–85.

595   "Surrender of the German High Seas Fleet." *Current History* 9 (Dec. 1918): 382–84; (Jan. 1919): 30–33.

596   Taussig, Joseph K. "Destroyer Experiences during the Great War." *U.S. Naval Institute Proceedings* 48 (Dec. 1922): 2015–40; 49 (Jan.–Mar. 1923): 39–69, 221–48, 383–408.

597   U.S. Congress. Senate. Committee on Naval Affairs. Hearings before a Subcommittee . . . : *Naval Investigation,* 2 vols. 66th Cong., 2d Sess., 1921.

598   U.S. Office of Naval Records and Library. *The Northern Barrage and Other Mining Activities.* Washington, D.C.: G.P.O., 1920.

599   ———. *The United States Naval Railway Batteries in France.* Washington, D.C.: G.P.O., 1922.

600   Whitaker, Herman. *Hunting the German Shark: The American Navy in the Undersea War.* New York: Century, 1918.

601   ———. "Our Toy Dreadnoughts." *Century* 96 (Oct. 1918): 797–804.

602   ———. "Sims' Circus: A Cruise with Our Destroyers Over There." *Independent* 94 (June 8, 1918): 358–59, 404–05.

603   Wilson, Henry B. *An Account of the Operations of the American Navy in France during the War with Germany.* N.p., 1919 (?).

J/Air Operations

General

604   Brown, Charles R. "The Development of Fleet Aviation during the World War." *U.S. Naval Institute Proceedings* 64 (Sept. 1938): 1297–303.

605 Felice, C. P., comp. "Air Operations in World War I." In "The Men and the Machines: A Chronological Treatise on the Growth of Air Power." *Air Power Historian* 5 (Jan. 1958): 37–53.

606 ——. "World War I—Early Phases." In "The Men and the Machines: A Chronological Treatise on the Growth of Air Power." *Air Power Historian* 4 (Oct. 1957): 192–206.

607 Goldberg, A., ed. "A History of the United States Air Force—1907–1957." *Air Force* 40 (Aug. 1957): 75–419.

608 Gorrell, Edgar S. *The Measure of America's World War Aeronautical Effort.* Northfield, Vermont: Norwich University, 1940.

609 Hudson, James J. *Hostile Skies: A Combat History of the American Air Service in World War I.* Syracuse: Syracuse University Press, 1968.

610 Mitchell, William. "The Air Service at the Argonne-Meuse." *World's Work* 38 (Sept. 1919): 552–60.

611 ——. "The Air Service at St. Mihiel." *World's Work* 38 (Aug. 1919): 360–70.

612 Norman, Aaron. *The Great Air War.* New York: Macmillan, 1968.

613 Patrick, Mason M. *The United States in the Air.* Garden City, New York: Doubleday, Doran, 1928.

614 Reynolds, Quentin J. *They Fought for the Sky: The Dramatic Story of the First War in the Air.* New York: Holt, Rinehart & Winston, 1957.

615 Sweetser, Arthur. *The American Air Service.* New York: Appleton, 1919.

616 Tips, Walter. "Air War: August–September 1918." *Military History of Texas and the Southwest* 12:2 (1975): 119–23.

617 Toulmin, Harry A., Jr. *Air Service, American Expeditionary Forces, 1918.* New York: Van Nostrand, 1927.

618 Turnbull, Archibald D., and Clifford L. Lord. *History of United States Naval Aviation:* New Haven: Yale University Press, 1949.

619 U.S. Army. A.E.F. Air Service. *Final Report of the Chief of Air Service, A.E.F. to the Commander in Chief, American Expeditionary Forces.* Washington, D.C.: G.P.O. 1921.

620 Van Wyen, Adrian O. *Naval Aviation in World War I.* Washington, D.C.: G.P.O., 1969.

Specific Accounts

621 Briand, Paul L., Jr. "A Fateful Tuesday, 1918: The Last Combat Flight of James Norman Hall." *Airpower Historian* 11 (Apr. 1964): 34– 38.

622 Edwards, Walter A. "The United States Naval Air Force in Action, 1917– 1918." *U.S. Naval Institute Proceedings* 48 (Nov. 1922): 1863– 82.

623 Frank, Sam H. "American Air Service Observation in World War I." Ph.D. dissertation, University of Florida, 1961.

624 Frey, Royal D. "A.E.F. Combat Airfields and Monuments in France." *American Aviation Historical Society Journal* 17 (Fall 1972): 194– 200.

625 ———. "Setting the Record Straight: The First of Many American Air-to-Air Victories." *Aerospace Historian* 21 (Fall 1974): 156– 59.

626 Gorrell, Edgar S. "An American Proposal for Strategic Bombing in World War I." *Air Power Historian* 5 (Apr. 1958): 102– 17.

627 Grant, Robert M. "Aircraft Against U-Boats." *U.S. Naval Institute Proceedings* 65 (June 1939): 824– 28.

628 Grey, Charles G. *The History of Combat Airplanes.* Northfield, Vermont: Norwich University, 1942.

629 Gurney, Gene. *Five Down and Glory: A History of the American Air Ace.* New York: Putnam's, 1958.

630 Hopper, Bruce C. "American Day Bombardment in World War I." *Air Power Historian* 4 (Apr. 1957): 87– 97.

631 Maurer, Maurer. "Another Victory for Rickenbacker." *Airpower Historian* 7 (Apr. 1960): 117– 24.

632 ———. "Flying with Fiorello: The U.S. Air Service in Italy, 1917– 1918." *Airpower Historian* 11 (Oct. 1964): 113– 18.

633 Melville, Phillips. "Piloti Americani in Italia— The U.S. Air Service in Italy, World War One." *American Aviation Historical Society Journal* 18 (Winter 1973): 229– 44; 19 (Spring 1974): 58– 62.

634 Naval Aviation War Book Committee. *Flying Officers of the U.S.N.* Washington, D.C.: Naval Aviation War Book Committee, 1919.

635 Paine, Ralph D. *The First Yale Unit: A Story of Naval Aviation, 1916– 1919.* 2 vols. Cambridge, Massachusetts: Riverside Press, 1925.

636 Rickenbacker, Edward V. "Baling Wire and Fabric Crates." *Airman* 1 (Aug. 1957): 8– 11.

637 Whitaker, Herman. "Eyes of the Destroyers." *Sunset* 41 (July 1918): 34– 36.

638 Whitehouse, Arch. "The Years of the Yammering Guns." *Aerospace Historian* 15 (Summer 1968): 12– 15.

K/Enemy Operations

Land

639 U.S. Army. A.E.F. *A Survey of German Tactics, 1918.* N.p.: Printed at the base printing plant, 29th Engineers, 1918.

640 U.S. General Staff. *Histories of Two Hundred and Fifty-One Divisions of the German Army Which Participated in the War (1914– 1918). . . .* Washington, D.C.: G.P.O., 1920.

Naval

641 Clark, William B. *When the U-Boats Came to America.* Boston: Little, Brown, 1929.

642 Gray, Edwyn A. *The Killing Time: The U-Boat War, 1914– 1918.* New York: Scribner's, 1972.

643 Herwig, Holger H., and David F. Trask. "The Failure of Imperial Germany's Undersea Offensive against World Shipping, February 1917– October 1918." *Historian* 33 (Aug. 1971): 611– 36.

644 James, Henry J. *German Submarines in Yankee Waters: First World War.* New York: Gotham House, 1940.

645 Merrill, James M. "Submarine Scare, 1918." *Military Affairs* 17 (Winter 1953): 181– 90.

646 Thomas, Lowell. *Raiders of the Deep.* Garden City, New York: Doubleday, Doran, 1928.

647 U.S. Office of Naval Records and Library. *German Submarine Activities on the Atlantic Coast of the United States and Canada.* Washington, D.C.: G.P.O., 1920.

L/Strategy, Command, and Administration

United States

648 *Appreciations of Frederick Paul Keppel by Some of His Friends.* New York: Columbia University Press, 1951.

649 Coffman, Edward M. "The American Military Generation Gap in World War I: The Leavenworth Clique in the A.E.F." In *Command and*

Commanders in Modern Warfare, edited by William Geffen. Colorado Springs: U.S. Air Force Academy, 1964.

650 ———. "The Battle against Red Tape: Business Methods of the War Department General Staff, 1917– 1918." *Military Affairs* 26 (Spring 1962): 1– 10.

651 ———. "Conflicts in American Planning: An Aspect of World War I Strategy." *Military Review* 43 (June 1963): 78– 90.

652 Edwards, H. W. "Harbord and Lejeune: A Command Precedent." *Marine Corps Gazette* 37 (July 1953): 12– 15.

653 Hammond, Paul Y. *Organizing for Defense: The American Military Establishment in the Twentieth Century.* Princeton: Princeton University Press, 1961.

654 Holley, I. B., Jr. "On History and Staff Work." *Air University Review* 21 (Jan.– Feb. 1970): 101– 08.

655 Lowry, Bullitt. "Pershing and the Armistice." *Journal of American History* 55 (Sept. 1968): 281– 91.

656 May, Ernest R. "The Development of Political-Military Consultation in the United States." *Political Science Quarterly* 70 (June 1955): 161– 80.

657 Nelson, Otto L. *National Security and the General Staff.* Washington, D.C.: Infantry Journal, 1946.

658 Pohl, James W. "The General Staff and American Defense Policy: The Formative Period, 1898– 1917." Ph.D. dissertation, University of Texas, 1967.

659 "Should the Army and Navy Be Muzzled? The Controversy between Admiral Sims and Secretary Daniels." *Outlook* 124 (Feb. 4, 1920): 187– 88.

660 Soule, George. "The Brain of the Army." *New Republic* 13 (Dec. 22, 1917): 203– 05.

661 Spector, Ronald. " 'You're Not Going to Send Soldiers Over There Are You!': The American Search for an Alternative to the Western Front, 1916– 1917." *Military Affairs* 36 (Feb. 1972): 1– 4.

662 U.S. Army. A.E.F. General Staff College. *Note Book for the General Staff Officer.* Paris: Imprimerie de Vaugirard, 1918.

663 U.S. Office of Naval Records and Library. *The American Naval Planning Section, London.* Washington, D.C.: G.P.O., 1923.

664 Williams, H. "The Naval Controversy between the Line and the Staff Corps." *North American Review* 208 (Nov. 1918): 736– 44.

Joint United States-Allies

665 Allard, Dean C. "Admiral William S. Sims and United States Naval Policy in World War I." *American Neptune* 35 (Apr. 1975): 97–110.

666 Blackburn, Forrest R. "The A.E.F. under Foreign Flags." *Military Review* 48 (May 1968): 56–65.

667 Churchill, Winston L. S. "Naval Organization: American and British." *Atlantic Monthly* 120 (Aug. 1917): 277–84.

668 Frothingham, Thomas G. "The Strategy of the World War and the Lessons of the Effort of the United States." *U.S. Naval Institute Proceedings* 47 (May 1921): 669–83.

669 Hankey, Sir Maurice P. A. *The Supreme Command: 1914–1918.* 2 vols. London: Allen & Unwin, 1961.

670 Hunter, Francis T. *Beatty, Jellicoe, Sims and Rodman: Yankee Gobs and British Tars, as Seen by an "Anglomaniac."* Garden City, New York: Doubleday, Page, 1919.

671 Klachko, Mary. "Anglo-American Naval Competition, 1918–1922." Ph.D. dissertation, Columbia University, 1962.

672 Lonergan, Thomas C. *It Might Have Been Lost!* New York: Putnam's, 1929.

673 Lyddon, William G. *British War Missions to the United States, 1914–1918.* New York: Oxford University Press, 1938.

674 Maurice, Sir Frederick. *Lessons of Allied Co-operation: Naval, Military, and Air, 1914–1918.* London: Oxford University Press, 1942.

675 Norton, Nile B. "The Multi-lateral Forces Experiment in World War I." *Rocky Mountain Social Science Journal* 2 (Oct. 1965): 77–84.

676 Sargent, Herbert H. *The Strategy on the Western Front (1914–1918).* Chicago: McClurg, 1920.

677 Shumate, Thomas D., Jr. "The Allied Supreme War Council, 1917–1918." Ph.D. dissertation, University of Virginia, 1952.

678 Trask, David F. *Captains and Cabinets: Anglo-American Naval Relations, 1917–1918.* Columbia: University of Missouri Press, 1972.

679 ——. *General Tasker Howard Bliss and the "Sessions of the World,"* 1919. Philadelphia: American Philosophical Society, 1966.

680 ——. *The United States in the Supreme War Council: American War Aims and Inter-Allied Strategy, 1917–1918.* Middletown, Connecticut: Wesleyan University Press, 1961.

M/Siberian Expedition

General

681 Bradley, John. *Allied Intervention in Russia.* New York: Basic Books, 1968.

682 Fike, Claude E. "The Influence of the Creel Committee and the American Red Cross on Russian-American Relations, 1917– 1919." *Journal of Modern History* 31 (June 1959): 93– 109.

683 ——. "The United States and Russian Territorial Problems, 1917– 1920." *Historian* 24 (May 1962): 331– 46.

684 Filene, Peter G. *Americans and the Soviet Experiment, 1917–1933.* Cambridge: Harvard University Press, 1967.

685 Guins, George C. "The Siberian Intervention, 1918– 1919." *Russian Review* 28 (Oct. 1969): 428– 40.

686 Kennan, George F. *Russia and the West under Lenin and Stalin.* Boston: Little, Brown, 1961.

687 ——. *Soviet-American Relations, 1917– 1920.* Vol. 1: *Russia Leaves the War.* Princeton: Princeton University Press, 1956.

688 ——. *Soviet-American Relations, 1917– 1920.* Vol. 2: *The Decision to Intervene.* Princeton: Princeton University Press, 1958.

689 Lasch, Christopher. "American Intervention in Siberia: A Reinterpretation." *Political Science Quarterly* 77 (June 1962): 205– 23.

690 ——. *The American Liberals and the Russian Revolution.* New York: Columbia University Press, 1962.

691 Maddox, Robert J. "Woodrow Wilson, the Russian Embassy, and Siberian Intervention." *Pacific Historical Review* 36 (Nov. 1967): 435– 48.

692 Poteat, George. "Analysis of the Role of David R. Francis in American-Russian Relations (May 1917– March 1918)." *New Scholar* 1 (Fall 1969): 200– 236.

693 Seal, Enoch, Jr. "Attitude of the United States toward the Russian Provisional Government, March 15 to November 7, 1917." *Southern Quarterly* 4 (Oct. 1965– 1966): 331– 47.

694 Trani, Eugene P. "Woodrow Wilson and the Decision to Intervene in Russia: A Reconsideration." *Journal of Modern History* 48 (Sept. 1976): 440– 61.

695 Unterberger, Betty M. "The Russian Revolution and Wilson's Far Eastern Policy." *Russian Review* 16 (Apr. 1957): 35– 46.

696 Worth, Robert D. *The Allies and the Russian Revolution: From the Fall of the Monarchy to the Peace of Brest Litovsk.* Durham: Duke University Press, 1954.

U.S. Military Operations

697 Ackerman, Carl W. *Trailing the Bolsheviki.* New York: Scribner's, 1919.

698 Dupuy, Richard E. *Perish by the Sword: The Czechoslovakian Anabasis and Our Supporting Campaigns in North Russia and Siberia, 1918–1920.* Harrisburg, Pennsylvania: Military Service Publishing, 1939.

699 Graves, William S. *America's Siberian Adventure, 1918–1920.* New York: Cape & Smith, 1931.

700 Halliday, Ernest M. *The Ignorant Armies.* New York: Harper, 1960.

701 Kindall, Sylvian G. *American Soldiers in Siberia.* New York: R. R. Smith, 1945.

702 McClellan, Edwin N. "American Marines in Siberia during the World War." *Marine Corps Gazette* 5 (June 1920): 173–81.

702a Maddox, Robert J. *The Unknown War with Russia: Wilson's Siberian Intervention.* San Rafael, California: Presidio Press, 1977.

703 Moore, Joel R.; Harry H. Mead; and Lewis E. Jahns; eds. *The History of the American Expedition Fighting the Bolsheviki: Campaigning in North Russia 1918–1919.* Detroit: Polar Bear Publishing, 1920.

704 Shapiro, Sumner. "Intervention in Russia (1918–1919)." *U.S. Naval Institute Proceedings* 99 (Apr. 1973): 52–61.

705 Stevenson, Charles S. "The Below-Zero Campaigns." *Army* 19 (Feb. 1969): 49–50.

706 Strakhovsky, L. I. *Intervention at Archangel.* Princeton: Princeton University Press, 1944.

707 Tolley, Kemp. "Our Russian War of 1918–1919." *U.S. Naval Institute Proceedings* 95 (Feb. 1969): 58–72.

708 Unterberger, Betty M. *America's Siberian Expedition, 1918–1920.* Durham: Duke University Press, 1956.

709 ———. "President Wilson and the Decision to Send American Troops to Siberia." *Pacific Historical Review* 24 (Feb. 1955): 63–74.

710 Westall, Virginia C. "A.E.F. Siberia—The Forgotten Army: Recollections of General Robert L. Eichelberger." *Military Review* 48 (Mar. 1968): 11–18.

711 White, John A. *The Siberian Intervention.* Princeton: Princeton University Press, 1950.

712 Williams, William A. "American Intervention in Russia, 1917–1920." In *Containment and Revolution,* edited by David Horowitz. Boston: Beacon, 1967.

N/U.S. Occupation of Germany

713 Allen, Henry T. *The Rhineland Occupation.* Indianapolis: Bobbs-Merrill, 1927.

714 Girard, Jolyan P. "Congress and Presidential Military Policy: The Occupation of Germany, 1919–1923." *Mid-America* 56 (Oct. 1974): 211–20.

715 Nelson, Keith L. *Victors Divided: America and the Allies in Germany, 1918–1923.* Berkeley: University of California Press, 1975.

O/Civil-Military Relations

716 Croly, Herbert. "Effect on American Institutions of Powerful Military and Naval Establishment." *Annals of the American Academy of Political and Social Science* 66 (July 1916): 157–72.

717 Schilling, Warner R. "Civil-Naval Politics in World War I." *World Politics* 7 (July 1955): 572–91.

P/Prisoners of War, U.S. and Enemy

718 Cameron, John S. *Ten Months in a German Raider: A Prisoner of War Aboard the Wolf.* New York: Doran, 1918.

719 Ellinwood, Ralph E. *Behind the German Lines: A Narrative of the Everyday Life of an American Prisoner of War.* New York: Knickerbocker, 1920.

720 Glidden, William B. "Internment Camps in America, 1917–1920." *Military Affairs* 37 (Dec. 1973): 137–41.

721 Hoffman, Conrad. *In the Prison Camps of Germany: A Narrative of "Y" Service among Prisoners of War.* New York: Association Press, 1920.

722 Isaacs, Edouard V. M. *Prisoner of the U-90.* Boston: Houghton Mifflin, 1919.

723 Markle, Clifford M. *A Yankee Prisoner in Hunland.* New Haven: Whitlock's Book Store, 1920.

724 O'Brien, Pat. *Outwitting the Hun: My Escape from a German Prison Camp.* New York: Harper, 1918.

725 Troyes, F. G. *A Captive on a German Raider*. New York: McBride, 1918.

726 Winant, Cornelius. *A Soldier's Manuscript*. Boston: Merrymount, 1929.

Q/U.S. Military Personnel

General

727 Allen, Frederick L. "The Lesson of 1917." *Harpers* 181 (Sept. 1940): 344– 53.

728 Baldwin, Fred G. "The American Enlisted Man in World War I." Ph.D. dissertation, Princeton University, 1964.

729 U.S. Adjutant General's Office. *The Personnel System of the United States Army*. 2 vols. Washington, D.C., 1919.

730 U.S. Department of the Army. Office of Military History. *History of Military Mobilization in the United States Army*. Vol. I: *Colonial Period– World War I*, by Marvin A. Kreidberg and Merton G. Henry. Washington, D.C., 1953.

Prebelligerency Preparedness Movement

731 Alger, George W. "Preparedness and Democratic Discipline." *Atlantic Monthly* 117 (Apr. 1916): 476– 86.

732 Breckinridge, Henry. "Universal Service as the Basis of National Unity and National Defense." *Proceedings of the Academy of Political Science* 6 (July 1916): 439– 40.

733 Clifford, John G. "Leonard Wood, Samuel Gompers, and the Plattsburg Training Camps." *New York History* 52 (Apr. 1971): 169– 89.

734 ——. "The Plattsburg Training Camp Movement, 1913– 1917." Ph.D. dissertation, Indiana University, 1969.

735 Ellis, Olin O., and E. B. Garey. *The Plattsburg Manual: A Handbook for Military Training*. 7th ed. New York: Century, 1917.

736 Finnegan, John P. *Against the Specter of a Dragon: The Campaign For American Military Preparedness, 1914– 1917*. Westport, Connecticut: Greenwood, 1975.

737 ——. "Military Preparedness in the Progressive Era, 1911– 1917." Ph.D. dissertation, University of Wisconsin, 1969.

738 Hagedorn, Hermann. *The Bugle that Woke America: The Saga of Theodore Roosevelt's Last Battle for His Country*. New York: John Day, 1940.

739 ——. *Leonard Wood: A Biography*. 2 vols. New York: Harper, 1931.

740   Herring, George C., Jr. "James Hay and the Preparedness Controversy, 1915– 1916." *Journal of Southern History* 30 (Nov. 1964): 383– 404.

741   Kellor, Frances A. *Straight America: A Call to National Service.* New York: Macmillan, 1916.

742   Krehbiel, Edward. "Cassandra—Voices of 'Preparedness.' " *Dial* 59 (Nov. 11, 1915): 416– 18.

743   Maxim, Hudson. *Defenseless America.* New York: Hearst's International Library, 1915.

744   Mooney, Chase C., and Martha E. Layman. "Some Phases of the Compulsory Military Training Movement, 1914– 1920." *Mississippi Valley Historical Review* 38 (Mar. 1952): 633– 56.

745   Perry, Ralph B. *The Plattsburg Movement: A Chapter of America's Participation in the World War.* New York: Dutton, 1921.

746   Reynolds, M. T. "The General Staff as a Propaganda Agency, 1908– 1914." *Public Opinion Quarterly* 3 (July 1939): 391– 408.

747   Sutton, Walter A. "Republican Progressive Senators and Preparedness, 1915– 1916." *Mid-America* 52 (July 1970): 155– 76.

748   Tinsley, William. "The American Preparedness Movement, 1913– 1916." Ph.D. dissertation, Stanford University, 1939.

749   U.S. Congress. Senate. Committee on Military Affairs. Hearings: *Preparedness for National Defense,* 64th Cong., 1st Sess., 1916.

750   Ward, Robert D. "The Origins and Activities of the National Security League, 1914– 1919." *Mississippi Valley Historical Review* 47 (June 1960): 51– 65.

751   Woll, Matthew. "Trades-Unionism and Military Training." *Proceedings of the Academy of Political Science* 6 (July 1916): 558– 69.

752   Wood, Leonard. *The Military Obligations of Citizenship.* Princeton: Princeton University Press, 1915.

Recruitment and Conscription

753   Albany County (New York). Home Defense Committee. *The World War: Selective Service in the County of Albany in the State of New York* (April 6, 1917– November 11, 1918). Albany: J. B. Lyon, 1922.

754   Bauer, William E., and J. P. Judge, comps. "Baltimore and the Draft." *An Historical Record.* Baltimore: Monumental Printing, 1919.

755   California. Adjutant General's Office. *Report of the Selective Service Administration of California.* Sacramento: California State Printing Office, 1922.

756   Chambers, John W. "Conscripting For Colossus: The Adoption of the Draft in the United States in World War I." Ph.D. dissertation, Columbia University, 1973.

757   Crowder, Enoch H. *The Spirit of Selective Service.* New York: Century, 1920.

758   Davis, Arthur K., ed. . . . *Virginia War Agencies, Selective Service and Volunteers.* Richmond: Virginia War History Commission, 1926.

759   Decker, Joe F. "Progressive Reaction to Selective Service in World War I." Ph.D. dissertation, University of Georgia, 1969.

760   Dickinson, John. *The Building of an Army: A Detailed Account of Legislation, Administration and Opinion in the United States, 1915–1920.* New York: Century, 1922.

761   Durr, Ernest, "The Training of Recruits." *U.S. Naval Institute Proceedings* 43 (Jan. 1917): 99–123.

762   Leach, Jack F. *Conscription in the United States: Historical Background.* Rutland, Vermont: Tuttle, 1952.

763   Lynn, John D. "The United States Marshal's Office in the World War." *Rochester Historical Society Publication Fund Series* 4 (1925): 133–89.

764   Ohl, John K. "Hugh S. Johnson and the Draft, 1917–1918." *Prologue* 8 (Summer 1976): 85–96.

765   Rinehart, Mary (R.). *The Altar of Freedom.* Boston: Houghton Mifflin, 1917.

766   Roosevelt, Franklin D. "What the Navy Can Do for Your Boy." *Ladies Home Journal* 34 (June 1917): 25.

767   Tryon, Warren S. "The Draft in World War I." *Current History* 54 (June 1968): 339–44, 368.

768   U.S. Congress. House. Committee on Military Affairs. Hearings: *Increase of the Military Establishment*, 65th Cong., 1st Sess., Apr. 7–17, 1917.

769   U.S. Congress. Senate. Committee on Military Affairs. Hearings: *Temporary Increase of the Military Establishment*, 65th Cong., 1st Sess., 1917.

770   ———. Hearings before a subcommittee: *Universal Military Training*, 64th Cong., 2d Sess., 1917.

771   U.S. Provost Marshal General. *Final Report to the Secretary of War on the Operations of the Selective Service System to July 15, 1919.* Washington, D.C.: G.P.O, 1920.

772   West Virginia. Department of Military Census and Enrollment. *Organization and the Execution of the Selective Service in the State of West Virginia.* Charleston, West Virginia: Tribune Printing, 1920 (?).

773   White, John P. "Organized Labor and Military Service." *Proceedings of the Academy of Political Science* 6 (July 1916): 625– 29.

774   Wood, Leonard. *Universal Military Training.* New York: P. F. Collier, 1917.

Training

775   Agard, Walter R. "Rookie's Reaction." *New Republic* 13 (Dec. 8, 1917): 147– 49.

776   "American Army Discipline as Spiritual Murder." *Literary Digest* 71 (Nov. 12, 1921): 29– 30.

777   [Crump, Irving.] *Conscript 2989: Experiences of a Drafted Man.* New York: Dodd, Mead, 1918.

778   Earle, Ralph. *Life at the U.S. Naval Academy: The Making of the American Naval Officer.* New York: Putnam's, 1917.

779   Empey, Arthur G. *First Call: Guide Posts to Berlin.* New York: Putnam's, 1918.

780   "Fifty Years Ago: Training to Make the World Safe for Democracy." *Michigan History* 52 (Winter 1968): 316– 26.

781   Finney, Robert T. "Early Air Corps Training and Tactics." *Military Affairs* 20 (Fall 1956): 154– 61.

782   Fox, Edward L. "Is the Soldier Coddled?" *Forum* 59 (Feb. 1918): 189– 202.

783   ——. "Life in the Training Camps." *Forum* 58 (Dec. 1917): 637– 48.

784   ——. "Our New National Army." *Forum* 59 (Jan. 1918): 21– 30.

785   Hungerford, Edward. "Making a Soldier Out of Johnnie." *Everybody's* 38 (Feb. 1918): 39– 43.

786   Ihlder, John. "Our New Cities: The Cantonments of the National Army: An Achievement of the City Planners." *Survey* 39 (Oct. 27, 1917): 88– 93.

787 Jackson, Orton P., and F. E. Evans. "The Training of a Man-o' War's Man." *St. Nicholas Magazine* 44 (July 1917): 833– 37.

788 Koch, Louis P. "Drill on the Campus: The Student's Army Training Corps, 1918." *Palimpsest* 56 (Nov.– Dec. 1975): 184– 91.

789 Lanier, Henry W. "Lest We Forget: What the Training Camps Did for Four Million Americans." *World's Work* 39 (Jan. 1920): 275– 79.

790 McCarthy, Timothy F. *"A Year at Camp Gordon": United States Army Cantonment No. 123.* Wilkes-Barre, Pennsylvania: Caxton Press, 1920.

791 McNutt, William S. *The Yanks Are Coming!* Boston: Page, 1918.

792 MacQuarrie, Hector. *How to Live at the Front: Tips for American Soldiers.* Philadelphia: Lippincott, 1917.

793 Nordhoff, Charles B. *The Fledgling.* Boston: Houghton Mifflin, 1919.

794 Odell, Joseph H. *The New Spirit of the New Army: A Message to the "Service Flag" Homes.* New York: Revell, 1918.

795 Pownall, Dorothy A. "A Girl Reporter at Camp Dodge." *Palimpsest* 47 (June 1966): 225– 56.

796 Sassé, Fred A. *Rookie Days of a Soldier.* St. Paul, Minnesota: W. G. Greene, 1924.

797 Schauffler, Edward R. "Bricks without Straw." *Infantry Journal* 42 (July– Aug. 1935): 341– 43.

798 Showalter, W. J. "America's New Soldier Cities." *National Geographic Magazine* 32 (Nov. 1917): 439– 76.

799 Stanley, Frederic L. *Perils of a Private: Sketches of Camp Life.* Boston: Small, Maynard, 1918.

800 Stockbridge, Frank P. "Single Men in Barracks." *World's Work* 35 (Mar. 1918): 502– 07.

801 Wright, George. "The Army at Work and Play. Sketches from the Cantonments." *Harpers* 137 (Aug. 1918): 369– 76.

Reserves and National Guard

802 Hill, Jim Dan. *The Minute Man in Peace and War: A History of the National Guard.* Harrisburg, Pennsylvania: Stackpole, 1964.

803 Kansas. Adjutant General's Office. *History and Roster of the Kansas State Guard, August 6, 1917– November 11, 1919.* Topeka: Kansas State Printing Plant, 1925.

Recreation and Morale of Servicemen *(See also VII, L, Government Regulation of Sex)*

804 [American Library Association.] *Report of the War Service Committee of the American Library Association, 1919.* Albany, New York: American Library Association, 1919.

805 Evans, James W., and Gardner L. Harding. *Entertaining the American Army: The American Stage and Lyceum in the World War.* New York: Association Press, 1921.

806 Galloway, Blanche. "A Woman among Ten Thousand Bluejackets." *American Library Association Bulletin* 12 (Sept. 1918): 223–25.

807 Gleaves, Albert. "Books and Reading for the Navy and What They Have Meant in the War." *American Library Association Bulletin* 13 (July 1919): 155–57, 349.

808 Janis, Elsie. *The Big Show: My Six Months with the American Expeditionary Forces.* New York: Cosmopolitan Book Corp., 1919.

809 ———. *So Far, So Good! An Autobiography.* New York: Dutton, 1932.

810 Lee, Joseph. "War Camp Community Service." *The Annals* 79 (Sept. 1918): 189–94.

811 Mayo, Margaret. *Trouping for the Troops: Fun-making at the Front.* New York: Doran, 1919.

812 Morgan, Joy E. "How the Camp Library Reaches Every Man." *American Library Association Bulletin* 12 (Sept. 1918): 233–36.

813 National Hostess House Committee. *Report of the Hostess House Committee.* New York: National Board of the Young Women's Christian Associations, War Work Council, 1919 (?).

814 Sprenger, James A., and F. S. Edmonds, eds. *The Leave Areas of the American Expeditionary Forces, 1918–1919: Records and Memories.* Philadelphia: John C. Winston, 1928.

815 U.S. Commission on Training Camp Activities (War Department). *Army Song Book.* Washington, D.C., 1918.

816 ———. *Camp Music Division of the War Department.* Washington, D.C.: G.P.O., 1919.

817 War Camp Community Service. *Handbook of War Camp Community Service, Policies, Fundamental Principles and Instructions.* New York: War Camp Community Service, 1918.

818 ———. *Retrospect: How a Nation Served Its Sons in Army and Navy through Organized Community Hospitality.* New York: War Camp Community Service, 1920.

819 "War Camp Community Service in North Carolina." *North Carolina Historical Review* 1 (Jan. 1924): 412–48.

820 Weller, Charles F. "Permanent Values in War Camp Community Service." *Survey* 41 (Dec. 7, 1918): 295–98.

Education (in Service) of Military Personnel

821 Colby, Elbridge. *Education and the Army.* Boston: Palmer, 1922.

822 Pugh, W. S. "Education and Sanitation Aboard Ship." *U.S. Naval Medical Bulletin* 13 (Apr. 1919): 254–66.

823 Spaeth, John D. *Camp Reader for American Soldiers: Lessons in Reading, Writing, and Spelling.* Atlanta: YMCA, National War Work Council, 1918.

824 Stokes, Anson P. *Educational Plans for the Army Abroad.* New York: Association Press, 1918.

825 U.S. Adjutant General's Office. *The Educational System of the United States Army: The Army as a National School.* Washington, D.C.: G.P.O., 1920.

826 U.S. Army. A.E.F. *Report of the American E.F. Art Training Center, Bellevue* (Seine-et-Oise, March–June, 1919). Paris: Frazier-Soye, 1919.

Military Justice

827 Lindley, John M. "A Soldier's Also a Citizen: The Controversy Over Military Justice in the U.S. Army, 1917–1920." Ph.D. dissertation, Duke University, 1974.

Military Police

828 Russell, Charles E. *Adventures of the D.C.I. Department of Criminal Investigation.* Garden City, New York: Doubleday, Page, 1924.

Military Journalism

829 Larson, Cedric. "American Army Newspapers in the World War." *Journalism Quarterly* 17 (June 1940): 121–32, 160.

830 ———. "Censorship of Army News During the World War, 1917–1918." *Journalism Quarterly* 17 (Dec. 1940): 313–23.

831   Pickett, Calder M. "A Paper for the Doughboys: *Stars and Stripes* in World War I." *Journalism Quarterly* 42 (Winter 1965): 60– 68.

832   Woollcott, Alexander. *The Command is Forward: Tales of the A. E. F. Battlefields as They Appeared in the Stars and Stripes.* New York: Century, 1919.

Language of U.S. Troops

833   Fraser, Edward, comp. *Soldier and Sailor Words and Phrases.* . . . Reprint. Detroit: Gale Research, 1968.

834   Lighter, Jonathan. "The Slang of the American Expeditionary Forces in Europe, 1917– 1919: An Historical Glossary." *American Speech* 47 (Spring– Summer 1972): 5– 144.

Military Medicine

835   Bailey, Pearce; Frankwood E. Williams; and Paul O. Komora. *Neuropsychiatry.* . . . Vol. 10 of *The Medical Department of the U.S. Army in the World War,* by U.S. Surgeon General's Office. Washington, D.C.: G.P.O., 1929.

836   Bainbridge, William S. *Report on Medical and Surgical Developments of the War.* Washington, D.C.: G.P.O., 1919.

837   Bancroft, W. D.; H. C. Bradley; et al. *Medical Aspects of Gas Warfare.* Vol. 14 of *The Medical Department of the U.S. Army in the World War,* by U.S. Surgeon General's Office. Washington, D.C.: G.P.O., 1926.

838   Barclay, Harold. *A Doctor in France, 1917– 1919: The Diary of Harold Barclay.* New York: Privately printed, 1923.

839   Beal, Howard W. *The Letters of Major Howard W. Beal, Headquarters, First Division, Medical Department.* Completed by Louise C. Hale. Paris: J. R. E. Guild, 1926.

840   Bispham, William N. *Training.* Vol. 7 of *The Medical Department of the U.S. Army in the World War,* by U.S. Surgeon General's Office. Washington, D.C.: G.P.O., 1927.

841   Bowen, A. S. *Activities Concerning Mobilization and Ports of Embarkation.* Vol. 4 of *The Medical Department of the U.S. Army in the World War,* by U.S. Surgeon General's Office. Washington, D.C.: G.P.O., 1928.

842   Brackett, Elliott G., et al. *Surgery.* Vol. 2, pt. 1 of *The Medical Department of the U.S. Army in the World War,* by U.S. Surgeon General's Office. Washington, D.C.: G.P.O., 1924.

843   Burrage, Thomas J. "An American World War Hospital Centre in France." *Military Surgeon* 80 (May 1937): 352– 60.

844 Callender, George R., and James F. Coupal. *Pathology of the Acute Respiratory Disease and of Gas Gangrene Following War Wounds.* Vol. 12 of *The Medical Department of the U.S. Army in the World War,* by U.S. Surgeon General's Office. Washington, D.C.: G.P.O., 1929.

845 Chamberlain, W. P., and F. W. Weed. *Sanitation. . . .* Vol. 6 of *The Medical Department of the U.S. Army in the World War,* by U.S. Surgeon General's Office. Washington, D.C.: G.P.O., 1926.

846 Church, James R. *The Doctor's Part: What Happens to the Wounded in War.* New York: Appleton, 1918.

847 Cornell, Corwin S. *A Knoxville Physician's Part in the World War: From the Diary of Major C. S. Cornell, M.D. 1917–1919.* Knoxville, Iowa: Knoxville Journal, 1935.

848 Crane, A. G. *Physical Reconstruction and Vocational Education.* Vol. 13, pt. 1 of *The Medical Department of the U.S. Army in the World War,* by U.S. Surgeon General's Office. Washington, D.C.: G.P.O., 1927.

849 Cushing, Harvey W. *From a Surgeon's Journal, 1915–1918.* Boston: Little, Brown, 1936.

850 Darnall, J. R. "War Service with an Evacuation Hospital." *Military Surgeon* 80 (Apr. 1937): 261–76.

851 Davenport, G. H., and A. G. Love. *Statistics . . . Army Anthropology.* Vol. 15, pt. 1 of *The Medical Department of the U.S. Army in the World War,* by U.S. Surgeon General's Office. Washington, D.C.: G.P.O., 1921.

852 Derby, Richard. *"Wade In, Sanitary!": The Story of a Division Surgeon in France.* New York: Putnam's, 1919.

853 Dunham, Edward K., et al. *Surgery.* Vol. 11, pt. 2 of *The Medical Department of the U.S. Army in the World War,* by U.S. Surgeon General's Office. Washington, D.C.: G.P.O., 1924.

854 Ford, J. H. *Administration: American Expeditionary Forces.* Vol. 2 of *The Medical Department of the U.S. Army in the World War,* by U.S. Surgeon General's Office. Washington, D.C.: G.P.O., 1927.

855 Grissinger, Jay W. *Medical Field Service in France.* Washington, D.C.: Association of Military Surgeons, 1928.

856 Hoppin, Laura B., ed. *History of the World War Reconstruction Aides. . . .* Millbrook, New York: W. Tydsley, 1933. [Occupational and physical therapists in U.S. Army hospitals.]

857 Ivy, Robert H. "The Influenza Epidemic of 1918: Personal Experience of a Medical Officer in World War I." *Military Medicine* 125 (Sept. 1960): 620–22.

858   Jarrett, G. Burling. "Field Hospital Matériel of the A.E.F." *Journal of the American Military History Foundation* 1 (Fall 1937): 133–34.

859   Keen, W. W. "Military Surgery in 1861 and in 1918." *The Annals* 80 (Nov. 1918): 11–22.

860   Love, Albert G. *Statistics . . . Medical and Casualty Statistics. . . .* Vol. 15, pt. 2 of *The Medical Department of the U.S. Army in the World War,* by U.S. Surgeon General's Office. Washington, D.C.: G.P.O., 1925.

861   ——. *War Casualties.* Carlisle Barracks, Pennsylvania: Medical Field Service School, 1931.

862   Lyle, H. H. M. "The Principles of Surgery, Hospitalization and the Evacuation of the Wounded in the Meuse-Argonne Offensive." *Military Surgeon* 84 (June 1939): 580–91.

863   Lynch, Charles; Joseph H. Ford; and Frank W. Weed. *Field Operations.* Vol. 8 of *The Medical Department of the U.S. Army in the World War,* by U.S. Surgeon General's Office. Washington, D.C.: G.P.O., 1925.

864   ——. Frank W. Weed; and Loy McAfee. *The Surgeon General's Office.* Vol. 1 of *The Medical Department of the U.S. Army in the World War,* by U.S. Surgeon General's Office. Washington, D.C.: G.P.O., 1923.

865   Porter, William T. *Shock at the Front.* Boston: Atlantic Monthly Press, 1918.

866   Roberts, Harold C. "The Road to the Rear." *Marine Corps Gazette* 22 (Nov. 1938): 25–26, 53–60.

867   Roth, William E. *Memoirs of a Private, 1917–1919.* Austin, Texas, 1960.

868   Russell, Frederick F. "Some Diseases Prevalent in the Army." In *The New World of Science,* edited by Robert M. Yerkes. Freeport, New York: Books for Libraries Press, 1969.

869   ——. "The War Service of the Medical Profession." In *The New World of Science,* edited by Robert M. Yerkes. Freeport, New York: Books for Libraries Press, 1969.

870   Siler, Joseph F. *Communicable and Other Diseases.* Vol. 9 of *The Medical Department of the U.S. Army in the World War,* by U.S. Surgeon General's Office. Washington, D.C.: G.P.O., 1928.

871   Stimson, Julia C. *The Army Nurse Corps.* Vol. 13, pt. 2 of *The Medical Department of the U.S. Army in the World War,* by U.S. Surgeon General's Office. Washington, D.C.: G.P.O., 1927.

872 ———. *Finding Themselves: The Letters of an American Army Chief Nurse in a British Hospital in France.* New York: Macmillan, 1918.

873 Strott, George G. *The Medical Department of the United States Navy with the Army and Marine Corps in France in World War I: Its Functions and Employment.* Washington, D.C.: Department of the Navy, Bureau of Medicine & Surgery, 1947.

874 Thompson, Dora E. "How the Army Nursing Service Met the Demands of War." *Twenty-fifth Annual Report of the National League of Nursing Education* (1919): 116.

875 Weed, Frank W. *Military Hospitals in the United States.* Vol. 5 of *The Medical Department of the U.S. Army in the World War,* by U.S. Surgeon General's Office. Washington, D.C.: G.P.O., 1923.

876 Wolfe, E. P. *Finance and Supply.* Vol. 3 of *The Medical Department of the U.S. Army in the World War,* by U.S. Surgeon General's Office. Washington, D.C.: G.P.O., 1928.

877 Young, Hugh H. *Hugh Young: A Surgeon's Autobiography.* New York: Harcourt, Brace, 1940.

R/Logistics

878 Chicago, Universty of. Graduate School of Business. *Quartermaster and Ordnance Supply: A Guide to the Principles of the Supply Service of the United States Army,* by Instructors of the Army Supply Service Course, the University of Chicago. Chicago: University of Chicago Press, 1917.

879 Claudy, Carl H. "Preparing the Navy Ashore: War Work of the Bureau of Yards and Docks." *Scientific American* 117 (Dec. 1, 1917): 416–17.

880 Crowell, Benedict, and Robert F. Wilson. *The Road to France . . . the Transportation of Troops and Military Supplies, 1917–1918.* Vols. 2, 3 of *How America Went to War.* New Haven: Yale University Press, 1921.

881 Dawes, Charles G. *A Journal of the Great War.* 2 vols. Boston: Houghton Mifflin, 1921.

882 Dyer, George P. "The Navy Supply Department in War Time." *U.S. Naval Institute Proceedings* 46 (Mar. 1920): 379–92.

883 Gleaves, Albert. *A History of the Transport Service: Adventures and Experiences of United States Transports and Cruisers in the World War.* New York: Doran, 1921.

884 Hagood, Johnson. *The Services of Supply: A Memoir of the Great War.* Boston: Houghton Mifflin, 1927.

885   Huston, James A. *The Sinews of War: Army Logistics, 1775–1953.* Washington, D.C.: G.P.O., 1966.

886   Kinney, William S. Construction Division in the First World War." *Quartermaster Review* 18:1 (1938): 23–28, 69–73.

887   "Life on a Transport." *Literary Digest* 55 (Sept. 22, 1917): 43–46.

888   Lipsett, Charles H. *U.S. War Surplus: Its Source and Distribution, 1917–1924.* New York: Atlas Publishing, 1924.

889   McLean, Ross H. "Troop Movements on the American Railroads during the Great War." *American Historical Review* 26 (Apr. 1921): 464–88.

890   Marcosson, Isaac F. *S.O.S. America's Miracle in France.* New York: Lane, 1919.

891   Pickell, James R. *Twenty-Four Days on a Troopship.* Chicago: Rosenbaum Review, 1919.

892   Powell, Edward A. *The Army Behind the Army.* New York: Scribner's, 1919.

893   Risch, Erna. *Quartermaster Support of the Army: A History of the Corps, 1775–1939.* Washington, D.C.: Office of the Quartermaster General, Quartermaster Historian's Office, 1962.

894   Scott, Albert L. "The Procurement of Quartermaster Supplies during the World War." *Historical Outlook* 11 (Apr. 1920): 133–38.

895   Shanks, David C. *As They Passed through the Port.* Washington, D.C.: Cary Publishing, 1927.

896   Sharpe, Henry G. *The Quartermaster Corps in the Year 1917 in the World War.* New York: Century, 1921.

897   U.S. General Staff. War Plans Division. Historical Branch. *Organization of the Service of Supply: American Expeditionary Forces.* Washington, D.C.: G.P.O., 1921.

898   U.S. Navy Department Bureau of Engineering. *History of the Bureau of Engineering, Navy Department, during the World War.* Washington, D.C.: G.P.O., 1922.

899   U.S. War Department. Purchase, Storage and Traffic Division. *Compilation of Supply Circulars and Supply Bulletins of the Purchase, Storage and Traffic Division, General Staff, War Department, Issued between April 24, 1918 and May 1, 1919.* Washington, D.C.: G.P.O., 1919.

900   *Who's Who in the Construction Division of the United States Army.* New York: Simmons-Boardman, 1920.

901   Wilgus, William J. *Transporting the A.E.F. in Western Europe, 1917–1919.* New York: Columbia University Press, 1931.

902   Wilson, R. F. "Feeding the American Army." *Century* 97 (Nov. 1918): 77–81.

S/Technology and Weapons

903   Brophy, Leo P. "Origins of the Chemical Corps." *Military Affairs* 20 (Winter 1956): 217–26.

904   ———; Wyndham D. Miles; and Reymond C. Cochrane. *The Chemical Warfare Service: From Laboratory to Field.* Washington, D.C.: Department of the Army, Office of the Chief of Military History, 1959.

905   Brown, Sevellon. *The Story of Ordnance in the World War.* Washington, D.C.: James William Bryan Press, 1920.

906   Burgess, George K. "Applications of Science to Warfare in France." *Scientific Monthly* 5 (Oct. 1917): 289–97.

907   Cianflone, Frank A. "The Eagle Boats of World War I." *U.S. Naval Institute Proceedings* 99 (June 1973): 76–80.

908   Crozier, William. *Ordnance and the World War: A Contribution to the History of American Preparedness.* New York: Scribner's, 1920.

909   DeVore, Ronald M. "Weapons: The Futuristic Nightmare of the Trenches." *Mankind* 5 (Feb. 1977): 42–43.

910   DeWeerd, Harvey A. "American Adoption of French Artillery: 1917–1918." *Journal of the American Military Institute* 3 (Summer 1939): 104–16.

911   Dooly, William G., Jr. *Great Weapons of World War I.* New York: Walker, 1969.

912   Duncan, Robert C. *America's Use of Sea Mines.* White Oak, Maryland: U.S. Naval Ordnance Laboratory, 1962.

913   Farrow, Edward S. *American Guns in the War with Germany.* New York: Dutton, 1920.

914   Fries, Amos A., and Clarence J. West. *Chemical Warfare.* New York: McGraw-Hill, 1921.

915   Fulton, Garland. "The General Climate for Technological Developments in Naval Aeronautics on the Eve of World War I." *Technology and Culture* 4 (Spring 1963): 154–64.

916   Furer, Julius A. "The 110 Foot Submarine Chasers and Eagle Boats." *U.S. Naval Institute Proceedings* 45 (May 1919): 753–67.

917　Green, Constance M.; Harry C. Thomson; and Peter C. Roots. *The Ordnance Department: Planning for War*. Washington, D.C.: Department of the Army, Office of the Chief of Military History, 1955.

918　Haviland, Jean. "American Concrete Steamers of the First and Second World Wars." *American Neptune* 22 (July 1962): 157–83.

919　Jackson, Orton P., and Frank E. Evans. *The Marvel Book of American Ships*. New York: Stokes, 1917.

920　Kennelly, A. E. "Advances in Signalling Contributed during the War." In *The New World of Science*, edited by Robert M. Yerkes. Freeport, New York: Books for Libraries Press, 1969.

921　Kevles, Daniel J. "Flash and Sound in the A.E.F.: The History of a Technical Service." *Military Affairs* 33 (Dec. 1969): 374–84.

922　Knappen, Theodore M. *Wings of War: An Account of the Important Contribution of the United States to Aircraft Invention, Engineering, Development and Production during the World War*. New York: Putnam's, 1920.

923　Lavine, Abraham L. *Circuits of Victory*. Garden City, New York: Doubleday, Page, 1921. [Telephones in war.]

924　Manning, Van H. *War Gas Investigations*. Bureau of Mines Bulletin 178–A. Washington, D.C.: G.P.O., 1919.

925　Nenninger, Timothy K. "The Development of American Armor, 1917–1940: The World War I Experience." *Armor* 78 (Jan.–Feb. 1969): 46–51.

926　Noyes, Arthur A. "The Supply of Nitrogen Products for the Manufacture of Explosives." In *The New World of Science*, edited by Robert M. Yerkes. Freeport, New York: Books for Libraries Press, 1969.

927　Nutting, William W. *The Cinderellas of the Fleet*. Jersey City: Standard Motor Construction Co., 1920. [Subchasers.]

928　Owen, Richard W. "Origins of Antiaircraft Artillery." *Antiaircraft Journal* 93 (Jan.–Feb. 1950): 37–40.

929　Preston, Antony. *Battleships of World War I: An Illustrated Encyclopedia of Battleships of All Nations, 1914–1918*. Harrisburg, Pennsylvania: Stackpole, 1972.

930　Reichmann, W. D. "American Warship Design." *Scientific American* 116 (Apr. 28, 1917): 421.

931　Reid, E. Emmett. "Reminiscences of World War I." *Armed Forces Chemical Journal* 9 (July–Aug. 1955): 37–39.

932 Senior, James K. "The Manufacture of Mustard Gas in World War I." *Armed Forces Chemical Journal* 12 (Sept.–Oct. 1958): 12–14+; (Nov.–Dec. 1958): 26–29.

933 Silverstone, Paul. *U.S. Warships of World War I.* Garden City, New York: Doubleday, 1970.

934 Stieglitz, Julius. "The New Chemical Warfare." *Yale Review* 7 (Apr. 1918): 493–511.

935 Stockbridge, Frank P. *Yankee Ingenuity in the War.* New York: Harper, 1920.

936 Sumrall, Robert F. "Ship Camouflage (WWI): Deceptive Art." *U.S. Naval Institute Proceedings* 97 (July 1971): 57–78.

937 Trowbridge, Augustus. "Sound-Ranging in the American Expeditionary Forces." In *The New World of Science,* edited by Robert M. Yerkes. Freeport, New York: Books for Libraries Press, 1969.

938 ———. "War Letters of Augustus Trowbridge, August 28, 1917 to January 19, 1919." *New York Public Library Bulletin* 43 (Aug. 1939): 591–617; (Sept. 1939): 645–66; (Oct. 1939): 725–38; (Nov. 1939): 830–44; (Dec. 1939): 901–14; 44 (Jan. 1940): 8–35; (Feb. 1940): 117–30; (Apr. 1940): 331–50.

939 U.S. Army. A.E.F. Engineer Department. *Report on Sound and Flash Ranging for Lieutenant Colonel A. Trowbridge* (1917–1919). Paris (?): 1918.

940 West, Clarence J. "The Chemical Warfare Service." In *The New World of Science,* edited by Robert M. Yerkes. Freeport, New York: Books for Libraries Press, 1969.

T/Doctrine—Strategic and Tactical

941 Greer, Thomas H. "Air Arm Doctrinal Roots, 1917–1918." *Military Affairs* 20 (Winter 1956): 202–16.

942 ———. *The Development of Air Doctrine in the Army Air Force 1917–1941.* Montgomery, Alabama: Air University Press, 1955.

943 Holley, I. B., Jr. *Ideas and Weapons: Exploitation of the Aerial Weapons by the United States during World War I: A Study in the Relationship of Technological Advance, Military Doctrine, and the Development of Weapons.* New Haven: Yale University Press, 1953.

U/Intelligence-related Activities

U.S. Military and Naval Intelligence

944 Churchill, Marlborough. "The Military Intelligence Division General Staff." *Journal of the United States Artillery* 52 (Apr. 4, 1920): 293–315.

945   Coulter, C. S. "Intelligence Service in the World War." *Infantry Journal* 20 (Apr. 1922): 376– 83.

946   Gowenlock, Thomas R., and Guy Murchie, Jr. *Soldiers of Darkness.* Garden City, New York: Doubleday, Doran, 1937.

947   Johnson, Thomas M. *Our Secret War: True American Spy Stories, 1917– 1919.* Indianapolis: Bobbs-Merrill, 1929.

948   Parish, John C. "Intelligence Work at First Army Headquarters." *Historical Outlook* 11 (June 1920): 213– 17.

949   Powe, Marc B. *The Emergence of the War Department Intelligence Agency: 1885– 1918.* Manhattan, Kansas: Military Affairs, 1975.

950   Rodman, Burton. "The Intelligent 27." *Cavalry Journal* 44:189 (1935): 31– 36.

951   Russell, Charles E. *True Adventures of the Secret Service.* Garden City, New York: Doubleday, Page, 1923.

952   Sweeney, Walter C. *Military Intelligence: New Weapon in War.* New York: Stokes, 1924.

Enemy Espionage and U.S. Counterespionage

953   Hall, William R., and Amos J. Peaslee. *Three Wars with Germany.* New York: Putnam's, 1944.

954   Kleist, Franz Rintglen von. *Dark Invader.* New York: Macmillan, 1933.

955   Landau, Henry. *The Enemy Within: The Inside Story of German Sabotage in America.* New York: Putnam's, 1937.

956   O'Brian, John Lord. "Uncle Sam's Spy Policies: Safeguarding American Liberty during the War." *Forum* 61 (Apr. 1919): 407– 16.

957   Strother, French. *Fighting Germany's Spies.* Garden City, New York: Doubleday, Page, 1918.

958   Wood, Eric F. *The Note-book of an Intelligence Officer.* New York: Century, 1917.

959   Yardley, Herbert O. *Secret Service in America: The American Black Chamber.* London: Faber & Faber, 1940.

960   Zimmer, George F. *K-7: Spies at War as Told to Burke Boyce.* New York: Appleton-Century, 1934.

Psychological Warfare

961 Blankenhorn, Heber. *Adventures in Propaganda: Letters from an Intelligence Officer in France*. Boston: Houghton Mifflin, 1919.

962 Bruntz, George G. *Allied Propaganda and the Collapse of the German Empire in 1918*. Stanford: Stanford University Press, 1938.

963 Whitehouse, Mrs. Vira (B.). *A Year as a Government Agent*. New York: Harper, 1920.

V/U.S. Troops and Other Nationals

Americans with Allied Units

964 Abbey, Edwin A. *An American Soldier: Letters of Edwin Austin Abbey*. Boston: Houghton Mifflin, 1918.

965 Adams, Briggs K. *The American Spirit*. Boston: Atlantic Monthly Press, 1918.

966 Brooks, Alden. *As I Saw It*. New York: Knopf, 1930.

967 ———. *Battle in 1918: Seen by an American in the French Army*. Paris: H. Jonquières, 1929.

968 [Bruno, Henry A.] *The Flying Yankee by "Flight"* [pseud.]. New York: Dodd, Mead, 1918.

969 Butters, Henry A. *Harry Butters, R.F.A. — "An American Citizen": Life and War Letters*. Edited by Mrs. Denis O'Sullivan. New York: Lane, 1918.

970 Chapin, Harold. *Soldier and Dramatist*. New York: Lane, 1916.

971 Chapin, William A. R. *The Lost Legion: The Story of the Fifteen Hundred American Doctors Who Served with the B.E.F. in the Great War*. Springfield, Massachusetts: Loring-Axtell, 1926.

972 Depew, Albert N. *Gunner Depew*. Chicago: Reilly & Britton, 1918.

973 Gallagher, Bernard J. "A Yank in the B.E.F." *American Heritage* 16 (June 1965): 18– 27, 101– 08.

974 Hall, James N. *Kitchener's Mob: The Adventures of an American in the British Army*. Boston: Houghton Mifflin, 1916.

975 Holmes, Robert D. *A Yankee in the Trenches*. Boston: Little, Brown, 1918.

976   Kautz, John I. *Trucking to the Trenches: Letters From France, June–November 1917.* Boston: Houghton Mifflin, 1918.

977   Kelly, Russell A. *Kelly of the Foreign Legion.* New York: Kennerley, 1917.

978   McClellan, Edwin N. "American Marines in the British Grand Fleet." *Marine Corps Gazette* 7 (June 1922): 147–68.

979   McCoy, Patrick T. *Kiltie McCoy: An American Boy with an Irish Name Fighting in France as a Scotch Soldier.* Indianapolis: Bobbs-Merrill, 1918.

980   Mack, Arthur J. *Shellproof Mack: An American's Fighting Story.* Boston: Small, Maynard, 1918.

981   *"Mademoiselle Miss." Letters from an American Girl Serving with the Rank of Lieutenant in a French Army Hospital at the Front.* Boston: Butterfield, 1916.

982   Merrill, Wainright. *A College Man in Khaki: Letters of an American in the British Artillery.* Edited by Charles M. Stearns. New York: Doran, 1918.

983   Morse, Edwin W. *America in the War: The Vanguard of American Volunteers in the Fighting Lines and in Humanitarian Service, August 1914–April 1917.* New York: Scribner's, 1919.

984   Pliska, Stanley R. "The 'Polish-American Army,' 1917–1921." *Polish Review* 10 (Summer 1965): 46–59.

985   Roberts, E. M. *A Fighting Flier: An American above the Lines in France.* New York: Harper, 1918.

986   Robinson, William J. *My Fourteen Months at the Front: An American Boy's Baptism of Fire.* Boston: Little, Brown, 1916.

987   Rockwell, Paul A. *American Fighters in the Foreign Legion, 1914–1918.* Boston: Houghton Mifflin, 1930.

988   ———. "Writings of the American Volunteers in the French Foreign Legion during the World War." *Ex Libris* 1 (Oct. 1923): 99–110.

989   Russel, William M. *A Happy Warrior: Letters of William Muir Russel, an American Aviator in the Great War, 1917–1918 . . . A Family Memorial.* Detroit: Saturday Night Press, 1919.

990   Seeger, Alan. *Letters and Diary of Alan Seeger.* New York: Scribner's, 1917.

991   Sheahan, Henry B. [Henry B. Beston, pseud.] *A Volunteer Poilu.* Boston: Houghton Mifflin, 1916.

992 Smith, Joseph S. *Over There and Back in Three Uniforms*. New York: Dutton, 1918.

993 Winslow, Carroll D. *With the French Flying Corps*. New York: Scribner's, 1917.

European Views of U.S. Forces

994 "Americans at the Second Battle of the Marne: From An Eye-witness Account of a German Officer." *New Jersey Historical Society Proceedings*, n.s. 7 (Apr. 1922): 145–48.

995 Chambrun, Jacques A. de P., Comte de. *The American Army in the European Conflict*. New York: Macmillan, 1919.

996 Edmonds, Sir James E., comp. *Military Operations: France and Belgium, 1918*. 5 vols. London: Macmillan, 1935–.

997 Foch, Ferdinand. *The Memoirs of Marshal Foch*. Garden City, New York: Doubleday, Doran, 1931.

998 Giehrl, Hermann Von. "The American Expeditionary Forces in Europe, 1917–1918." *Infantry Journal* 19 (Dec. 1921): 630–37; 20 (Jan.–Mar. 1922): 18–23, 140–49, 292–303.

999 ———. "Battle of the Meuse-Argonne." *Infantry Journal* 19 (Aug.–Nov. 1921): 131–38, 264–70, 376–84, 534–40.

1000 Kennett, Lee. "The A.E.F. through French Eyes." *Military Review* 52 (Nov. 1972): 3–11.

1001 Otto, Ernst. *The Battle at Blanc Mont (October 2 to October 10, 1918)*. Translated by Martin Lichtenberg. Annapolis: U.S. Naval Institute, 1930.

1002 ———. "The Battles for the Possession of Belleau Wood, June 1918." *U.S. Naval Institute Proceedings* 54 (Nov. 1928): 941–62.

1003 Terraine, John. *Douglas Haig: The Educated Soldier*. London: Hutchinson, 1963.

1004 Viereck, George S., and A. Paul Maerker-Branden. *As They Saw Us: Foch, Ludendorff and Other Leaders Write Our War History*. Garden City, New York: Doubleday, Doran, 1929.

1005 Walton, Robert C. *Over There: European Reaction to Americans in World War I*. Itasca, Illinois: F. E. Peacock, 1972.

U.S. Servicemen View the Allies

1006 Woollcott, Alexander. "Them Damned Frogs." *North American Review* 210 (Oct. 1919): 490–98.

W/American Auxiliaries

General

1007   American Military Hospital No. 1: Report . . . September 1, 1916 to December 31, 1917. New York (?), 1918 (?).

1008   Anderson, Isabel W. *Zigzagging.* Boston: Houghton Mifflin, 1918.

1009   Ashe, Elizabeth H. *Intimate Letters from France and Extracts from the Diary of Elizabeth Ashe, 1917–1919.* San Francisco: Bruce Brough Press, 1931.

1010   Bakewell, Charles M. *The Story of the American Red Cross in Italy.* New York: Macmillan, 1920.

1011   Baldwin, Marian. *Canteening Overseas, 1917–1919.* New York: Macmillan, 1920.

1012   Bradley, Amy O. *Back of the Front in France.* Boston: Butterfield, 1918.

1013   Davison, Henry P. *The American Red Cross in the Great War, 1917–1919.* New York: Russell Sage Foundation, 1943.

1014   Dulles, Foster R. *The American Red Cross: A History.* New York: Harper, 1950.

1015   Eddy, George Sherwood. *With Our Soldiers in France.* New York: Association Press, 1917.

1016   Farnam, Ruth. *Nation at Bay: What an American Woman Saw and Did in Suffering Serbia.* Indianapolis: Bobbs-Merrill, 1918.

1017   Frazer, Elizabeth. *Old Glory and Verdun, and Other Stories.* New York: Duffield, 1918.

1018   Gaines, Ruth L. *Helping France: The Red Cross in the Devastated Area.* New York: Dutton, 1919.

1019   ———. *Ladies of Grécourt: The Smith College Relief Unit in the Somme.* New York: Dutton, 1920.

1020   ———. *A Village in Picardy.* New York: Dutton, 1918.

1021   Harris, Frederick, ed. *Service with Fighting Men: An Account of the Work of the American Young Men's Christian Associations in the World War.* 2 vols. New York: Association Press, 1922.

1022   Harrison, Carter H. *With the American Red Cross in France, 1918–1919.* Chicago: Seymour, 1947.

1023 Hunt, Edward E. *War Bread: A Personal Narrative of the War and Relief in Belgium.* New York: Holt, 1916.

1024 Irvine, Alexander. *A Yankee with the Soldiers of the King.* New York: Dutton, 1923.

1025 Jones, Rufus M. *A Service of Love in Wartime: American Friends Relief Work in Europe, 1917–1919.* New York: Macmillan, 1920.

1026 Kellogg, Paul U. "The Expanding Demands for War Relief in Europe." *The Annals* 79 (Sept. 1918): 9–23.

1027 Kimmel, Stanley P. "Crucifixion: The Experiences of a Red Cross Ambulance Driver in France." *Overland,* n.s. 75 (Jan.–Apr. 1920): 36–40, 158–62, 236–40, 277–82.

1028 Kramer, Harold M. *With Seeing Eyes: The Unusual Story of an Observant Thinker at the Front.* Boston: Lathrop, Lee & Shepard, 1919.

1029 Livingston, St. Clair, and Ingebord Steen-Hansen. *Under Three Flags: With the Red Cross in Belgium, France and Serbia.* London: Macmillan, 1916.

1030 Lovejoy, Esther P. *Certain Samaritans.* New York: Macmillan, 1927.

1031 Mayo, Katherine. *"That Damn Y": A Record of Overseas Service.* Boston: Houghton Mifflin, 1920.

1032 [Morse, Katherine D.] *The Uncensored Letters of a Canteen Girl.* New York: Holt, 1920.

1033 Mortimer, Maud. *A Green Tent in Flanders.* Garden City, New York: Doubleday, Page, 1917.

1034 O'Shaughnessy, Edith L. *My Lorraine Journal.* New York: Harper, 1918.

1035 Poling, Daniel A. *Huts in Hell.* Boston: Christian Endeavor World, 1918.

1036 Prentice, Sartell. *Padre: A Red Cross Chaplain in France.* New York: Dutton, 1919.

1037 Putnam, Elizabeth C. *On Duty and Off.* Cambridge, Massachusetts: Riverside Press, 1919.

1038 *A Red Triangle Girl in France.* New York: Doran, 1918.

1039 Root, Esther S., and Marjorie Crocker. *Over Periscope Pond: Letters from Two American Girls in Paris, October 1916–January 1918.* Boston: Houghton Mifflin, 1918.

1040   Sears, Herbert M. *Journal of a Canteen Worker: A Record of Service with the American Red Cross in Flanders.* Boston: Merrymount, 1919.

1041   Shortall, Katherine. *A "Y" Girl in France.* Boston: Badger, 1919.

1042   Slusser, Thomas H. *Letters to Her, 1917–1919.* Chicago, 1937.

1043   Smith, Fred B. *Observations in France.* New York: Association Press, 1918.

1044   Stidger, William L. *Soldier Silhouettes on Our Front.* New York: Scribner's, 1918.

1045   Thayer, George B. *Army Influence over the Y.M.C.A. in France.* N.p., 1919 (?).

1046   Toland, Edward D. *The Aftermath of Battle: With the Red Cross in France.* New York: Macmillan, 1916.

1047   U.S. American National Red Cross. War Council. *The Work of the American Red Cross during the War: A Statement of Finances and Accomplishments, July 1, 1917 to February 28, 1919.* Washington, D.C.: American Red Cross, 1919.

1048   Van Schaick, John. *The Little Corner Never Conquered: The Story of the American Red Cross Work for Belgium.* New York: Macmillan, 1922.

1049   Warren, Harold L. *With the YMCA in France.* New York: Revell, 1919.

1050   West, William B. *The Fight for the Argonne: Personal Experiences of a "Y" Man.* New York: Abingdon, 1919.

1051   Whitehair, Charles W. *Out There.* New York: Appleton, 1918.

1052   ———. *Pictures Burned into My Memory.* Akron, Ohio: Saalfield, 1918.

1053   [Young Men's Christian Associations. National War Work Council.] *Summary of World War Work of the American Y.M.C.A.* New York, 1920.

American Ambulance Volunteers

1054   Ambulance Field Service. *Diary of Section VIII: American Ambulance Field Service.* Boston: T. Todd, 1917.

1055   Bodfish, Robert W. *A History of Section 647: United States Army Ambulance Service with the French Army.* Worcester, Massachusetts: Stobbs Press, 1919.

1056 Bradley, Amy O. *Back of the Front in France: Letters from Amy Owen Bradley, Motor Driver of the American Fund for French Wounded.* Boston: Butterfield, 1918.

1057 Bryan, Julien H. *"Ambulance 464": Encore des Blessés.* New York: Macmillan, 1918.

1058 [Buswell, Leslie], ed. *Ambulance No. 10: Personal Letters from the Front.* Boston: Houghton Mifflin, 1916.

1059 *Camion Letters from American College Men: Volunteer Drivers of the American Field Service in France, 1917. . . .* New York: Holt, 1918.

1060 Clark, Glen W., ed. *"Lest We Forget": A History of Section 503 of the U.S. Army Ambulance Service with the French Army.* Philadelphia: Westminster Press, 1920.

1061 Coyle, Edward R. *Ambulancing on the French Front.* New York: Britton, 1918.

1062 Dexter, Mary. *In the Soldier's Service: War Experiences of Mary Dexter, England, Belgium, France, 1914– 1918.* Edited by her mother. Boston: Houghton Mifflin, 1918.

1063 Fenton, Charles A. "American Ambulance Drivers in France and Italy, 1914– 1918." *American Quarterly* 3 (Winter 1951): 326– 43.

1064 Florez, C. de. *"No. 6": A Few Pages from the Diary of an Ambulance Driver.* New York: Dutton, 1918.

1065 *Friends of France: The Field Service of the American Ambulance Described by Its Members.* Boston: Houghton Mifflin, 1916.

1066 Gibson, Preston. *Battering the Boche.* New York: Century, 1918.

1067 Gray, Andrew. "The American Field Service." *American Heritage* 26 (Dec. 1974): 58– 63, 88– 92.

1068 *History of the American Field Service in France: "Friends of France," 1914– 1917.* 3 vols. Boston: Houghton Mifflin, 1920.

1069 Howe, Mark A. De Wolfe, ed. *The Harvard Volunteers in Europe: Personal Records of Experience in Military, Ambulance, and Hospital Service.* Cambridge: Harvard University Press, 1916.

1070 Imbrie, Robert W. *Behind the Wheel of a War Ambulance.* New York: McBride, 1918.

1071 Millen, De Witt C. *Memoirs of 591 in the World War.* Ann Arbor: D. C. Millen, 1932. [591st *Section Sanitaire.*]

1072   Orcutt, Philip D. *The White Road of Mystery: The Note-book of an American Ambulancier.* New York: Lane, 1918.

1073   Piatt, Andrew A. "The Genesis of the American Ambulance Service with the French Army, 1915– 1917." *Military Surgeon* 57 (Oct. 1925): 363– 77.

1074   Rice, Philip S. *An Ambulance Driver in France.* Wilkes-Barre, Pennsylvania, 1918.

1075   Shively, George J., ed. *Records of S.S.U. 585.* New York: E. L. Hildreth, 1920.

1076   Stevenson, William Y. *At the Front in a Flivver.* Boston: Houghton Mifflin, 1917.

1077   ——. *From Poilu to Yank.* Boston: Houghton Mifflin, 1918.

1078   Williams, Paul B. *United States Lawn Tennis Association and the World War.* N.p., n.d. [603d *Section Sanitaire.*]

X/Military Statistics

1079   [Ayres, Leonard P.] *The War with Germany: A Statistical Survey.* Washington, D.C.: G.P.O., 1919.

1080   Gosnell, H. A. "World War Losses of the United States Navy." *U.S. Naval Institute Proceedings* 63 (May 1937): 630– 34.

1081   U.S. Adjutant General's Office. *Summary of Casualties in the A.E.F.* Washington, D.C.: G.P.O., 1919.

1082   U.S. Navy Department. *American Ship Casualties of the World War.* Washington, D.C.: G.P.O., 1923.

VI/Unit Histories

We have generally followed the order of World War I U.S. Army units used by Charles Dornbusch in his *Histories of American Army Units: World War I and II and Korean Conflict, with Some Earlier Histories.* (entry no. 7) Types of units are listed alphabetically; within each type, units are ordered by number, and subdivisions of numbered units follow the larger unit. Titles are *not* alphabetized within units.

A/Army Ground Forces

General Classification

1083   U.S. Army War College. Historical Section. *Order of Battle of the United States Land Forces in the World War: 1917–1919.* 4 vols. Washington, D.C.: G.P.O., 1931–1949.

Ambulance Companies

1084   [Fitzhugh, Robert S., et al.] *The History and La-trine Rumor of Ambulance Company 33.* Newark, New Jersey: Essex Press, 1920.

1085   Chaskel, Walter. *History of Ambulance Company No. 105 (Former Fourth New York Ambulance Company), 102nd Sanitary Train, 27th Division, U.S.A.* Syracuse: Quality Print Shop, 1919.

1086   *History of Ambulance Company Number 139.* Kansas City, Kansas: E. R. Callender, 1919 (?).

1087   Schmitz, John J. *One Hundred and Forty-third Ambulance Company, 1917–1919, Amex Forces, United States Army.* Paris: Herbert Clarke, 1920 (?).

1088   [Graham, Milton P.], ed. *History of Ambulance Company No. 161, A.E.F., 1917–1919.* Aberdeen, Washington: Welsh-Richards, 1919.

1089   Davis, Delbert M. *307 at Home and in France.* Garden City, New York: Country Life Press, 1919.

1090 History of 308th Ambulance Company, 302d Sanitary Train, 77th Division, American Expeditionary Forces. N.p., 1919.

1091 [Hicks, William P., Jr.], ed. Three-eleven: Being a Collection of Prose and Verse Contributed by Members of the Company. N.p., 1919 (?).

1092 A History of the 361 Ambulance Company, 316 Sanitary Train, 91 "Wild West" Division. . . . N.p., 1919 (?).

Ammunition Trains

1093 [Hussey, Robert F.], ed. United States First Ammunition Train. Coblenz: Görres-Druckerei, 1919.

1094 1917–1918–1919: 102nd, Yesterday, To-day and Tomorrow. . . . Laval: Imprimerie L. Barneoud et cie, 1919. [102d Ammunition Train.]

1095 DeLong, Thomas F., comp. A History and Roster of the 103rd Ammunition Train. Allentown, Pennsylvania: 103rd Publishing Co., 1920.

1096 Acker, John. Thru the War with Our Outfit: Being a Historical Narrative of the 107th Ammunition Train. Sturgeon Bay, Wisconsin: Door County Publishing Co., 1920.

1097 Loomis, Ernest L., comp. History of the 304th Ammunition Train. Boston: Badger, 1920.

1098 Underhill, Edwin H. How It Happened and Other Poems. (?), Texas: Reimer Co., 1919. [History of 311th Ammunition Train written in verse.]

Artillery Park

1099 [McEvoy, A.L.], comp. History of Army Artillery Park, First Army, A.E.F., France. Oakland: Bennett & Morehouse, 1919.

Armies

1100 Report of the First Army, American Expeditionary Forces: Organization and Operations. Fort Leavenworth, Kansas: General Service Schools Press, 1923.

1101 U.S. Army. First Army. Report of the First Army, American Expeditionary Forces: Organization and Operations. Fort Leavenworth, Kansas: General Service Schools Press, 1923.

1102 U.S. Army War College. Historical Section. The Genesis of the American First Army. . . . Washington, D.C.: G.P.O., 1938.

1103 Adams, James G. Review of the American Forces in Germany. Coblenz, 1921. [2d Army.]

Balloon Section

1104 Ovitt, Spaulding W., ed. *The Balloon Section of the American Expeditionary Forces.* New Haven: Tuttle, Morehouse & Taylor, 1919.

Base Hospitals

1105 U.S. Army. A.E.F. Base Hospital No. 4. *"Album de la Guerre."* Cleveland: Scientific Illustrating Studios, 1919.

1106 [Clymer, George], ed. *The History of U.S. Army Base Hospital No. 6 and Its Part in the American Expeditionary Forces.* Boston, 1924.

1107 *Base Hospital No. 9, A.E.F.: A History of the Work of the New York Hospital Unit during Two Years of Active Service: Written by the Padre.* New York, 1920.

1108 U.S. Army. A.E.F. Base Hospital No. 10. *History of the Pennsylvania Hospital Unit (Base Hospital No. 10, U.S.A.) in the Great War.* New York: P. B. Hoeber, 1921.

1109 *History of Base Hospital No. 18, American Expeditionary Forces.* Baltimore: Base Hospital No. 18 Association, 1919.

1110 Swan, John M., and Mark Heath. *A History of United States Army Base Hospital No. 19. . . .* Rochester: Wegman-Walsh Press, 1922.

1111 Munger, Donna B. "Base Hospital 21 and the Great War." *Missouri Historical Review* 70 (Apr. 1976): 272–90.

1112 Kaletzki, Charles H., ed. *Official History of U.S.A. Base Hospital No. 31 of Youngstown, Ohio and Hospital Unit "G" of Syracuse University.* Syracuse: Craftsman Press, 1919.

1113 Hitz, Benjamin D., ed. *A History of Base Hospital 32 (Including Unit R).* Indianapolis, 1922.

1114 [Pitts, Edmund M.; William T. Bauer; and Malcolm G. Sausser], eds. *Base Hospital 34 in the World War.* Philadelphia: Lyon & Armor, 1922.

1115 [Cooper, Alice E.], ed. *A History of the United States Army Base Hospital No. 36. . . .* Detroit, 1922.

1116 Coplin, W. M. L. *American Red Cross Base Hospital No. 38 in the World War.* Philadelphia, 1923.

1117 Combs, Josiah H. *Siege of Salisbury Court Which Chronicles the Feat of Base Hospital 40 Winning the War.* Lexington, Kentucky: Hurst & Byars, 1923.

1118   [Cabell, Julian M.] A Brief Sketch of Base Hospital No. 41, by the Commanding Officer. Washington, D.C., 1925.

1119   [Geisinger, Joseph F.], ed. History of U.S. Army Base Hospital No. 45 in the Great War (Medical College of Virginia Unit). Richmond, Virginia: William Byrd Press, 1924.

1120   On Active Service with Base Hospital 46, U.S.A., Mar. 20, 1918 to May 25, 1919. Portland, Oregon: Arcady Press, 1919 (?).

1121   Matheson, Martin. 48: An Informal and Mostly Pictorial History of U.S. Base Hospital 48, 1918–1919. New York: Veterans U.S. Base Hospital No. 48, 1939.

1122   History of Base Hospital Number Fifty-three, Advance Section, Services of Supply. Langres, Haute-Marne: 29th Engineers Printing Plant, 1919.

1123   A History of U.S.A. Base Hospital No. 115. . . . Memphis, Tennessee: Toof, 1919 (?).

Cavalry

1124   Harmon, Ernest N. "The Second Cavalry in the Meuse-Argonne." Cavalry Journal 31 (Jan. 1922): 10–18.

1125   ———. "The Second Cavalry in the St. Mihiel Offensive." Cavalry Journal 30 (July 1921): 282–89.

1126   Perry, Redding F. "The 2d Cavalry in France." Cavalry Journal 37 (Jan. 1928): 27–41.

1127   New Jersey Cavalry. 102d Regiment. History of the Essex Troop, 1890–1925. Newark, New Jersey: Essex Troop Armory, 1925.

Coast Artillery

1128   Ninth Coast Artillery Corps. The Minute Men of '17. . . . N.p.: Memorial and Property Committee of the Ninth Artillery Corps, 1922.

1129   Regimental History: 19th Regiment Army Artillery (C.A.C.), Fort MacArthur, California, 1918. Los Angeles: Times-Mirror, 1918.

1130   Roster and History of Battery "D," 35th Regiment, Coast Artillery. Fort Monroe, Virginia. . . . N.p., 1919 (?).

1131   [47th Coast Artillery Regiment.] Story of the Forty Seventh. . . . Baltimore: George W. King Printing, 1919.

1132   Cutler, Frederick M. The 55th Artillery (C.A.C.) in the American Expeditionary Forces, France 1918. Worcester, Massachussetts: Commonwealth Press, 1920.

1133 Dupuy, Richard Ernest. *With the 57th in France*. Brooklyn: Our Army, Inc., 1930.

1134 [Grace, James L.] *A Brief History of the 2nd Battalion, 57th Artillery C.A.C., 31st Brigade, Army Artillery, First Army, From July 20, 1917 to January 15, 1919.* N.p., 1919.

1135 *History of the 58th U.S. Artillery, C.A.C., American Expeditionary Forces*. New York, 1919 (?).

1136 [McClinton, H. L.], ed. *Ye Batterie Booke Battery B, Sixty-third Artillery (C.A.C.), American Expeditionary Forces*. N.p., 1919 (?).

1137 Ashton, John L., et al., eds. *F, 63.* Tacoma, Washington, 1919. [63d Coast Artillery Regiment.]

1138 *The History of Battery E, 66th Artillery, C.A.C.* Westerly, Rhode Island: Utter Co., 1919.

1139 [Elder, Bowman], comp. *An Illustrated History of the 71st Artillery (C.A.C.). . . .* Indianapolis: William H. Burford, 1920 (?).

Corps

1140 *Records of the World War: Field Orders 2d Army Corps*. Washington, D.C.: G.P.O., 1921.

1141 U.S. General Staff. War Plans Division. Historical Branch. *Operations of the 2d American Corps in the Somme Offensive, August 8 to November 11, 1918. . . .* Washington, D.C.: G.P.O., 1920.

Engineers (General)

1142 Collins, Francis A. *The Fighting Engineers: The Minute Men of Our Industrial Army*. New York: Century, 1918.

1143 Fiske, Harold C. "A Division Engineer at the Front." *Military Engineer* 20 (Sept. 1928): 408– 12.

1144 *Historical Report of the Chief Engineer: Including All Operations of the Engineer Department, American Expeditionary Forces, 1917– 1919.* Washington, D.C.: G.P.O., 1919.

1145 Parsons, William B. *The American Engineers in France*. New York: Appleton, 1920.

1146 Tomlin, Robert K. *American Engineers Behind the Battle Lines of France*. New York: McGraw-Hill, 1918.

1147 U.S. Army. A.E.F. Engineer Department. *Historical Report of the Chief Engineer, 1917– 1919.* Washington, D.C.: G.P.O., 1919.

Engineer Units

1148 [Farrell, Thomas F.], ed. *A History of the First U.S. Engineers.* . . . Coblenz, 1919.

1149 *History of Company "F," First U.S. Engineers, 1917–1918–1919.* Montabaur: G. Sauerborn, 1919 (?).

1150 [Burton, Allan.] *A History of the Second Regiment of Engineers, United States Army, from Its Organization in Mexico, 1916, to Its Watch on the Rhine, 1919.* Cologne: M. DuMont Schauberg, 1919.

1151 U.S. Army. 2d Engineers. *The Official History of the Second Regiment of Engineers and Second Engineer Train: United States Army, in the World War.* San Antonio: San Antonio Printing, 1920.

1152 *Columbia to the Rhine: Being a Brief History of the Fourth Engineers.* . . . Wald: Westdeutsche Grossdruckerei, 1919.

1153 Adams, Donald B. "Fore and Aft of the Infantry: The 6th Engineers in the American Offensives of 1918." *Military Engineer* 13 (Nov.-Dec. 1921): 470–73.

1154 *History of the Sixth Engineers: By Its Men.* New York: Knickerbocker, 1920.

1155 *"The Carpathians": Tenth Engineers (Forestry), A.E.F., 1917–1919.* Washington, D.C., 1940.

1156 [Boughton, Van Tuyl.] *History of the Eleventh Engineers, United States Army . . . February 3, 1917, to May 8, 1919.* . . . New York: Little & Ives, 1926.

1157 [Lincoln, Leopold L.], ed. *Company C, Eleventh Engineers: A History.* Indianapolis: Hollenbeck Press, 1919.

1158 Laird, John A. *History of the Twelfth Engineers, U.S. Army.* St. Louis: Buxton & Skier, 1919.

1159 Warmer, L. E. *History of the 13th Engineers (Railway), U.S.A., 1917–1918–1919: With the American Forces in France.* Fleury-sur-Aire, 1919.

1160 [Henderson, Robert G.], ed. *History of the Fourteenth Engineers, U.S. Army, from May 1917 to May 1919.* . . . Boston: Atlantic Printing, 1923.

1161 [Wilkins, Oliver], ed. *The Company Fund:* . . . *Company D of the Fifteenth Engineers.* . . . N.p., 1919 (?).

1162 Reilly, John E. *History of F Company, 15th Engineers, American Expeditionary Forces, 1917–1919.* Pittsburgh: Bletchers-Anchors, 1919.

1163 Sixteenth Engineers Veterans Association, comp. *History of the Sixteenth Engineers (Railway), American Expeditionary Forces, 1917–1919.* Detroit: La Salle Press, 1939.

1164 Wiley, Hugh, ed. *The Eighteenth Engineers, A.E.F. France, 1917–1919.* Berkeley, 1959.

1165 *Ninth Company, Twentieth Engineers Forestry, A.E.F.: Its Story by Its Men.* Lodi, California: Lodi Printing & Rubber Stamp Co., 1919.

1166 [Simmons, Perez, and A. H. Davies], eds. *Twentieth Engineers, France, 1917–1918–1919.* Portland, Oregon: Twentieth Engineers Publishing Association, 1920.

1167 [Gilbert, W. F., and William J. Garren], eds. *An Historical and Technical Biography of the Twenty-first Engineers, Light Railway, United States Army. . . .* New York: McConnell Printing Co., 1919.

1168 [Ellington, W. B.], ed. *Company "A," Twenty-Third Engineers, A.E.F.* Chicago: Geographical Publishing Co., 1920.

1169 *"C" Company: Our Book, of the Company, for the Company, by the Company: "C" Company 23rd Regiment of United States Highway Engineers, in the United States and France, November 1917 to June 1919.* Kansas City, Missouri, 1922.

1170 [Lee, Charles H.], ed. *History of the Twenty-Sixth Engineers (Water Supply Regiment), in the World War, September 1917–March 1919.* N.p., published by the regiment, 1920 (?).

1171 [Ingalls, W. R.], ed. *History of the 27th Engineers, U.S.A., 1917–1919.* New York: Association of the 27th Engineers, 1920.

1172 Hinman, Jesse R. *Ranging in France with Flash and Sound. . . .* Portland, Oregon: Dunham Printing Co., 1919. [29th Engineers, 2d Battalion.]

1173 Studley, George M. *History of the 31st Railway Engineers of the A.E.F.* Berkeley, 1941.

1174 Johnston, Clarence D. *Engineer Depots in the American Expeditionary Forces.* Châteauroux: P. Mellottee, 1919. [34th Engineers.]

1175 Clement, Don L. *But We Built the Cars: A Record of the Work Done by the 35th Engineers, U.S.A., in France.* New York: Redfield-Kendrick-Odell, 1922.

1176 Brown, Herbert C. *History of E Company, 37th Engineers.* Boston: George H. Ellis, 1919.

1177 Peterson, William L. *Company History "D," 55th Engineers, American Expeditionary Forces.* Minneapolis: Augsburg Publishing Co., 1919.

1178   Macomber, Alexander, and Meade Brunet, comps. *The 56th Engineers in the World War.* Albany, New York: Brandow, 1920.

1179   Davis, Robert M. *The History of Company C, 57th Engineers during the World War, 1918– 1919.* N.p., 1919 (?).

1180   *The 101st U.S. Engineers (1st Corps Cadets) in Foreign Service.* Boston, 1919.

1181   *The Story of B Company, 101st Engineers. . . .* N.p., 1919 (?).

1182   Swann, Carroll J. *My Company.* Boston: Houghton Mifflin, 1919. [101st Engineers.]

1183   U.S. Army. 101st Engineers. *The Story of "E" Company, 101st Engineers, 26th Division.* Boston: Walton Advertising & Printing, 1919.

1184   Weaver, Frederic N., and Philip N. Sanborn. *The Story of F Company, 101st regiment, U.S. Engineers: An Informal Narrative.* Boston: T. O. Metcalf, 1924.

1185   Andrews, James H.; J. S. Bradford; and Charles Elcock. *Soldiers of the Castle: A History of Company B . . . 103rd Engineers, 28th Division, A.E.F.* Philadelphia: Hoeflich Printing House, 1929.

1186   Engineers Club of Trenton, comp. *Trenton's Own Company of Engineers.* Trenton, 1922 (?). [104th Engineers.]

1187   Pratt, Joseph H. "Diary of Colonel Joseph Hyde Pratt, Commanding 105th Engineers, A.E.F." *North Carolina Historical Review* 1 (Jan.– Oct. 1924): 35– 70, 210– 36, 344– 80, 475– 540; 2 (Jan.– Apr. 1925): 117– 24, 269– 99.

1188   Sullivan, Willard P., and H. S. Tucker, comps. *The History of the 105th Regiment of Engineers: Divisional Engineers of the "Old Hickory" (30th) Division.* New York: Doran, 1919.

1189   *The Operations of the 106th Regiment of Engineers in France. . . .* Paris: Leon Dauer, 1919.

1190   Rankin, Edward P. *The Santa Fe Trail Leads to France: A Narrative of Battle Service of the 110th Engineers (35th Division) in the Meuse-Argonne Offensive.* Kansas City, Missouri: Dick Richardson Co., 1933.

1191   U.S. Army. 113th Engineers. *Overseas Castle.* Nancy: Berger-Levrault, 1919. [113th Engineers.]

1192   [Wittkamp, Frank F.], ed. *. . . Souvenir Castle: 113th Engineers, Camp Shelby, Mississippi.* Hattiesburg, Mississippi: Dever Printing, 1918.

1193 [Shields, Mark A.], ed. *The History of the 116th Engineers, First Depot Division, American Expeditionary Forces, France.* Angers: Caserne Desjardins, 1918.

1194 Sadler, Edwin J., ed. *California Rainbow Memories: A Pictorial Review of the Activities of the 2nd Battalion: 117th Engineers during the World War.* Los Angeles, 1925.

1195 [Irvine, E. S. J.], ed. *A Regimental Biography of the Two Hundred and Tenth Engineers, Tenth Division, United States Army.* Camp A. A. Humphreys, Virginia: Printed at the Vocational School, 1920.

1196 [Slosser, Gaius J.], ed. *History of the 212th Engineers, 1918– 1919.* . . . N.p., 1919.

1197 . . . *213th Engineers, Camp Lewis, Washington.* Seattle: Gateway Printing, 1918.

1198 U.S. Army 214th Engineers. *Two Hundred Fourteenth Engineers, 14th Division, Camp Custer, Michigan.* Battle Creek, Michigan: Gage Printing Co., 1919.

1199 U.S. Army 301st Engineers. *The Three Hundred and First Engineers: A History, 1917– 1919.* . . . Boston: Houghton Mifflin, 1920.

1200 [Crawford, Gilbert H., et al.], eds. *The 302d Engineers: A History.* New York (?), 1919 (?).

1201 [Roth, Joseph P., and R. L. Wheeler], comps. *History of Company "E," 303d Engineers of the 78th Division, 1917– 1919.* Rochester, New York: J. P. Smith, 1919.

1202 U.S. Army 304th Engineers. *The Official History of the Three Hundred and Fourth Engineer Regiment, Seventy-ninth Division, U.S.A. during the World War.* Lancaster, Pennsylvania: Steinman & Foltz, 1920.

1203 Floyd, Frank T. *Company "F" Overseas.* . . . Pittsburgh: Pittsburgh Printing Co., 1921 (?). [305th Engineers.]

1204 *Roster and History, 306th Regiment of Engineers and 306th Engineer Train.* . . . Columbia, South Carolina: State Co., 1920 (?).

1205 U.S. Army. 308th Engineers. *With the 308th Engineers from Ohio to the Rhine and Back, 1917– 1919.* Cleveland, 308th Engineers Veterans Association, 1923.

1206 Parsons, G. C. "The 313th Engineer Regiment in France." *Military Engineer* 18 (Nov. 1926): 453– 57.

1207 Haswell, William S., and C. S. Stevenson. *A History of Company A—314th Engineers, 89th Division.* N.p., 1920 (?).

1208   [Martin, Paul A.] Company "B," 314th Engineers. . . . Chicago: Foster, 1919.

1209   History of Company D—314 Engineers. Trier: Schlaar & Dathe, 1919.

1210   [Hixson, Merrel E.], comp. From Funston to the Rhine with "E" Company. . . . Trier: J. Lintz, 1919. [314th Engineers, A.E.F.]

1211   The History of the 316th Engineers: A Record of Military Operations, from August 1917 to April 1919. N.p., 1919.

Evacuation Hospitals

1212   The History of Evacuation Hospital Number 6, United States Army, 1917–1919. Poughkeepsie, New York, 1931.

1213   Pottle, Frederick A. Stretchers: The Story of a Hospital Unit on the Western Front. New Haven: Yale University Press, 1929. [8th Evacuation Hospital.]

1214   Shipley, Arthur M., and Agnes T. Considine. The Officers and Nurses of Evacuation Eight. New Haven: Yale University Press, 1929.

1215   [Bachman, Walter J.] Souvenir Roster and History of Evacuation Hospital No. 15 with the Story of Verdun and the Argonne Drive. N.p., 1919.

Field Artillery

1216   Hess, Dudley. "Going Thru" with a Golden Spoon: An Illustrated Story of 52nd Brigade, Field Artillery, American Expeditionary Forces. New York, 1919 (?).

1217   Price, William G. Activities and Citations of the 53rd Artillery Brigade, Twenty-eighth Division, United States Army, World War, 1914–1918. Chester, Pennsylvania: Chester Times, 1919.

1218   Chandler, Walter. The 55th Field Artillery Brigade, Thirtieth Division, American Expeditionary Forces. Memphis, Tennessee: Jno. R. Kinnie Co., 1919.

1219   Bacon, William J., ed. History of the Fifty-fifth Field Artillery Brigade . . . 1917, 1918, 1919. Nashville: Benson Printing Co., 1920.

1220   Harlow, Rex F. Trail of the 61st: A History of the 61st Field Artillery Brigade during the World War, 1917–1919. Oklahoma City: Harlow Publishing, 1919.

1221   A History of the Sixty-sixth Field Artillery Brigade. . . . Denver: Smith-Brooks Printing Co., 1919 (?).

1222 Russell, Richard M. *The 151st Field Artillery Brigade.* Boston: Cornhill, 1919.

1223 DeVarila, Osborne. *The First Shot For Liberty. . . .* Philadelphia: John C. Winston, 1918. [6th Field Artillery Regiment, Battery C.]

1224 U.S. Army. 6th Field Artillery. *A History of the Sixth Regiment, Field Artillery, First Division.* Coblenz: Görres-Druckerei, 1919 (?).

1225 *History of the Seventh Field Artillery (First Division, A.E.F.), World War, 1917–1919.* New York: Little & Ives, 1929.

1226 Roosevelt, Kermit. *War in the Garden of Eden.* New York: Scribner's, 1919. [7th Field Artillery Regiment.]

1227 [Day, Clifford L.] *A History of Operations and Activities of the 1st Battalion, 10th Field Artillery in the World War, 1914–1918.* Coblenz, 1919.

1228 Hayes, Casey. "Operations of the 2nd Battalion, 10th Field Artillery in the Second Battle of the Marne." *Field Artillery Journal* 14 (Sept. 1924): 443–50.

1229 Anderson, J. W. "With the Tenth Field Artillery at the Second Battle of the Marne." *Field Artillery Journal* 13 (Sept. 1923): 375–83.

1230 Duff, James L. *The Eleventh Field Artillery.* Dijon: Imprimerie Darantière, 1919.

1231 [Cortelyou, K. M. Escott, and W. B. Williamson], eds. *From Arizona to the Huns: Battery "C," 11th F. A.* Dijon: V. P. Berthier, 1919.

1232 Foster, Pell W. *A Short History of Battery "B," 12th Field Artillery, Second Division in the World War.* New York: Evening Post Job Printing Office, 1921.

1233 Wahl, George D. "Battery 'B' of the Twelfth Field Artillery during the Late War." *Field Artillery Journal* 14 (Jan.–June 1924): 15–30, 131–43, 221–36.

1234 Upson, William H. *Me and Henry and the Artillery.* Garden City, New York: Doubleday, Doran, 1928. [13 Field Artillery Regiment.]

1235 Cone, Anthony D. *E Battery Goes to War: Being Extracts from the Wartime Diary of First Sergeant Anthony D. Cone, Battery E, 15th Field Artillery, Second (Regular) Division, U.S. Army.* Washington, D.C., 1929.

1236 [Gerhart, Harry S.], ed. *History of the 19th Regiment Field Artillery Replacement Depot, Camp Jackson, S.C.* Columbia, South Carolina: State Co., 1919.

1237 Stevenson, Kenyon, comp. *History of the Twenty-first Field Artillery, from Date of Organization, June 1, 1917 to February 22, 1919.* Luxembourg: Imprimerie Art. Dr. M. Huss, 1919 (?).

1238 Tierney, Dudley R. *The Seventy-seventh Field Artillery Goes to War, 1917–1919.* N.p., 1919 (?).

1239 Carter, Russell G. *The 101st Field Artillery, A.E.F., 1917–1919.* Boston: Houghton Mifflin, 1940.

1240 *A Short History and Photographic Record of the 101st Field Artillery, 1917. . . .* Cambridge: Harvard University Press, 1918.

1241 *Being the Narrative of Battery A of the 101st Field Artillery. . . .* Cambridge, Massachusetts: Brattle Press, 1919.

1242 Washburn, Slater. *One of the D [Yankee Division.]* Boston: Houghton Mifflin, 1919. [101st Field Artillery.]

1243 *History of the One Hundred Second Field Artillery, July 1917–April 1919.* Boston: Lawrence Press, 1927.

1244 *A Short History and Photographic Record of the 102nd U.S. Field Artillery. . . .* Cambridge: Harvard University Press, 1918.

1245 Sirois, Edward D., and William McGinnis. *Smashing through "the World War" with Fighting Battery C, 102nd F.A., 26th Division, Yankee Division, 1917–1918–1919.* Salem, Massachusetts: Meek Press, 1919.

1246 La Branche, Ernest E. *An American Battery in France.* Worcester, Massachusetts: Belisle Printing & Publishing, 1923. [Battery E, 102d Field Artillery.]

1247 Mozley, George. *Our Miracle Battery.* Lowell, Massachusetts: Sullivan Brothers, 1920. [Battery F, 102d Field Artillery.]

1248 Chaffee, Everitte St. J. *The Egotistical Account of an Enjoyable War.* Providence (?), 1951. [103d Field Artillery.]

1249 Kernan, W. F., and Henry T. Samson. *History of the 103rd Field Artillery (Twenty-sixth Division, A.E.F.), World War, 1917–1919.* Providence: Remington Printing Co., 192?

1250 McKenna, Frederick A., ed. *Battery "A," 103rd Field Artillery in France.* Providence: Livermore & Knight Co., 1919.

1251 *History of Battery B, One Hundred Third Field Artillery, Twenty-sixth Division with Pictorial Supplement.* Providence: E. L. Freeman, 1922.

1252 Samson, Henry T., and George C. Hull. *The War Story of C Battery, One Hundred and Third U.S. Field Artillery, France 1917–1919.* Norwood, Massachusetts: Plimpton Press, 1920.

1253 Herzog, Stanley J. *The Fightin' Yanks . . . Battery F, 103rd Field Artillery, 26th or Yankee Division.* Stamford, Connecticut: Cunningham Print, 1922.

1254 ———. *Helmets, Second Battle of the Marne.* Stamford, Connecticut: Bell Press, 1930. [103d Field Artillery.]

1255 *The 104th Field Artillery in the Great War, 1917– 1919.* N.p., 1919.

1256 *The War Book of One Hundred and Sixth Regiment Field Artillery, United States Army, 1917– 1919.* New York: Nation Press, 1919.

1257 *A Short History and Illustrated Roster of the 107th Field Artillery, U.S.N.G. . . .* Philadelphia: Edward Stern, 1918.

1258 Jacobsen, A. Wilmot, and J. Carroll Mansfield. *The Blue and Gray: A Story of Battery D, 110th Field Artillery.* Baltimore: Norman T. A. Munder & Co., 1919 (?).

1259 *Battery E of the 110th Field Artillery: A Record of Service and Fellowship Here and "Over There."* Baltimore: Kohn & Pollock, 1919.

1260 Lord, Russell. *Captain Boyd's Battery, A.E.F.* Ithaca, New York: Atkinson Press, 1920. [110th Field Artillery Regiment, Battery F.]

1261 Seal, Henry F. *"Numquam non Paratus": . . . History of the 111th Field Artillery Regiment. . . .* Richmond: Adjutant General of Virginia, 1953.

1262 [Fletcher, A. L.] *History of the 113th Field Artillery, 30th Division.* New York: Wynkoop Hallenbeck Crawford, 1920.

1263 Jacks, Leo V. *Service Record: By an Artilleryman.* New York: Scribner's, 1928. [119th Field Artillery.]

1264 [Penner, Carl; Frederic Samond; and H. M. Appel], eds. *The 120th Field Artillery Diary, 1880– 1919.* Milwaukee: Hammesmith-Kortmeyer, 1928.

1265 [Casey, Robert J.] *The Cannoneers Have Hairy Ears: A Diary of the Front Lines.* New York: Sears, 1927. [124th Field Artillery Regiment.]

1266 Bucklew, Leslie L. *The "Orphan Battery" and Operations, 128th U.S. Field Artillery. . . .* Cleveland: Howard M. White, 1921.

1267 Daniels, Jonathan. *The Man of Independence.* Philadelphia: Lippincott, 1950. [Harry S Truman in 129th Field Artillery Regiment.]

1268 Lee, Jay M. *The Artilleryman: The Experiences and Impressions of an American Artillery Regiment in the World War, 129th F.A., 1917– 1919.* Kansas City, Missouri: Spencer Printing, 1920.

1269   McLean, William P. My Story of the 130th F.A., A.E.F. Topeka: Boys' Industrial School, 1920.

1270   Kirtley, Lorin E. The Liaison: A History of Regimental Headquarters Company, One Hundred Thirty Fourth U.S. Field Artillery. Dayton: Otterbein Press, 1919.

1271   Witt, Fred R. Riding to War with "A": A History of Battery "A" of the 135th Field Artillery. Cleveland: C. Hauser, 1919.

1272   Coffin, Louis, and Cameron H. Sanders. A History of the Third Field Artillery, Ohio National Guard which Served through the World War, 1917, 1918, 1919, as the 136th F.A. Regiment, U.S.A. . . . Cincinnati: Montel Press, 1928.

1273   Moorhead, Robert L. The Story of the 139th Field Artillery, American Expeditionary Forces. Indianapolis: Bobbs-Merrill, 1920.

1274   Davis, Paul M., and H. K. Clay, History of Battery "C," 148th Field Artillery, American Expeditionary Forces. . . . Colorado Springs: Out West, 1919.

1275   Being the Story of a Light Field Artillery Battery from Illinois during the World War. Chicago: Gunthorp-Warren Printing Co., 1930. [149th Field Artillery Regiment.]

1276   Canright, Eldon J. "Some War-time Letters." Wisconsin Magazine of History 5 (Dec. 1921): 171– 200; (Mar. 1922): 301– 19. [149th Field Artillery.]

1277   Gilmore, William E. "History of Headquarters Company, One Hundred and Forty-ninth Field Artillery, from June 30, 1917 to May 10, 1919." Illinois Historical Society Journal 17 (Apr. 1924): 21– 143.

1278   Kilner, Frederick R. Battery E in France, 149th Field Artillery, Rainbow (42nd) Division. Chicago: Advertising Co., 1919.

1279   Langille, Leslie. Men of the Rainbow. Chicago: O'Sullivan Publishing House, 1933. [149th Field Artillery.]

1280   MacArthur, Charles. War Bugs. Garden City, New York: Doubleday, Doran, 1929. [149th Field Artillery.]

1281   Straub, Elmer F. A Sergeant's Diary in the World War: The Dairy of an Enlisted Member of the 150th Field Artillery (Forty-second [Rainbow] Division), October 27, 1917 to August 7, 1919. Indianapolis: Indiana Historical Commission, 1923.

1282   Sherwood, Elmer W. Diary of a Rainbow Veteran: Written at the Front. Terre Haute, Indiana: Moore-Langen, 1929. [150th Field Artillery.]

1283 ———. *Rainbow Hoosier.* Indianapolis: Printing Arts Co., 1922. [150th Field Artillery.]

1284 Collins, Louis L. . . . *History of the 151st Field Artillery, Rainbow Division.* St. Paul. Minnesota War Records Commission, 1924.

1285 Leach, George E. *War Diary [by] George E. Leach, Colonel, 151st Field Artillery, Rainbow Division.* Minneapolis: Pioneer Printers, 1923.

1286 *The 302nd Field Artillery, United States Army.* Cambridge, Massachusetts: Cosmos Press, 1919.

1287 *G.P.F. Book: Regimental History of the Three Hundred and Third Field Artillery.* N.p., 1921.

1288 Howard, James M. *The Autobiography of a Regiment: A History of the 304th Field Artillery in the World War.* New York: Privately printed, 1920.

1289 Camp, Charles W. *History of the 305th Field Artillery.* Garden City, New York: Country Life Press, 1919.

1290 *In France with Battery F, 305th F.A.* N.p., 1919.

1291 [306th Field Artillery History Staff.] *The History of the 306th Field Artillery.* . . . New York: Knickerbocker, 1920.

1292 *Hickoxy's Army: Being a Sort of a History of Headquarters Company, 306th Field Artillery, 77th Division, A.E.F.* New York: Little & Ives, 1920.

1293 [Field, Francis L., and G. H. Richards], eds. *The Battery Book: A History of Battery "A," 306 F.A.* New York: De Vinne Press, 1921.

1294 *"C" Battery Book, 306th F.A., 77th Division, 1917–1919.* Brooklyn: Braunworth & Co., 1920.

1295 *History of the 307th Field Artillery, September 6, 1917–May 16, 1919.* N.p., 1919.

1296 *History of "A" Battery, 308th Field Artillery, 153rd Field Artillery Brigade, 78th Division.* N.p., 1919.

1297 Binder, Raymond S. *A History of Battery "C," 308th Field Artillery, 78th Division, American Expeditionary Forces.* N.p., 1919.

1298 McCarthy, William E. *Memories of the 309th Field Artillery.* Rochester, New York: Henry Connolly Printing Co., 1920.

1299 Bachman, William E. *The Delta of the Triple Elevens: The History of Battery D, 311th Field Artillery, United States Army, American Expeditionary Forces.* Hazleton, Pennsylvania: Standard-Sentinel Print, 1920.

1300   [Crowell, Thomas I., Jr.], ed. *A History of the 313th Field Artillery*, *U.S.A.* New York: Thomas Y. Crowell, 1920.

1301   *History of the 314th Field Artillery*. N.p., 1919 (?).

1302   McElroy, John L. *War Diary of John Lee McElroy, 1st Lieutenant*, *315th Field Artillery, 155th Brigade. . . .* Camden, New Jersey: Haddon Press, 1929.

1303   *The 316th Field Artillery*. Chicago: Rogers & Hall, 1920 (?).

1304   *History of the 322d Field Artillery*. New Haven, 1920.

1305   Colyer, Charles M. *The History of the 323rd Regiment of Field Artillery. . . .* Cleveland: Britton Print, 1920.

1306   Wideman, Ernest G.; Sherlock A. Herrick; and Carl Shem; comps. *History of Battery E, 323rd Field Artillery. . . .* Cleveland: Ward & Shaw, 1921.

1307   Riggs, McDonald H., and Rutherford H. Platt, Jr. *A History of Battery F, 323d Field Artillery*. Cleveland: Privately printed by J. B. Dempsey, 1920.

1308   Ashburn, Thomas Q. *History of the 324th Field Artillery, United States Army*. New York: Doran, 1920.

1309   *The Trail of Battery D, Three Hundred and Twenty-fourth Heavy Field Artillery, American Expeditionary Forces. . . .* Marietta, Ohio: Hyde Brothers, 1919.

1310   Barry, Edward W., ed. *Doings of Battery B, . . . 328th Field Artillery, American Expeditionary Forces*. Grand Rapids: Dean-Hicks Co., 1920.

1311   *331st Field Artillery, United States Army, 1917–1919*. Chicago: Rogers Print Co., 1919.

1312   *The Blackhawk Howitzer*. Chicago: R. R. Donnelley & Sons, 1919. [333 Field Artillery Regiment.]

1313   Forbes, Jerome R., ed. *September Nineteen Seventeen–January Nineteen Nineteen: . . . . 338th U.S. Field Artillery. . . .* St. Paul, Minnesota: Pioneer Co., 1921 (?).

1314   *Regimental History Three Hundred and Forty-First Field Artillery, Eighty-ninth Division of the National Army*. Kansas City, Missouri: Union Bank Note Co., 1920.

1315   Chubb, Robert W. *Regimental History, 342nd Field Artillery, 89th Division*. New York: 342d Field Artillery, Regimental Historian, 1921.

1316 Scott, Charles M. *Activities of the 343rd Field Artillery, 90th Division, United States Army.* Germany, 1919.

1317 Ross, William O., and Duke L. Slaughter, comps. *With the 351st in France.* Baltimore: Afro-American Co., 1919 (?).

Field Hospitals

1318 Hoyt, Charles B., ed. *The Story, the History of Field Hospital 139 of Topeka, Kansas, in the Great War, 1917–1918–1919.* Topeka: Jones & Birch, 1919 (?).

1319 Yates, Stanley. *History of the 163rd Field Hospital, American Expeditionary Forces.* Seattle: Moulton Printing Co., 1936.

1320 George, Herbert. *The Challenge of War.* New York: Vantage Press, 1966. [165th Field Hospital.]

1321 *A Record of the 362nd Field Hospital Company, 316th Sanitary Train, 91st Division, United States Army.* N.p., 1919 (?).

1322 Hill, Howard. *Facts and Fancies of 363d Field Hospital Company, 316th Sanitary Train, 91st Division, U.S.A., 1917–1919.* Portland, Oregon: Kleist & Co., 1919 (?).

1323 [Binswanger, Alvin O., et al.], eds. *Chronological History of the 364th Field Hospital Company.* Portland, Oregon: Press of Portland Printing House Co., 1929.

Field Signal Battalions

1324 *A Record of the Activities of the Second Field Signal Battalion, First Division.* Cologne: J. P. Bachem, 1919.

1325 Mohr, Harold O. *The Service Record: le Journal des Exploits du Compagnie C, 303rd Field Signal Battalion.* Chicago, 1919.

1326 *The History of Company C, 304th Field Signal Battalion, U.S. Army, American Expeditionary Forces.* Philadelphia: Shade Printing Co., 1920.

1327 [Shryer, Davis M.], ed. *Company C, 305th Field Signal Battalion, October Nineteen Seventeen to June Nineteen Nineteen.* N.p., 1919.

1328 [Selby, Herbert E.; J. E. Shimmin; and Harold V. Kelly], comps. *313th Field Signal Battalion History . . . during the World War.* Des Moines: Welch Publishing Co., 1939.

Gas Regiments

1329 Addison, James T. *The Story of the First Gas Regiment.* Boston: Houghton Mifflin, 1919.

1330 Langer, William L. *Gas and Flame in World War I.* New York: Knopf, 1965.

1331 ———, and Robert B. MacMullin. *With "E" of the First Gas.* Brooklyn: Holton Printing Co., 1919.

General Hospitals

1332 *History and Roster of the United States Army General Hospital No. 16.* New Haven: Yale University Press, 1919.

Infantry Brigades

1333 Crawford, Charles. *Six Months with the 6th Brigade.* Kansas City, Missouri: E. B. Barnett, 1927.

1334 *History of the 7th Infantry Brigade during the World War, 1918.* Cologne: M. Dumont Schauberg, 1919.

1335 Rupp, Roland L., comp. *Our Last Fight: An Actual Account of the Men and Work of the Signal Detachment of the 158th Infantry Brigade in the Final Drive North of Verdun.* Richmond, Virginia: Cussons, May, 1920.

Infantry Divisions

1336 Butler, Alban B., Jr. *"Happy Days!": A Humorous Narrative in Drawings of the Progress of American Arms, 1917–1919.* New York: Coward-McCann, 1929. [1st Division.]

1337 Miller, Henry R. *The First Division.* Pittsburgh: Crescent Press, 1920.

1338 Society of the First Division, comp. . . . *History of the First Division during the World War: 1917–1919.* Philadelphia: John C. Winston, 1922.

1339 Bogert, George D. *"Let's Go!": 10 Years' Retrospect of the World War.* San Francisco: Press of H. S. Crocker Co., 1927. [1st Division.]

1340 American Battle Monuments Commission. *1st Division: Summary of Operations in the World War.* Washington, D.C.: G.P.O., 1944.

1341 Bundy, Omar. "The Second Division at Château-Thierry." *Everybody's* 40 (Mar. 1919): 9–20.

1342 Spaulding, Oliver L., and John W. Wright. *The Second Division, American Expeditionary Forces in France: 1917–1919.* New York: Hillman Press, 1937.

1343 American Battle Monuments Commission. *2d Division: Summary of Operations in the World War.* Washington, D.C.: G.P.O., 1944.

1344   U.S. General Staff. War Plans Division. Historical Branch. *Blanc Mont (Meuse-Argonne-Champagne)*. Washington, D.C.: G.P.O., 1922. [2d Division.]

1345   [Hemenway, Frederic V.], comp. *History of the Third Division United States Army in the World War for the Period December 1, 1917 to January 1, 1919*. Andernach-on-the-Rhine, 1919.

1346   Dickman, Joseph T. *The Great Crusade: A Narrative of the World War*. New York: Appleton, 1927. [3d Division.]

1347   American Battle Monuments Commission. *3d Division: Summary of Operations in the World War*. Washington, D.C.: G.P.O., 1944.

1348   Linberger, C. W. *The Fourth Division in the World War: A Book of Illustrations from Photographs*. Los Angeles: Times-Mirror, 1919.

1349   Bach, Christian A., and Henry N. Hall. *The Fourth Division: Its Services and Achievements in the World War. . . .* Garden City, New York: Country Life Press, 1920.

1350   American Battle Monuments Commission. *4th Division: Summary of Operations in the World War*. Washington, D.C.: G.P.O., 1944.

1351   [Stevenson, Kenyon], comp. *The Official History of the Fifth Division U.S.A. . . . 1917–1919*. Washington, D.C.: Society of the Fifth Division, 1919.

1352   Records of the World War. *Field Orders, 1918, 5th Division*. Washington, D.C.: G.P.O., 1921.

1353   American Battle Monuments Commission. *5th Division: Summary of Operations in the World War*. Washington, D.C.: G.P.O., 1944.

1354   Fell, Edgar T., comp. *History of the Seventh Division, United States Army, 1917–1919*. Philadelphia: Printed by H. Moore, 1927.

1355   American Battle Monuments Commission. *7th Division: Summary of Operations in the World War*. Washington, D.C.: G.P.O., 1944.

1356   [Van Deusen, G. L. and W. G. Muller], comps. *Official History of the Thirteenth Division, 1918–1919*. Tacoma, Washington: R. W. Hulbert, 1919.

1357   Whitney, Parkhurst L., ed. *Camp Travis and Its Part in the World War*. New York: E. B. Johns, 1919. [18th Division.]

1358   Benwell, Harry A. *History of the Yankee Division*. Boston: Cornhill, 1919. [26th Infantry Division.]

1359   Albertine, Connell. The Yankee Doughboy. Boston: Branden Press, 1968. [26th Infantry Division.]

1360   Colby, Elbridge. "The March of the 26th." Infantry Journal 47 (Sept.–Oct. 1940): 462–74.

1361   Ford, Bert. The Fighting Yankees Overseas. Boston: N. E. McPhail, 1919, [26th Infantry Division.]

1362   George, Albert E., and E. H. Cooper. Pictorial History of the Twenty-sixth Division, United States Army. . . . Boston: Ball Publishing Co., 1920.

1363   Sibley, Frank P. With the Yankee Division in France. Boston: Little, Brown, 1919. [26th Infantry Division.]

1364   Taylor, Emerson G. New England in France, 1917–1919: A History of the Twenty-sixth Division, U.S.A. Boston: Houghton Mifflin, 1920.

1365   American Battle Monuments Commission. 26th Division: Summary of Operations in the World War. Washington, D.C.: G.P.O., 1944.

1366   Starlight, Alexander, comp. The Pictorial Record of the 27th Division. New York: Harper, 1919.

1367   Clarke, William F. Over There with O'Ryan's Roughnecks. Seattle: Superior Publishing, 1968. [27th Division.]

1368   O'Ryan, John F. The Story of the 27th Division. 2 vols. New York: Wynkoop Hallenbeck Crawford, 1921.

1369   American Battle Monuments Commission. 27th Division: Summary of Operations in the World War. Washington, D.C.: G.P.O., 1944.

1370   Gilbert, Eugene. The 28th Division in France. Nancy: Berger-Levrault, 1919.

1371   Proctor, Henry G. The Iron Division: National Guard of Pennsylvania in the World War. . . . Philadelphia: Winston, 1919. [28th Infantry Division.]

1372   Pennsylvania in the World War: An Illustrated History of the Twenty-eighth Division. 2 vols. Pittsburgh: States Publications Society, 1921.

1373   Martin, Edward, comp. The Twenty-eighth Division: Pennsylvania's Guard in the World War. 5 vols. Pittsburgh: 28th Division Publishing Co., 1923–1924.

1374   American Battle Monuments Commission. 28th Division: Summary of Operations in the World War. Washington, D.C.: G.P.O., 1944.

1375 Cutchins, John A. *History of the Twenty-Ninth Division: "Blue and Gray," 1917–1919.* Philadelphia: MacCalla & Co., 1921.

1376 *Source Book: Operations of the 29th Division, East of the Meuse River, October 8th to 30th, 1918.* Fort Monroe, Virginia: Coast Artillery School, 1922.

1377 American Battle Monuments Commission. *29th Division: Summary of Operations in the World War.* Washington, D.C.: G.P.O., 1944.

1378 Murphy, Elmer A., and Robert S. Thomas. *The Thirtieth Division in the World War.* Lepanto, Arkansas: Old Hickory Publishing Co., 1936.

1379 American Battle Monuments Commission. *30th Division: Summary of Operations in the World War.* Washington, D.C.: G.P.O., 1944.

1380 Wisconsin War History Commission. *The 32nd Division in the World War, 1917–1919.* Milwaukee: Wisconsin Printing, 1920.

1381 Garlock, Glenn R. *Tales of the Thirty-Second.* West Salem, Wisconsin: Badger Publishing, 1927.

1382 Pearson, LeRoy. "Major General William G. Haan." *Michigan History* 9 (Jan. 1925): 3–16. [Commander, 32d Division.]

1383 American Battle Monuments Commission. *32d Division: Summary of Operations in the World War.* Washington, D.C.: G.P.O., 1944.

1384 Stearns, Gustav. *From Army Camps and Battle Fields.* Minneapolis: Augsburg Publishing, 1919. [32d Division.]

1385 Huidekoper, Frederic L. *The History of the 33rd Division, A.E.F.* 4 vols. Springfield: Illinois State Historical Library, 1921.

1386 *Illinois in the World War: An Illustrated History of the Thirty-third Division.* . . . 2 vols. Chicago: States Publications Society, 1921.

1387 Lawrence, Andrea. " 'Over There' With the Thirty-third Division." *Illinois History* 19 (Apr. 1966): 150–51.

1388 American Battle Monuments Commission. *33d Division: Summary of Operations in the World War.* Washington, D.C.: G.P.O., 1944.

1389 Hay, Donald D. "Machine Guns, 35th Division, Meuse-Argonne Operation, Sept. 26–Oct. 1, 1918." *Infantry Journal* 40 (May–June 1933): 193–206.

1390 Hoyt, Charles B. *Heroes of the Argonne: An Authentic History of the Thirty-fifth Division.* Kansas City, Missouri: F. Hudson Publishing Co., 1919.

1391 Kenamore, Clair. "The 35th Division in the Vosges Mountains." *Cavalry Journal* 30 (Apr. 1921): 105–11.

1392 ———. *From Vauquois Hill to Exermont: A History of the Thirty-fifth Division of the United States Army.* St. Louis, Missouri: Guard Publishing Co., 1919.

1393 Carter, Robert L. *Pictorial History of the 35th Division.* Kansas City, Missouri, 1933.

1394 American Battle Monuments Commission. *35th Division: Summary of Operations in the World War.* Washington, D.C.: G.P.O., 1944.

1395 Chastaine, Ben H. *Story of the 36th: The Experiences of the 36th Division in the World War.* Oklahoma City: Harlow Publishing, 1920.

1396 American Battle Monuments Commission. *36th Division: Summary of Operations in the World War.* Washington, D.C.: G.P.O., 1944.

1397 Cole, Ralph D., and W. C. Howells. *The Thirty-seventh Division in the World War: 1917–1918.* 2 vols. Columbus, Ohio: Thirty-seventh Division Veterans Association, 1926–1929.

1398 Koons, Jack, and Don Palmer. *Billets and Bullets of 37th Division: Cartoons and Ragtime. . . .* Cincinnati: Bacharach Press, 1919.

1399 American Battle Monuments Commission. *37th Division: Summary of Operations in the World War.* Washington, D.C.: G.P.O., 1944.

1400 *History of the Fortieth (Sunshine) Division . . . 1917–1919.* Los Angeles: C. S. Hutson, 1920.

1401 Tomkins, Raymond S. *The Story of the Rainbow Division.* New York: Boni & Liveright, 1919. [150th Field Artillery.]

1402 Sherwood, Elmer W. *Diary of a Rainbow Veteran: Written at the Front.* Terre Haute, Indiana: Moore-Langen, 1929. [150th Field Artillery.]

1403 Reilly, Henry J. *Americans All, The Rainbow at War: Official History of the 42nd Rainbow Division in the World War.* Columbus, Ohio: F. J. Heer, 1936.

1404 Wolf, Walter B. *A Brief Story of the Rainbow Division.* New York: Printed by Rand McNally, 1919.

1405 American Battle Monuments Commission. *42d Division: Summary of Operations in the World War.* Washington, D.C.: G.P.O., 1944.

1406 [Adler, J. O.], ed. *History of the Seventy-seventh Division, August 25 1917–November 11, 1918.* New York: W. H. Crawford Printers, 1919.

1407 McKeogh, Arthur. *The Victorious 77th Division (New York's Own) in the Argonne Fight.* New York: Eggers, 1919.

1408 ———. *Over the 77th's War Ground.* . . . New York (?), 1929.

1409 Alexander, Robert. *Memories of the World War, 1917–1918.* New York: Macmillan, 1931. [77th Division.]

1410 American Battle Monuments Commission. *77th Division: Summary of Operations in the World War.* Washington, D.C.: G.P.O., 1944.

1411 Cochrane, I. L., ed. *Pictorial History of the 78th Division in France.* . . . Moorestown, New Jersey: I. L. Cochrane, 1920.

1412 Meehan, Thomas F., ed. *History of the Seventy-eighth Division in the World War, 1917–1918–1919.* New York: Dodd, Mead, 1921.

1413 American Battle Monuments Commission. *78th Division: Summary of Operations in the World War.* Washington, D.C.: G.P.O., 1944.

1414 Kleber, Brooks E. "The 78th Division Uses Gas in the Meuse-Argonne." *Armed Forces Chemical Journal* 14 (Jan.–Feb. 1960): 40.

1415 [Malcolm, Gilbert, and J. M. Cain.] *79th Division Headquarters Troop: A Record.* N.p., 1920 (?).

1416 [History Committee, 79th Division Association], comp. *History of the Seventy-ninth Division, A.E.F., during the World War: 1917–1919.* Lancaster, Pennsylvania: Steinman & Steinman, 1922.

1417 American Battle Monuments Commission. *79th Division: Summary of Operations in the World War.* Washington, D.C.: G.P.O., 1944.

1418 Young, Rush S. *Over the Top with the 80th by a Buck Private.* Washington, D.C., 1933.

1419 American Battle Monuments Commission. *80th Division: Summary of Operations in the World War.* Washington, D.C.: G.P.O., 1944.

1420 ———. *81st Division: Summary of Operations in the World War.* Washington, D.C.: G.P.O., 1944.

1421 *Official History of 82nd Division, American Expeditionary Forces: "All American" Division.* Indianapolis: Bobbs-Merrill, 1920.

1422 Wright, Henry B. *Soldiers of Oakham, Massachusetts, in the Great War of 1914–1918.* Oakham, Massachusetts: Oakham Historical Society, 1919. [82d Division.]

1423 American Battle Monuments Commission. *82nd Division: Summary of Operations in the World War.* Washington, D.C.: G.P.O., 1944.

1424 [Little, John G.] *The Official History of the Eighty-sixth Division.* Chicago: States Publishing Society, 1921.

1425 *The 88th Division in the World War of 1914–1918.* New York: Wynkoop Hollenbeck Crawford, 1919.

1426 Larson, Edgar J. O., comp. *Memoirs of France and the Eighty-eighth Division.* . . . Minneapolis: Webb, 1920.

1427 [Masseck, C. J.], comp. *Official Brief History of the 89th Division, U.S.A., 1917–1918–1919.* N.p., 1919.

1428 English, George H., Jr. *History of the 89th Division, U.S.A.* Denver: Smith-Brooks Printing Co., 1920.

1429 *Report on the St. Mihiel Offensive: 89th Division, September 12–13, 1918.* Fort Leavenworth, Kansas: Army Service Schools Press, 1919.

1430 American Battle Monuments Commission. *89th Division: Summary of Operations in the World War.* Washington, D.C.: G.P.O., 1944.

1431 Wythe, George. *A History of the 90th Division.* New York: 90th Division Association, 1920.

1432 American Battle Monuments Commission. *90th Division: Summary of Operations in the World War.* Washington, D.C.: G.P.O., 1944.

1433 Henderson, Alice P. *The Ninety-first: The First at Camp Lewis.* . . . Tacoma, Washington: J. C. Barr, 1918.

1434 *The Story of the 91st Division.* San Mateo, California: 91st Division Publication Committee, 1919.

1435 American Battle Monuments Commission. *91st Division: Summary of Operations in the World War.* Washington, D.C.: G.P.O., 1944.

1436 ———. *92nd Division: Summary of Operations in the World War.* Washington, D.C.: G.P.O., 1944.

1437 "The Ninety-Second Division in Action." *Southern Workman* 48 (Jan. 1919): 41–43.

1438 American Battle Monuments Commission. *93d Division: Summary of Operations in the World War.* Washington, D.C.: G.P.O., 1944.

1439 Mason, Monroe, and Arthur Furr. *The American Negro Soldier with the Red Hand of France.* Boston: Cornhill, 1920. [93d Division.]

Infantry Regiments

1440 Brown, William. *The Adventures of An American Doughboy.* . . . Compiled and arranged from his notes by Birdeena Tuttle. Tacoma, Washington, 1919. [Company F, 9th Infantry.]

1441 *The Ninth U.S. Infantry in the World War. . . .* Neuwied: L. Heusersche Buchdruckerei, 1919.

1442 Wood, Lambert A. *His Job: Letters Written by a 22-year-old Lieutenant in the World War to His Parents and Others in Oregon.* Portland, Oregon: Metropolitan Press, 1932. [9th Infantry.]

1443 Vail, Glenn H. *Lest We Forget: A Personal Narrative of the Prowess of the 9th Infantry While "Over There."* N.p., n.d.

1444 *Twelfth U.S. Infantry 1798– 1919: Its Story —By Its Men.* New York: Knickerbocker, 1919.

1445 *The Story of the Sixteenth Infantry in France,* by the regimental chaplain. Montabaur-Frankfurt am Main: Martin Flock, 1919.

1446 Chastaine, Ben H. *History of the 18th U.S. Infantry, First Division, 1812– 1919.* New York: Hymans, 1920.

1447 Evarts, Jeremiah M. *Cantigny: A Corner of the War.* New York: Scribner's, 1938. [18th Infantry.]

1448 Caygill, Harry W. "Operations of Company M, 23rd Infantry (Second Division) in the Attack on Vaux, July 1– 2, 1918." *Infantry Journal* 40 (Mar.– Apr. 1933): 131– 36.

1449 McCrossen, Bernard J. *Diary of the Machine Gun Company, 23rd Infantry, Second Division, 1917– 1919.* Vallendar-Rhine: Hartmann Brothers, 1919.

1450 *The Twenty-sixth Infantry in France,* by the regimental adjutant. Montabaur-Frankfurt am Main: Martin Flock, 1919.

1451 *The Story of the Twenty-eighth Infantry in the Great War.* Coblenz (?), 1919.

1452 Butts, Edmund L. *The Keypoint of the Marne and Its Defense by the 30th Infantry.* Menasha, Wisconsin: Banta, 1930.

1453 Lovejoy, Clarence E. *The Story of the Thirty-Eighth.* Coblenz: Görres-Druckerei, 1919. [38th Infantry.]

1454 Williams, Cleon L. "Operations of the First Platoon, Company B, 38th Infantry (3rd Division) in the Aisne-Marne Offensive, from July 18 to July 22." *Infantry Journal* 40 (Sept.– Oct. 1933): 331– 34.

1455 Wooldridge, Jesse W. *The Rock of the Marne: A Chronological Story of the 38th Regiment, U.S. Infantry.* Columbia: University of South Carolina Press, 1920.

1456 Fretwell, Frank M. *The Rock of the Marne: A Narrative of the Military Exploits of General Ulysses Grant McAlexander at the Second Battle of the Marne.* Seattle, 1923. [38th Infantry.]

1457   Wooldridge, Jesse W. *The Grants of the Marne: A Story of McAlexander and His Regiment.* Salt Lake City: Seagull Press, 1923. [38th Infantry.]

1458   [Cole, Robert B., and Barnard Eberlin], eds. *The History of the 39th U.S. Infantry during the World War.* New York: J. D. McGuire, 1919.

1459   *A History and Photographic Record of the 43rd U.S. Infantry.* San Antonio: San Antonio Printing, 1918.

1460   Pollard, James E. *The Forty-seventh Infantry: A History, 1917, 1918, 1919.* Saginaw, Michigan: Seeman & Peters, 1919.

1461   *The Gold Chevron: A History of the Fifty-third U.S. Infantry.* N.p., 1919 (?).

1462   Mabry, Gregory, comp. *Recollections of a Recruit: An Official History of the Fifty-fourth U.S. Infantry.* New York: Schilling Press, 1919.

1463   Whitehead, Lawrence E. *Memoirs of the World War.* St. Louis: Stewart Scott Printing Co., 1925 [55th Infantry.]

1464   [Hymans, H. I., and G. H. Altekruse.] *A History and Photographic Record of the 57th U.S. Infantry.* San Antonio: San Antonio Printing, 1918.

1465   [Morrow, George L.] *The Fifty-eighth Infantry in the World War: 1917–1918–1919.* N.p.: 58th Infantry History Association, 1919.

1466   Howe, Dan D. "Operations of Company H, 60th Infantry, in the Meuse-Argonne Offensive, October 11–14, 1918." *Infantry Journal* 40 (Nov.–Dec. 1933): 405–10.

1467   Wrentmore, Ernest L. *In Spite of Hell.* New York: Greenwich Book Publishers, 1958. [60th Infantry.]

1468   *History of the Sixtieth U.S. Infantry, 1917–1919.* N.p., n.d.

1469   *A History of the Sixty-third U.S. Infantry, 1917–1919.* New York: Published by members of the 63d Infantry, 1920.

1470   Duane, James T. *Dear Old "K."* Boston: Thomas Todd, 1922. [101st Infantry.]

1471   Shine, William F. "With Company E, 101st Infantry, in the World War." *Medford Historical Register* 30 (Dec. 1927): 77–85.

1472   [Maher, Augustin F.] *When Connecticut Stopped the Hun: Battle of Seicheprey, April 20–21, 1918. . . .* New Haven: S. Z. Field, 1919. [102d Infantry.]

1473   Hills, Ratcliffe M. *The War History of the 102d Regiment, United States Infantry. . . .* Hartford, Connecticut, 1924.

1474 Strickland, Daniel W. *Connecticut Fights: The Story of the 102nd Regiment.* New Haven: Quinnipiack Press, 1930.

1475 *History of the 103rd Infantry, 1917–1919.* Boston: H. I. Hymans, 1919.

1476 Westbrook, Stillman F. *Those Eighteen Months, October 9, 1917– April 8, 1919.* Hartford, Connecticut: Case, Lockwood & Brainard, 1934. [104th Infantry.]

1477 *A Short History and Illustrated Roster of the 105th Infantry, United States Army.* Philadelphia: Edward Stern, 1918.

1478 Sutliffe, Robert S., comp. *Seventy-First New York in the World War.* New York: Little & Ives, 1922. [105th Infantry.]

1479 *A Short History and Illustrated Roster of the 106th Infantry, United States.* Philadelphia: Edward Stern, 1918.

1480 Hansen, Harold C., ed. *Historical Sketch of the Seventh Regiment, National Guard of New York.* New York, 1918. [107th Infantry.]

1481 Mitchell, Harry T. *Company L, 107th Infantry, 54th Infantry Brigade, 27th Division, American Expeditionary Forces, 1917–1919.* N.p., 1919 (?).

1482 *History of Company "E," 107th Infantry, 54th Brigade, 27th Division, U.S.A. (National Guard, New York) 1917–1919.* New York: War Veterans Association, 1920.

1483 Jacobson, Gerald F., comp. *History of the 107th Infantry, U.S.A.* New York: De Vinne, 1920.

1484 Leland, Claude G. *From Shell Hole to Chateau with Company T.* New York: Society of Ninth Company Veterans, 7th Regiment, N.Y.N.G., 1950. [107th Infantry.]

1485 *A Short History and Illustrated Roster of the 108th Infantry, United States Army.* Philadelphia: Edward Stern, 1918.

1486 *A Short History and Illustrated Roster of the 110th Infantry (10th Pennsylvania Infantry) United States, 1917.* Philadelphia: Edward Stern, 1918.

1487 Lutz, Earle. *The 110th Infantry in the World War.* Haddonfield, New Jersey, 1919.

1488 *A Short History and Illustrated Record of the First Regiment, Pennsylvania Infantry, National Guard, United States.* Philadelphia: Edward Stern, 1918. [110th Infantry.]

1489 *History of the 110th Infantry (10th Pennsylvania) of the 28th Division, U.S.A., 1917–1919.* Pittsburgh: Association of the 110th Infantry, 1920.

1490   A Short History and Illustrated Roster of the 111th Infantry, U.S., Formerly 18th Pennsylvania Infantry, N.G.U.S. Philadelphia: Edward Stern, 1918.

1491   Cooper, George W. Our Second Battalion: The Accurate and Authentic History of the Second Battalion, 111th Infantry. Pittsburgh: Second Battalion Book Co., 1920.

1492   Hoffman, Robert C. I Remember the Last War. York, Pennsylvania: Strength & Health Publishing Co., 1940. [111th Infantry.]

1493   A Short History and Illustrated Roster of the 112th Infantry, Army of the United States. Philadelphia: Edward Stern, 1918.

1494   Murrin, James A. With the 112th in France: A Doughboy's Story of the War. Philadelphia: Lippincott, 1919.

1495   [Reynolds, Frederick C.], ed. 115th Infantry, U.S.A., in the World War. Baltimore, Read-Taylor, 1920.

1496   Woodcock, Amos W. W. Golden Days. Salisbury, Maryland: Salisbury Advertiser, 1951. [115th Infantry.]

1497   Davis, Arthur K., ed. Virginia Military Organizations in the World War. Richmond: Virginia War History Commission, 1927. [116th Infantry and others.]

1498   [Waller, Samuel G.] A Brief History of the 116th Infantry, 29th Division, American Expeditionary Forces, October 4, 1917 to June 1, 1919. Richmond, Virginia: William Byrd Press, 1919.

1499   Seal, Henry F., ed. "Ever Forward": World War I, 1917–1919: History of the 116th U.S. Infantry Regiment. Richmond: Virginia Department of Military Affairs, 1953.

1500   History of the 118th Infantry, American Expeditionary Force [sic.], France. Columbia, South Carolina: State Co., 1919.

1501   [Conway, Coleman B., and George A. Shuford], comps. History 119th Infantry, 60th Brigade, 30th Division, U.S.A., Operations in Belgium and France, 1917–1919. Wilmington, North Carolina: Wilmington Chamber of Commerce, 1920.

1502   Walker, John O. Official History of the 120th Infantry, "3rd North Carolina," 30th Division. . . . Lynchburg, Virginia: J. P. Bell Co., 1919.

1503   Gansser, Emil B. History of the 126th Infantry in the War with Germany. Grand Rapids: Dean-Hicks Co., 1920.

1504   ———. On the Battlefields of France in 1918. Grand Rapids, Michigan, 1958. [126th Infantry.]

1505 Schmidt, Paul W. *Company C, 127th Infantry in the World War: A Story of the 32nd Division and a Complete History of the Part Taken by Company C.* Sheboygan, Wisconson: Press Publishing Co., 1919.

1506 [Manly, Claude C.] *History of Company K, 127th Infantry, 32nd Division (Kosciusko Guard), Wisconsin National Guard, 1874–1924.* Milwaukee: Quality Press, 1924.

1507 Baker, Horace L. *Argonne Days: Experiences of a World War Private on the Meuse-Argonne Front. . . .* Aberdeen, Mississippi: Aberdeen Weekly, 1927. [128th Infantry.]

1508 Peterson, Ira L. "Journal of a World War Veteran." *Wisconsin Magazine of History* 8 (Dec. 1924): 199–220; (Mar. 1925): 328–48. [128th Infantry.]

1509 Sanborn, Joseph B. *The 131st U.S. Infantry (First Infantry Illinois National Guard) in the World War: Narrative-Operations-Statistics.* Chicago, 1919.

1510 Corning, Walter D. *The Yanks Crusade: A Book of Reminiscences.* Chicago, 1927. [131st Infantry.]

1511 Haterius, Carl E., comp. *Reminiscences of the 137th U.S. Infantry.* Topeka: Crane, 1919.

1512 Mechem, Kirke. *"Cooty Bill."* Topeka: Capper Printing Co., 1919. [137th Infantry.]

1513 Fels, Daniel M. *History of "A" Company, 138th Infantry.* St. Louis: Woodward & Tiernan, 1919 (?).

1514 Kenamore, Clair. *The Story of the 139th Infantry.* St. Louis: Guard Publishing Co., 1920.

1515 Edwards, Evan A. *From Doniphan to Verdun: The Official History of the 140th Infantry.* Lawrence, Kansas: World Co., 1920.

1516 *In Memoriam, Albert Craig Funkhouser, Company F, 144 Infantry, 36th Division, Paul Taylor Funkhauser, Company B, 7th Machine Gun Battalion, 3rd Division.* Evansville, Indiana, 1919.

1517 [Cadwallader, William.] *Major Conelly's Front Line Fighters, France and Belgium: Glorious Record, First Battalion, 148th Infantry, 37th Division.* Cleveland: L. S. Conelly, 1919.

1518 Duffy, Frances P., *Father Duffy's Story. . . .* New York: Doran, 1919. [165th Infantry.]

1519 Hogan, Martin J. *The Shamrock Battalion of the Rainbow: A Story of the "Fighting Sixty-ninth."* New York: Appleton, 1919. [165th Infantry.]

1520 Reppy, Alison. *Rainbow Memories: Character Sketches and History of the First Battalion, 166th Infantry, 42nd Division, American Expeditionary Forces.* New York: Carey Printing, 1919.

1521 Cheseldine, Raymond M. *Ohio in the Rainbow: Official Story of the 166th Infantry, 42nd Division in the World War.* Columbus, Ohio: F. J. Heer, 1924.

1522 Amerine, William H. *Alabama's Own in France.* New York: Eaton & Gettinger, 1919. [167th Infantry.]

1523 Peterson, William J., and John Taber. "The Story of the 168th Infantry." *Palimpsest* 48 (Apr. 1967): 145– 208.

1524 Robb, Winfred E. *The Price of Our Heritage: In Memory of the Heroic Dead of the 168th Infantry.* Des Moines: American Lithographing & Printing, 1919.

1525 Stewart, Lawrence O. *Rainbow Bright.* Philadelphia: Dorrance, 1923. [168th Infantry.]

1526 Taber, John H. *The Story of the 168th Infantry.* 2 vols. Iowa City: State Historical Society of Iowa, 1925.

1527 Tucker, William J. *Not All Ashes.* Dallas: Southwest Press, 1941. [168th Infantry.]

1528 Tiebout, Frank B. *A History of the 305th Infantry.* New York: 305th Infantry Auxiliary, 1919.

1529 306th Infantry Association. *History of the 306th Infantry.* New York: 306th Infantry Association, 1935.

1530 Rainsford, Walter K. *From Upton to the Meuse with the Three Hundred and Seventh Infantry. . . .* New York: Appleton, 1920.

1531 Klausner, Julius, comp. *Company B, 307th Infantry. . . .* New York: American Legion, Burke-Kelly Post No. 172, 1920.

1532 [Adams, John W., and Lee C. McCollum.] *"Our Company" by Two Bucks.* Seattle: Lumberman Printing, 1919. [308th Infantry.]

1533 Fuller, Hurley E. " 'Lost Battalion' of the 77th Division." *Infantry Journal* 28 (June 1926): 597– 608. [308th Infantry.]

1534 Hussey, Alexander T., and R. M. Flynn. *The History of Company E, 308th Infantry (1917– 1919).* New York: Knickerbocker, 1919.

1535 McCollum, Lee C. *History and Rhymes of the Lost Battalion by "Buck Private" McCullom.* Columbus, Ohio: L. C. McCullom, 1929. [308th Infantry.]

1536 Maddox, Robert J. "Ordeal of the 'Lost Battalion.' " *American History Illustrated* 10 (Dec. 1975): 22–33. [308th Infantry.]

1537 Swindler, Henry O. "The So-Called Lost Battalion." *American Mercury* 15 (Nov. 1928): 257–65. [308th Infantry.]

1538 Miles, L. Wardlaw. *History of the 308th Infantry, 1917–1919.* New York: Putnam's, 1927.

1539 Johnson, Thomas M., and Fletcher Pratt. *The Lost Battalion.* Indianapolis: Bobbs-Merrill, 1938. [308th Infantry.]

1540 Schurman, Jacob G., Jr. *A History of the 309th Regiment of Infantry, 78th Division.* New York, 1919 (?).

1541 *A History of the Three Hundred Tenth Infantry, Seventy-eighth Division, U.S.A., 1917–1919.* New York: Association of the 310th Infantry, 1919.

1542 [Dyke, Harold D.] *Headquarters Company, 310th Infantry, U.S.A.* N.p., 1919.

1543 *Company F, 310th Infantry: A Brief History, August 29, 1917–June 5, 1919.* New York: Wynkoop Hallenbeck Crawford, 1919.

1544 Eberlin, Barnard. *History of the 311th Infantry (78th Division).* Flavigny-sur-Ozerain, 1919.

1545 Colonna, Benjamin A. *The History of Company B, 311th Infantry, in the World War.* Freehold, New Jersey: Transcript Printing House, 1922.

1546 *A History of the Three Hundred and Twelfth Infantry in France.* New York: Three Hundred and Twelfth Infantry Association, 1919.

1547 Morgan, George R. *Company "E," 312th Infantry, 78th Division in France, May 19, 1918 to May 31, 1919.* Greenville, South Carolina: A. K. Magill, 1919.

1548 *History, Company C, 312.* Newark, New Jersey: Loges-Wiener, 1919. [312th Infantry.]

1549 Muller, E. Lester. *The 313th of the 79th in the World War.* Baltimore: Meyer & Thalheimer, 1919. [313th Infantry.]

1550 Thorn, Henry C., Jr. *History of the 313th U.S. Infantry: "Baltimore's Own."* New York: Wynkoop Hallenbeck Crawford, 1920.

1551 Joel, Arthur H. *Under the Lorraine Cross.* East Lansing, Michigan, 1921. [314th Infantry.]

1552   Historical Board of the 315th Infantry. *The Official History of the 315th Infantry, U.S.A.* Williamsport, Pennsylvania: Penn Grit Publishing, 1920.

1553   *History of Company F, 316th Infantry, 79th Division, A.E.F., in the World War, 1917– 1918– 1919.* Philadelphia: Company F, Association of the 316th Infantry, 1930.

1554   [Glock, Carl E.] *History of the 316th Regiment of Infantry in the World War, 1918.* Philadelphia: Biddle-Deemer Printing Co., 1930.

1555   [Anson, Eldred.] *Overseas Diary of Company "G," 317th Infantry, France, June 1918– June 1919.* New York (?), 1919 (?).

1556   Shaw, Arthur F., comp. *Company "K," 317th Infantry . . . September 1917 to June 1919.* Grand Rapids, Michigan: White Printing, 1919.

1557   *History of the 318th Infantry Regiment of the 80th Division, 1917– 1919.* Richmond, Virginia: William Byrd Press, 1919.

1558   Young, Rush S. *Over the Top with the 80th: By a Buck Private, 1917– 1919.* N.p., 1933.

1559   Peck, Josiah C. *The 319th Infantry, A.E.F.* Paris: Herbert Clarke, 1919 (?).

1560   [Herr, Charles R.] *Company F, History, 319th Infantry.* Somerville, New Jersey: Unionist-Gazette Association, 1920.

1561   Williams, Ashby. *Experiences of the Great War: Artois, St. Mihiel, Meuse-Argonne.* Roanoke, Virginia: Stone Printing, 1919. [320th Infantry.]

1562   [Westlake, Thomas H.] *History of the 320th Infantry Abroad.* New York: McGraw Phillips, 1923.

1563   Stringfellow, John S. *Hell! No! This and That: A Narrative of the Great War.* Boston: Meador, 1936. [320th Infantry.]

1564   Johnson, Clarence W. *The History of the 321st Infantry with a Brief Historical Sketch of the 81st Division.* Columbia, South Carolina: R. L. Bryan, 1919.

1565   *Story of the 325th.* Bordeaux: A. Saugnac & E. Drouillard, 1919. [325th Infantry.]

1566   Sparks, George M., ed. *The 327th under Fire: History of the 327th Infantry, 82nd Division, in the World War.* Fitzgerald, Georgia, 1919.

1567   *History of the Three Hundred and Twenty-eighth Regiment of Infantry, Eighty-second Division, American Expeditionary Forces, United States Army. . . .* Atlanta, Georgia: Foote & Davies, 1922 (?).

1568 [Hart, Walter C.], ed. *The Company Log from September 7, 1917, to May 2, 1919.* Cleveland: Britton Printing, 1920. [332d Infantry.]

1569 Lettau, Joseph L. *In Italy with the 332nd Infantry.* Youngstown, Ohio: J. L. Lettau, 1921.

1570 *Ohio Doughboys in Italy.* Atlantic City: Soldiers & Sailors Bulletin, 1921.

1571 York, Dorothea. *The Romance of Company "A," 339th Infantry, A.N.R.E.F.* Detroit: McIntyre Printing, 1923. [See also V, M/Siberian Expedition.]

1572 Richardson, Chalmer O. *Here Comes the Band!: Unofficial History of the 345th Infantry Band in the Great War.* North Platte, Nebraska: Hemphill Printery, 1928.

1573 *The 346th Infantry Historical Notes, 1917–1919.* Nantes: Imprimerie du Commerce, 1919.

1574 Fiske, Proctor M., ed. *History of the Three Hundred Fiftieth Regiment of U.S. Infantry, Eighty-eighth Division, American Expeditionary Forces.* Cedar Rapids: Laurance Press, 1919.

1575 Brantner, Cecil F. *351st Infantry.* St. Paul, Minnesota: Randall Co., 1919.

1576 Dienst, Charles F., et al. *History of the 353rd Infantry Regiment, 89th Division, National Army, September 1917–June 1919.* Wichita: 353d Infantry Society, 1921.

1577 [McGrath, John F.], comp. *War Diary of 354th Infantry . . . 89th Division.* Trier: J. Lintz, 1920 (?).

1578 [Jones, Carlisle L.], ed. *History and Roster of the 355th Infantry, 89th Division.* Lincoln: Society of the 355th Infantry, 1919 (?).

1579 Kyle, Homer L. "The 355th Infantry (Nebraska) Regiment in the World War." *Nebraska History* 20 (Oct.–Dec. 1939): 292–97.

1580 [Ross, James H., and N. B. Heath], comps. *History of Company E, 355th Infantry, A.E.F.* Omaha: Waters-Barnhardt Printing, 1919 (?).

1581 Marshall, Conrad H. *History of "M" Company, 357th Infantry, 1917–1919.* Carnegie, Oklahoma: Carnegie Herald, 1919.

1582 Emmett, Chris. *Give 'way to the Right: Serving with the A.E.F. in France.* San Antonio: Naylor, 1934. [359th Infantry.]

1583 *A Short History and Photographic Record of the 360th Infantry, Texas Brigade . . . 1918.* San Antonio: San Antonio Printing, 1918.

1584 Olson, Zenas A. *Following Fighting "F" . . . 361st Infantry, 91st Division. . . .* LaChapelle-Montligeon (Orne): Imprimerie de Montligeon, 1919.

1585 Romeo, Giuseppe. *Diary of Private Giuseppe L. Romeo, Company E, 361st Infantry, 91st Division, A.E.F., during the War.* Tacoma, Washington: T. V. Copeland, 1919.

1586 [Burton, Harold H.], ed. *600 Days' Service: A History of the 361st Infantry Regiment of the United States Army.* Portland, Oregon: James, Kern & Abbot, 1921.

1587 Wilson, Bryant, and Lamar Tooze. *With the 364th Infantry in America, France, and Belgium.* New York: Knickerbocker, 1919.

1588 Ross, Warner A. *My Colored Battalion.* Chicago: Warner A. Ross, 1920. [365th Infantry.]

1589 Grof, William S. "Henry Johnson Was a Fighting Man." *Soldiers* 30 (Apr. 1975): 10– 11. [369th Infantry.]

1590 Little, Arthur W. *From Harlem to the Rhine: The Story of New York's Colored Volunteers.* New York: Covici, Friede, 1936. [369th Infantry.]

1591 "Not One of the Famous 369th Was Ever Taken Alive." *Literary Digest* 60 (Mar. 15, 1919): 94– 96.

1592 Bradden, William S. *Under Fire with the 370th Infantry (8th I.N.G.) A.E.F. . . . Memoirs of the World War.* Chicago (?), William S. Bradden, 1927 (?).

1593 Deckard, Percy E. *List of Officers Who Served with the 371st Infantry and Headquarters, 186th Infantry Brigade during the World War and Also My Experience in the World War, with Memoirs of France and Service in the Medical Detachment of 371st Infantry.* Allegany, New York: Allegany Citizen, 1929.

1594 Heywood, Chester D. *Negro Combat Troops in the World War: The Story of the 371st Infantry.* Reprint. New York: AMS Press, 1969.

Machine Gun Battalions

1595 *History of the 2nd Machine Gun Battalion, First Division.* New York: Hymans, 1920.

1596 Westover, Wendell. *Suicide Battalions.* New York: Putnam's, 1929. [4th Machine Gun Battalion.]

1597 *In Memoriam, Albert Craig, Funkhouser, Company F, 144 Infantry, 36th Division, Paul Taylor Funkhouser, Company B, 7th Machine Gun Battalion, 3rd Division.* Evansville, Indiana, 1919.

1598 Mendenhall, John R. "The Fist in the Dyke." *Infantry Journal* 43 (Jan.– Feb. 1936): 13– 23. [7th Machine Gun Battalion.]

1599 [Dethlefs, Louis C.] *History 12th Machine Gun Battalion, 8th Infantry Brigade, Fourth Division, December 1917 to July 1919.* Coblenz: Druckerei Hartmann, 1919.

1600 [O'Neil, R. E.], ed. *The History of the 20th Machine Gun Battalion. . . .* Kansas City, Missouri: Franklin Hudson Publishing Co., 1920.

1601 Wainwright, Philip S., ed. *History of the 101st Machine Gun Battalion.* Hartford, Connecticut: 101st Machine Gun Battalion Association, 1922.

1602 Havlin, Arthur C. *The History of Company A, 102d Machine Gun Battalion Twenty-sixth Division, A.E.F.* Boston: Privately printed for H. C. Rodd & Associates, 1928.

1603 McCarthy, Robert J. *A History of Troop A, Cavalry, Connecticut National Guard and Its Service in the Great War as Company D, 102d Machine Gun Battalion.* New Haven (?): Tuttle, Morehouse & Taylor, 1919.

1604 Whitney, Stanton. *Squadron A in the Great War, 1917– 1918.* New York: Squadron A Association, 1923. [105th Machine Gun Battalion.]

1605 Kuhn, Walter R., ed. *. . . The Narrative of Company A, 106th Machine Gun Battalion, 27th Division, United States Army, in the "Great War."* New York: Patterson Press, 1919.

1606 Baker, Leslie S. *The Company History: The Story of Company B, 106th Machine Gun Battalion, 27th Division, U.S.A.* New York: Published by the company, 1920.

1607 *History and Rhymes of Our Boys in the Great War,* by Buck Private O'Neil. N.p., 1926. [Company B, 108th Machine Gun Battalion.]

1608 Nolan, James B. *The Reading Militia in the Great War.* Reading, Pennsylvania: F. A. Woerner, 1921. [Company D, 15th Machine Gun Battalion; Company B, 108th Machine Gun Battalion; Company D, 150th Machine Gun Battalion.]

1609 Tydings, Millard E. *The Machine Gunners of the Blue and Gray Division. . . .* Aberdeen, Maryland: Hartford Printing & Publishing Co., 1920. [Company B, 108th Machine Gun Battalion.]

1610 *History of 124th Machine Gun Battalion, 66th Brigade, 33rd Division, A.E.F.* Luxembourg, 1919.

1611 Weber, Walter W. *History of the 129th Machine Gun Battalion, 35th Division, A.E.F., 1917– 1919.* N.p., 1919.

1612   Tousley, Clyde E. T., ed. *War Record and History of the 136th Machine Gun Battalion, 37th Division, U.S. Army, 1917–1919*. N.p., 1919.

1613   Ellis, Allan B. *A Brief History of Appleton's "Old Company G" (Company A, 150th Machine Gun Battalion): With the Rainbow Division in the Great War*. Appleton, Wisconsin: Meyer Press, 1919.

1614   Smith, Henry W. *A Story of the 305th Machine Gun Battalion, 77th Division, A.E.F.* New York: Modern Composing Room, 1941.

1615   Minder, Charles F. *This Man's War: The Day-by-day Record of an American Private on the Western Front*. New York: Pevensey, 1931. [306th Machine Gun Battalion.]

1616   *History of the 309th Machine Gun Battalion. . . .* Dijon: Imprimerie J. Delorne, 1919.

1617   *History of the 347th Machine Gun Battalion. . . .* Oakland: Horwinski Co., 1923 (?).

Military Motor Corps

1618   *How Minnesota Gave to the United States: The First Military Motor Corps*. Minneapolis, Bancroft Printing, 1919.

Military Police

1619   *History of the 26th Military Police in France, 1917–1919*. Boston: Thomas Todd, 1919.

1620   Schwensen, Kai. *The History of the 102nd M.P.* New York: Call Printing, 1919.

1621   [Dundas, Wendell A.] *Company B, 109 Military Police*. Omaha, 1919 (?).

Pioneer Infantry

1622   Davis, Chester W. *The Story of the First Pioneer Infantry, U.S.A.* Utica, New York: Kirkland Press, 1920.

1623   *54th Pioneer Infantry with the Army of Occupation, Third U.S. Army, Germany, 1918*. N.p., 1919.

1624   *Fifty-sixth Pioneer Infantry (First Maine Heavy Field Artillery) with the Army in Occupation in Germany, New Year, 1919*. N.p., 1919.

1625   *History of the 59th Pioneer Infantry, 1918–1919. American Expeditionary Forces*. Toul: Imprimerie Lemaire, 1919.

1626   Crum, Earl L. *History of the Sixty-second Pioneer Infantry, Camp Wadsworth, S.C.* Spartanburg, South Carolina: Band & White, 1919.

1627   Bliss, Paul S. *Victory: History of the 805th Pioneer Infantry, American Expeditionary Forces.* St. Paul, Minnesota, 1919.

Supply Units

1628   Morris, Otho A. *A Brief History and Names and Addresses of Former Members of Company F, 111th Supply Train as Attached to the 36th Division, U.S. Army from October 15, 1917, to June 17, 1919.* Kerrville, Texas: Mountain Sun, 1920.

1629   Hollingsworth, Roy D. *10,000 Miles with 125th Infantry Supply Train.* Port Huron, Michigan, 1932.

1630   Bernet, Milton E. *The Three Hundred and Fourteenth Motor Supply Train in the World War.* . . . St. Louis, 1919.

1631   *Printing to Beat the Huns: An Illustrated Description of the Part Played by the 317th Supply Company and the Central Printing Plant in the Winning of the Great War, Paris, 1917–1919.* Paris, 1919.

Telegraph Battalions

1632   *The 401st Telegraph Battalion in the World War.* . . . N.p., 1919 (?).

1633   Schauble, Peter L. *The First Battalion: The Story of the 406th Telegraph Battalion, Signal Corps, U.S. Army.* Philadelphia, 1921.

1634   Moore, Charles H., ed. *Memories of the "411th" Telegraph Battalion 1917–1919, in the World War.* Reno, Nevada, 192?

1635   Smith, Joseph M. *History of the 412th Battalion, U.S. Signal Corps.* . . . St. Louis, Missouri, 1929. [412 Telegraph Battalion.]

Trench Artillery

1636   Ottosen, Peter H., ed. *Trench Artillery, A.E.F.: The Personal Experiences of Lieutenants and Captains of Artillery Who Served with Trench Mortars.* Boston: Lathrop, Lee & Shepard, 1931.

B/Air Units

General

1637   Maurer, Maurer. "The 1st Aero Squadron—1913–1917." *Air Power Historian.* 4 (Oct. 1957): 207–12.

1638   Wells, R., et al. "The 1st Aero Squadron U.S.A.S." *American Aviation Historical Society Journal* 13 (Fall 1968): 228–29; (Winter 1968): 296–97; 14 (Spring 1969): 51–54; (Fall 1969): 211–16.

1639   Tyler, John C. *Selections from the Letters and Diary of John Cowperthwaite Tyler from August, 1917 to September, 1918.* Arranged by his mother. Camden, New Jersey: Haddon Craftsmen, 1938. [11th Aero Squadron.]

1640   Clapp, Frederick M. *A History of the 17th Aero Squadron . . . December, 1918.* Garden City, New York: Country Life Press, 1920.

1641   Barth, Clarence G. *History of the Twentieth Aero Squadron. . . .* Winona, Minnesota: Winona Labor News, 1919 (?).

1642   Sloan, James J. "The 25th Aero Squadron." *American Aviation Historical Society Journal* 7 (Spring 1962): 17– 35; (Summer 1962): 126– 30; 8 (Spring 1963): 31– 38.

1643   Morse, Daniel P., Jr. *The History of the 50th Aero Squadron.* New York: Blanchard Press, 1920.

1644   [*Roster of the 53rd Spruce Squadron and an Account of Its Work and Camp.*] N.p., 1918.

1645   Piesbergen, Clarence F. *Overseas with an Aero Squadron.* Belleville, Illinois: News-Democrat Printing, 1919. [86th Aero Squadron.]

1646   Crosby, Wilson G. *Fletcher Ladd McCordic, 1st Lieutenant, 88th Aero Squadron, A.E.F., 1891– 1919.* Chicago, 1921.

1647   Carver, Leland M.; Gustaf A. Lindstrom; and A. T. Foster. *The Ninetieth Aero Squadron, American Expeditionary Forces. . . .* Hinsdale, Illinois, 1920.

1648   Kenney, George C. *History of the 91st Aero Squadron, Air Service, U.S.A.* Coblenz: Gebruder Breuer, 1919.

1649   Coolidge, Hamilton. *Letters of an American Airman . . . 1917– 1918.* Boston: Norwood, Plimpton Press, 1919. [94th Aero Squadron.]

1650   Rickenbacker, Edward V. *Fighting the Flying Circus.* Philadelphia: Lippincott, 1919. [94th Aero Squadron.]

1651   Blodgett, Richard A. *Life and Letters of Richard Ashley Blodgett, First Lieutenant, United States Air Service.* Boston: MacDonald & Evans, 1919 (?). [95th Aero Squadron.]

1652   Buckley, Harold. *Squadron 95: An Intimate History of the 95th Squadron.* Paris: Obelisk Press, 1933.

1653   Russel, William M. *A Happy Warrior: Letters of William Muir Russel, an American Aviator in the Great War, 1917– 1918. . . . A Family Memorial.* Detroit: Saturday Night Press, 1919. [95th Aero Squadron.].

1654   *113th Squadron (Engineers) Air Service, Aircraft Production: A Pictorial History of the Largest Squadron in the World, 1918– 1919.* N.p., 1919.

1655·   Hart, Percival G. *History of the 135th Aero Squadron from July 25 to November 11, 1918.* Chicago, 1939.

1656 *Captain Walter H. Schultze, the Peace Messenger, 1893–1919: In Memoriam.* N.p., 1925. [138th Aero Squadron.]

1657 Rogge, Robert E. "A History of the 148th Aero Squadron." *Airpower Historian* 9 (July 1962): 157–65.

1658 Taylor, William P., and F. L. Irvin, comps. *History of the 148th Aero Squadron, Aviation Section, U.S. Army Signal Corps, A.E.F., B.E.F., 1917–1918.* Reprint. Manhattan, Kansas: Military Affairs/Aerospace Historian Publishing Series, 1957.

1659 *History of "The Black Cat Squadron": 174th Aero Squadron, 1917–1919.* N.p., 1919 (?).

1660 *The History of the Four Hundred and Sixty-third Aero Squadron. . . .* N.p., 1919 (?).

1661 *History 484th Aero Squadron, American Expeditionary Forces.* Hampton, Virginia: Houston Printing & Publishing House, 192?

1662 [Norton, Thomas F., et al.], eds. *639th Aero Squadron Book. . . .* Berkeley: Lederer, Street & Zeus, 1920.

1663 Louser, Herman W., ed. *The Propeller: Dedicated to the Members of the 804th Aero Squadron. . . .* Harrisburg, Pennsylvania: Courier Press, 1919.

1664 Kauffman, Alvin E. *The Lost Squadron: Being the Swan Song of the 839th Aero Outfit. . . .* York, Pennsylvania: Kyle Printing Co., 1919.

1665 Hartney, Harold E. *Up and At 'Em.* Harrisburg, Pennsylvania: Stackpole, 1940. [1st Pursuit Group, including 27th, 94th, 95th, 147th, 185th night pursuit and 4th air park squadrons.]

1666 [Law, Hugo B.], ed. *A History of the Second Army Air Service.* Nancy: Berger-Levrault, 1919.

1667 [Yarwood, Bertram H.], ed. *Overseas Dreams: Second Provisional Wing.* Houston: Gulfport Printing Co., 1919. [190th, 191st, 343d Aero Squadrons.]

1668 *Sixth Detachment, U.S.A., Detroit, Michigan, A.S.A.P.* Detroit: Franklin Press, 191? [Bureau of Aircraft Production Detachment.]

Lafayette Escadrille and Lafayette Flying Corps (103d Aero Squadron)

1669 Biddle, Charles J. *The Way of the Eagle.* New York: Scribner's, 1919.

1670 Chapman, Victor. *Victor Chapman's Letters from France.* New York: Macmillan, 1917.

1671   Drew, Sidney R. *Life and Letters of Sidney Rankin Drew.* Edited by Mrs. Sidney Drew. New York: Cheltenham Press, 1921.

1672   Flammer, Philip M. "Lufbery: Ace of the Lafayette Escadrille." *Airpower Historian* 8 (Jan. 1961): 13– 22.

1673 ———. "The Myth of the Lafayette Escadrille." *Aerospace Historian* 22 (Mar. 1975): 23– 28.

1674 ———. "Tragedy and Triumph: The Story of Edmond C. C. Genet." *Airpower Historian* 11 (Apr. 1964): 39– 44.

1675   Genet, Edmond C. C. *War Letters of Edmond Genet: The First American Aviator Killed Flying the Stars and Stripes.* Edited by Grace E. Channing. New York: Scribner's, 1918.

1676   Hall, Bert, and John J. Niles. *One Man's War: The Story of the Lafayette Escadrille.* New York: Holt, 1929.

1677   Hall, James N. *High Adventure.* Boston: Houghton Mifflin, 1918.

1678 ———, and Charles B. Nordhoff, eds. *The Lafayette Flying Corps.* Boston: Houghton Mifflin, 1920.

1679   Hennessy, Juliette A. "The Lafayette Escadrille — Past and Present." *Air Power Historian* 4 (July 1957): 150– 60.

1680   Knight, Clayton, and K. S. Knight. *We Were There with the Lafayette Escadrille.* New York: Grosset & Dunlap, 1961.

1681   McConnell, James R. *Flying for France with the American Escadrille at Verdun.* Garden City, New York: Doubleday, Page, 1917.

1682   Mason, Herbert M., Jr. *The Lafayette Escadrille.* New York: Random House, 1964.

1683   [Parsons, Edwin C.] *The Great Adventure: The Story of the Lafayette Escadrille.* Garden City, New York: Doubleday, Doran, 1937.

1684   Prince, Norman. *Norman Prince: A Volunteer Who Died for the Cause He Loved.* Boston: Houghton Mifflin, 1917.

1685   Rockwell, Paul A., ed. *War Letters of Kiffin Yates Rockwell.* Garden City, New York: Country Life Press, 1925.

1686   Shaffer, Walter J. "Do It Yourself Flying . . . One Man's Recollections of the Lafayette Escadrille." *Aerospace Historian* 17 (Summer– Fall 1970): 83– 87.

1687   Thenault, Georges. *The Story of the Lafayette Escadrille.* Boston: Small, Maynard, 1921.

1688 Turner, George E. *George Evans Turner, Jr.: Flight Log and War Letters.* New York: Whitney Press, 1936.

1689 Wellman, William A. *Go, Get 'Em!* Boston: Page, 1918.

1690 Whitehouse, Arch. *Legion of the Lafayette.* Garden City, New York: Doubleday, 1962.

C/Naval Units

1691 *History of the U.S.S. Leviathan.* New York: Brooklyn Eagle, 1919.

D/Marine Corps Units

1692 Akers, Herbert H., comp. *History of the Third Battalion, Sixth Regiment, U.S. Marines.* Hillsdale, Michigan: Akers, Macritchie, Hurlbut, 1919.

1693 Waller, L. W. T., Jr. "Machine Guns of the Fourth Brigade." *Marine Corps Gazette* 5 (Mar. 1920): 1–31.

1694 Curtis, Theodore J. *History of the Sixth Machine Gun Battalion, Fourth Brigade, U.S. Marines, Second Division, and Its Participation in the Great War.* Neuwied: Sixth Machine Gun Battalion, 1919.

1695 Emmons, Roger M. "The First Marine Aviation Force." *Cross and Cockade Journal* 6 (Summer–Fall 1965): 173–86, 272–92.

VII/The War and American Society

A/General Works

1696 Churchill, Allen. *Over Here!: An Informal Re-Creation of the Home Front in World War I.* New York: Dodd, Mead, 1968.

1697 Shotwell, James T. "The Social History of the War." *Columbia University Quarterly* 21 (Oct. 1919): 284–97.

1698 Sullivan, Mark. *Over Here, 1914–1918.* Vol. 5 of *Our Times: The United States 1900–1925.* New York: Scribner's, 1933.

B/Comparison Studies (The War and Other Societies)

1699 Feldman, Gerald D. *Army, Industry, and Labor in Germany, 1914–1918.* Princeton: Princeton University Press, 1966.

1700 Gide, Charles, ed. *The Effects of the War upon French Economic Life.* Oxford: Clarendon Press, 1923.

1701 Hirst, Francis W. *The Consequences of the War to Great Britain.* Reprint. New York: Greenwood Press, 1968.

1702 Marwick, Arthur. *The Deluge: British Society and the First World War.* Boston: Little, Brown, 1965.

1703 ———. *War and Social Change in the Twentieth Century: A Comparative Study of Britain, France, Germany, Russia and the United States.* New York: St. Martin's Press, 1975.

1704 Mendelssohn-Bartholdy, Albrecht. *The War and German Society: The Testament of a Liberal.* New Haven: Yale University Press, 1937.

1705 Mitrany, David. *The Effect of the War in Southeastern Europe.* New Haven: Yale University Press, 1936.

1706 Thayer, John A. *Italy and the Great War: Politics and Culture, 1870–1915.* Madison: University of Wisconsin Press, 1964.

1707 Williams, John. *The Home Fronts: Britain, France and Germany, 1914–1918.* London: Constable, 1972.

C/Collections

1708 Trask, David F., ed. *World War I at Home: Readings on American Life, 1914–1920.* New York: John Wiley, 1970.

D/State and Local Studies

General

1709 Anderson, Claude H. "The Civic Work of State Councils of Defense." *National Municipal Review* 7 (Sept. 1918): 472–83.

1710 Scherer, James A. B. *The Nation at War.* New York: Doran, 1918.

Alphabetically by State, County, and City

1711 Alabama. State Council of Defense. *Report of the Alabama Council of Defense Covering Its Activities from May 17, 1917 to December 31, 1918.* Montgomery: Brown Printing, 1919.

1712 Hart, Hastings H. *Social Problems of Alabama: A Study of the Social Institutions and Agencies of the State of Alabama as Related to Its War Activities.* Montgomery, 1918.

1713 Arizona. State Council of Defense. *A Report of the Activities of the Arizona State Council of Defense from Formation April 18, 1917 to Dissolution June 1919.* Phoenix: Republican Print Shop, 1919.

1714 Arkansas. State Council of Defense. *Report of the Arkansas State Council of Defense, May 22, 1917 to July 1, 1919.* Little Rock (?), 1919 (?).

1715 Daley, Edith. *War History of Santa Clara County.* San Jose (?): Santa Clara Historical Society, 1919. [California.]

1716 Connecticut. State Council of Defense. *Report of the Connecticut State Council of Defense, December 1918.* Hartford, 1919.

1716a Fraser, Bruce. "Yankees at War: Social Mobilization on the Connecticut Homefront, 1917–1918." Ph.D. dissertation, Columbia University, 1976.

1717 Hornik, Anna. *Danbury and Our Boys in the World War.* Danbury, Connecticut, 1923.

1718 District of Columbia. Council of Defense. *Report of the District Council of Defense, Washington, D.C., June 9, 1917 to June 30, 1919.* Washington, D.C.: G.P.O., 1919.

1719 O'Malley, Frank W. *The War-whirl in Washington.* New York: Century, 1918. [District of Columbia.]

1720 Patten, Anna B. *Washington in Wartime: Poems and Verse.* Washington, D.C., 1919.

1721 Ripley, G. Peter. "Intervention and Reaction: Florida Newspapers and United States Entry into World War I." *Florida Historical Quarterly* 49 (Jan. 1971): 255–67.

1722 Jones, John. *World War History of Troup County, Georgia.* Atlanta: Webb & Vary, 1919.

1723 Ready, Milton R. "Georgia's Entry into World War I." *Georgia Historical Quarterly* 52 (Sept. 1968): 256–64.

1724 Toomey, Joseph M. *Georgia's Participation in the World War and the History of the Department of Georgia, the American Legion.* Macon: J. W. Burke, 1936.

1725 Kuykendall, Ralph S. *Hawaii in the World War.* Honolulu: Historical Commission of the Territory of Hawaii, 1928.

1726 McLeod, G. Duncan. *Twin Falls County in the World War.* Ogden, Utah: A. L. Scoville Press, 1920. [Idaho.]

1727 Currey, Josiah S. *Illinois Activities in the World War.* 3 vols. Chicago: T. B. Pook, 1921.

1728 Illinois. State Council of Defense. *Final Report of the State Council of Defense of Illinois, 1917–1918–1919.* Chicago (?), 1919.

1729 Jenison, Marguerite E., ed. *War Documents and Addresses.* Springfield: Illinois State Historical Library, 1923.

1730 ——. *The War-time Organization of Illinois.* Springfield: Illinois State Historical Library, 1923.

1731 Pease, Marguerite J. "Illinois in World War I." *Illinois History* 19 (Apr. 1966): 147–49.

1732 Zimmerman, Henry W. *His Story of Bethalto.* Bethalto, Illinois, 1921.

1733 Knox County, Illinois. *The Honor Roll, 1917–1918–1919: Being a Record of What was Done in Knox County in Those Three Eventful Years and Who Did It.* Galesburg, Illinois: Wagoner Printing, 1920.

1734   Pierson, Edward E., and J. L. Hasbrouck, eds. *McLean County, Illinois, in the World War, 1917–1918.* Bloomington, Illinois: McLean County Publishing Co., 1921 (?).

1735   Cummins, Cedric C. *Indiana Public Opinion and the World War, 1914–1917.* Indianapolis: Indiana Historical Bureau, 1945.

1736   Cox, Ora E. *Cass County in the World War.* Logansport, Indiana, 1928. [Indiana.]

1737   Blatt, Heiman K., comp. *Sons of Men: Evansville's War Record.* Evansville, Indiana: A. P. Madison, 1920.

1738   Hancock County, Indiana. Council of Defense. *Hancock County, Indiana, in the World War.* Greenfield, Indiana: Board of Commissioners of Hancock County, 1921.

1739   Hayworth, Clarence V. *History of Howard County in the World War.* Indianapolis: W. B. Burford, 1920. [Indiana.]

1740   Cottman, George S. *Jefferson County in the World War.* Madison, Indiana: Jefferson County Historical Society, 1920. [Indiana.]

1741   Wycoff, Minnie E., ed. *Ripley County's Part in the World War, 1917–1918: Compiled under the Direction and Censorship of the Ripley County Historical Society.* Batesville, Indiana, 1920. [Indiana.]

1742   Brown, Earl S. *A History of Switzerland County's Part in the World War.* Connersville, Indiana: Express Printing, 1919. [Indiana.]

1743   [Hansen, Marcus L.] *The Writing of War History in Iowa.* Iowa City: State Historical Society, 1919.

1744   *The History of Iowa's Part in the World War.* Iowa City: State Historical Society, 1919.

1745   Shambaugh, Bertha M. *Organized Speaking in Iowa during the War.* Iowa City: State Historical Society, 1918.

1746   Eilers, Tom D., ed. *Buena Vista's Part in the World War: One Iowa County's Record of Service and Sacrifice.* Storm Lake, Iowa: T. D. Eilers, 1920.

1747   Cram, Ralph W., ed. *History of the War Activities of Scott County, Iowa, 1917–1918.* Davenport, Iowa: State Council of National Defense, 1919.

1748   Kansas. State Council of Defense. *History of the Kansas State Council of Defense,* by Frank W. Blackmar. Topeka: State Printing Plant, 1921.

1749   Morehouse, George P. "Kansas as a State of Extremes, and Its Attitude during the World War." *Kansas Historical Society Collection* 15 (1923): 231– 78.

1750   Henney, Fred K., ed. *Reno's Response: History of Reno County's War Work Activities during the World War, 1917– 1918.* Hutchinson, Kansas, 1921 (?). [Kansas.]

1751   Wilson, John E. *Russell County in the War.* Topeka: Coper Printing, 1921. [Kansas.]

1752   Kentucky. State Council of Defense. *Report of the Activities of the Kentucky Council of Defense to January 1, 1920.* Frankfort, Kentucky: State Journal Co., 1920.

1753   Beer, William. "Louisiana State War Activities." *Mississippi Valley Historical Association Proceedings* 10, pt. 1, (1920): 108– 11.

1754   Historical Records Survey. Louisiana. *Inventory of the Records of World War Emergency Activities in Louisiana, 1916– 1920.* University: Louisiana State University, Department of Archives, 1942.

1755   Costrell, Edwin. *How Maine Viewed the War, 1914– 1917.* Orono: Printed at University of Maine Press, 1940.

1756   Maine. Adjutant General's Office. *Report of the Adjutant General of the State of Maine for the Period of the World War, 1917– 1919.* 2 vols. Augusta, 1929.

1757   Danforth, Florence W. *Somerset County in the World War.* Lewiston, Maine: Journal Printshop & Bindery, 1920. [Maine.]

1758   Maryland. State Council of Defense. *Report of Maryland Council of Defense to the Governor and General Assembly of Maryland.* Indianapolis (?), 1920.

1759   Maryland. War Records Commission. *Maryland in the World War, 1917– 1919: Military and Naval Service Records.* 2 vols. Baltimore: Maryland War Records Commission, 1933.

1760   Lyman, George H. *The Story of the Massachusetts Committee on Public Safety, February 10, 1917– November 21, 1918.* Boston: Wright & Potter Printing, 1919.

1761   Sherburne, John H. "Massachusetts in the World War (1914– 1919)." In *Commonwealth History of Massachusetts,* edited by Albert B. Hart. 2 vols. New York: States History Co., 1930.

1762   Fuess, Claude M., ed. *Andover, Massachusetts, in the World War.* Andover: Andover Press, 1921.

1763 Bedford, Massachusetts. *Bedford in the World War, 1917–1919.* In *Annual Reports of the Officers of the Town of Bedford.* Boston, 1928.

1764 Zack, Charles. *Holyoke in the Great War.* Holyoke, Massachusetts: Transcript Publishing, 1919.

1765 Waters, Thomas F. *Ipswich in the World War.* Salem, Massachusetts: Ipswich Historical Society, 1920. [Massachusetts.]

1766 Atkinson, Minnie. *Newburyport in the World War.* Newburyport, Massachusetts: News Publishing Co., 1938.

1767 South Hadley, Massachusetts. *South Hadley, Massachusetts, in the World War.* Holyoke, Massachusetts: Anker Printing, 1932.

1768 Landrum, Charles H. "Michigan in the Great War." *Michigan History* 4 (Apr. 1920): 478–84.

1769 ———. "Michigan War Legislation, 1919." *Michigan History* 5 (Jan. 1921): 228–67.

1770 Holbrook, Franklin F., and Livia Appel. *Minnesota in the War with Germany.* 2 vols. St. Paul: Minnesota Historical Society, 1928, 1932. [Vol. 2 edited by Solon J. Buck.]

1771 Jenson, Carol. "Loyalty as a Political Weapon: The 1918 Campaign in Minnesota." *Minnesota History* 43 (Summer 1972): 42–57.

1772 Minnesota. Commission of Public Safety. *Report of the Minnesota Commission of Public Safety.* St. Paul: L. F. Dow, 1919.

1773 Nelson, Arthur M., comp. *Martin County in the World War, 1917–1919.* Fairmont, Minnesota: Sentinel Publishing Co., 1920. [Minnesota.]

1774 Wentsel, Claude E., ed. *Newman County, Minnesota, in the World War.* Ada, Minnesota: Pfund & Wentsel, 1922.

1775 *Polk County, Minnesota, in the World War.* Ada, Minnesota: C. E. Wentsel, 1922.

1776 Holbrook, Franklin F., ed. *St. Paul and Ramsey County in the War of 1917–1918.* St. Paul, Minnesota: Ramsey County War Records Commission, 1929.

1777 Crighton, John C. *Missouri and the World War, 1914–1917: A Study in Public Opinion.* Columbia: University of Missouri, 1947.

1778 Lueker, Erwin L. "The Stance of Missouri in 1917." *Concordia Historical Institute Quarterly* 40 (Oct. 1967): 119–26.

1779 Missouri. State Council of Defense. *Final Report of the Missouri Council of Defense.* . . St. Louis: Curran Printing, 1919.

1780 Mitchell, Franklin D. "The Re-election of Irreconcilable James A. Reed." *Missouri Historical Review* 60 (July 1966): 416– 35.

1781 Shoemaker, Floyd C. "Missouri and the War." *Missouri Historical Review* 12 (Oct. 1917): 22– 31; (Jan. 1918): 90– 110; (Apr. 1918): 180– 94; (July 1918): 240– 57; 13 (Oct. 1918): 1– 35; (July 1919): 319– 60.

1782 Lowitt, Richard. "Senator Norris and the 1918 Campaign." *Pacific Northwest Quarterly* 57 (July 1966): 113– 19. [Nebraska.]

1783 New Hampshire. Committee on Public Safety. *The New Hampshire Committee on Public Safety, Personnel: List of Committees Record of Organized Work, Financial Statement.* Concord: Rumford Press, 1922.

1784 Sterling, Adaline W. *The Book of Englewood.* New York, 1922. [New Jersey.]

1785 Schmidt, Hubert G. "Hunterdon County in the First World War." *New Jersey Historical Society Proceedings* 72 (Apr. 1954): 103– 35; (July 1954): 184– 203; (Oct. 1954): 248– 69.

1786 Wall, John P. *New Brunswick, New Jersey, in the World War, 1917– 1918.* New Brunswick: S. M. Christie Press, 1921.

1787 Souder, Harry J. *Vineland, and Vinelanders in the World War.* Vineland, New Jersey: Channon-Souder Co., 1922.

1788 Bloom, Lansing B., et al. "New Mexico in the Great War." *New Mexico Historical Review* 1 (Jan. 1926): 3– 22; (Apr. 1926): 103– 34; (July 1926): 231– 64; (Oct. 1926): 400– 433; 2 (Jan. 1927): 3– 26.

1789 Cohen, Harry, comp. *Albany's Part in the World War.* Albany, New York: General Publishing, 1919.

1790 Auburn (New York). Mayor's Defense Committee. *Report of the Mayor's Defense Committee, Auburn, New York, 1917– 1919.* Auburn, 1920.

1791 Sweeney, Daniel J., ed. *History of Buffalo and Erie County, 1914– 1919.* Buffalo, New York, 1920.

1792 Columbia County, New York. Home Defense Committee. *Columbia County in the World War.* Albany, New York: J. B. Lyon, 1924.

1793 Rider, Edward C. *Franklin County, New York, in the World War.* Franklin County Board of Supervisors, 1926.

1794 [Christman, Franklin W.], comp. *Herkimer County in the World War, 1916– 1918.* Little Falls, New York: Journal & Courier Co., 1927. [New York.]

1795 [Wicks, Perry S.], comp. *War Record of the Town of Islip, Long Island, New York . . . 1917–1918.* Bay Shore, New York, 1921.

1796 Reeves, George W. *Jefferson County in the World War.* Watertown, New York, 1920. [New York.]

1797 Patmore, Arthur C. *Monroe in the World War.* Monroe, New York: Monroe Gazette, 1921.

1798 Dunphy, Edward P. *Newburgh in the World War. . . .* Newburgh, New York: Newburgh World War Publishing Co., 1924.

1799 Pallen, Condé B., ed. *New Rochelle: Her Part in the Great War.* New Rochelle, New York (?): W. C. Tindall, 1920.

1800 New York (City). Mayor's Committee on National Defense. *The Mayor's Committee on National Defense. . . .* New York: De Vinne, 1918.

1801 [Foreman, Edward R.], ed. *World War Service of Rochester and Monroe County, New York.* 3 vols. Rochester: Published by the city, 1924–1930.

1802 [Ives, Chauncey.] *The "World War" History of the Village of Rye, 1917–1918.* New York: Knickerbocker, 1923. [New York.]

1803 North, Arthur W. *Walton World War History. . . .* Walton, New York: Reporter Press, 1922.

1804 Lockwood, Louisa C. *The World War History of the City of White Plains 1917–1918. . . .* White Plains, New York, 1926.

1805 Harrison, Emmett De V., comp. *Yates County in the World War, 1917–1918.* Penn Yan, New York: E. D. Harrison, 1921. [New York.]

1806 Yonkers, New York. *Yonkers in the World War. . . .* Norwood, Massachusetts: Plimpton Press, 1922.

1807 Breen, William J. "The North Carolina Council of Defense during World War I, 1917–1918." *North Carolina Historical Review* 50 (Jan. 1973): 1–31.

1808 Clark, Walter, Jr. "North Carolina in the World War." *Proceedings of the 25th Annual Session of the North Carolina Bar Association* (1923): 57–72.

1809 Daughters of the American Revolution. North Carolina. Craighead-Dunlap Chapter, Wadesboro, comp. *Anson County in the World War, 1917–1919. . . .* Raleigh: Edwards & Broughton, 1929.

1810 Ohio. State Council of Defense. *Annual Report. . . 1917–1918–.* Columbus, 1918–.

1811 ———. *A History of the Activities of the Ohio Branch, Council of National Defense, 1917–1919: How Ohio Mobilized Her Resources for the War.* Columbus: F. J. Heer, 1919.

1812 Koch, Felix J. *Cincinnati Sees It Thru: The Camera's Story of How the Great World War Came to the Queen of the West.* Cincinnati: Meyer Engraving, 1917.

1813 Benton, Elbert J. "The Cleveland World War Machine." *Ohio Archeological and Historical Quarterly* 38 (July 1929): 448–74.

1814 Cleveland (Ohio). Mayor's Advisory War Committee. *Cleveland in the War.* Cleveland: "Harris" Printing & Engraving, 1919.

1815 Snider, Van A. *Fairfield County in the World War.* Lancaster, Ohio: Mallory Printing, 1926. [Ohio.]

1816 Hilton, O. A. "The Oklahoma Council of Defense and the First World War." *Chronicles of Oklahoma* 20 (1942): 18–42.

1817 Lutter, Martin H. "Oklahoma and the World War, 1914–1917: A Study in Public Opinion." Ph.D. dissertation, University of Oklahoma, 1961.

1818 Leader, John. *Oregon through Alien Eyes.* Portland: J. K. Gill, 1922.

1819 Pennsylvania. State Council of Defense. *An Outline of the Wartime Activities of the Pennsylvania Council of National Defense.* Philadelphia (?), 1919.

1820 Philadelphia. War History Committee. *Philadelphia in the World War, 1914–1919.* New York: Wynkoop Hallenbeck Crawford, 1922.

1821 Murdock, Frank R. "Some Aspects of Pittsburgh's Industrial Contribution to the World War." *Western Pennsylvania Historical Magazine* 4 (Oct. 1921): 214–23.

1822 Clifford, Edmund L. *Schuylkill County, Pennsylvania, in the World War.* Pottsville, Pennsylvania: Press of J. H. Zerbey Newspapers, 1931.

1823 Hall, Clifford J., and John P. Lehn, eds. *York County and the World War.* York, Pennsylvania, 1920.

1824 Hart, Hastings H. *The War Program of the State of South Carolina.* New York: Russell Sage Foundation, 1918.

1825 South Carolina. State Council of Defense. *The South Carolina Handbook of the War.* N.p., n.d.

1826 Hanson, Joseph M. *South Dakota in the World War, 1917–1919.* Pierre, South Dakota: State Historical Society, 1940.

1827 Baines, May, ed. *Houston's Part in the World War.* Houston, 1919.

1828 [Goddard, Benjamin], comp. *Pertinent Facts on Utah's Loyalty and War Record.* Salt Lake City: Bureau of Information, 1918.

1829 Utah. State Council of Defense. *Utah in the World War.* Salt Lake City: Arrow Press, 1924.

1830 Cushing, John T., and Arthur F. Stone, eds. *Vermont in the World War, 1917–1919.* Burlington, Vermont: Free Press Printing Co., 1928.

1831 Davis, Arthur K., ed. *Virginia Communities in War Times.* 2 vols. Richmond: Virginia War History Commission, 1926–1927.

1832 ———. *Virginia War History in Newspaper Clippings.* Richmond: Virginia War History Commission, 1924.

1833 Hodges, Leroy. "Virginia War Economy and Budget System." *Proceedings of the Academy of Political Science* 8 (1918–1920): 50–53.

1834 Washington (State). State Council of Defense. *Report of the State Council of Defense to the Governor of Washington Covering Its Activities during the War, June 16, 1917 to January 9, 1919.* Olympia, Washington: F. M. Lamborn, 1919.

1835 Mason, William H. *Snohomish County in the War.* Everett, Washington: Mason Publishing Co., 1927(?). [Washington.]

1836 Hart, Hastings H. *A Suggested Program for the Executive State Council of Defense of West Virginia.* New York: Russell Sage Foundation, 1917.

1837 Falk, Karen. "Public Opinion in Wisconsin during World War I." *Wisconsin Magazine of History* 25 (June 1942): 389–407.

1838 Holmes, Frederick L. *Wisconsin's War Record.* Madison: Capital Publishing, 1919.

1839 Pixley, Rutherford. *Wisconsin in the World War. . . .* Milwaukee: Wisconsin War History Co., 1919.

1840 Ruth, Harry S. *Ashland County, Wisconsin, in the World War, 1917–1919.* Boston: Chapple Publishing, 1928.

1841 Haight, Walter L. *Racine County in the World War: A History.* Racine, Wisconsin: Western Printing & Lithographing, 1920.

E/Economic Mobilization

General

1842 Ayres, Leonard P. *Business in Two War Periods.* Cleveland: Cleveland Trust Co., 1945.

1843 Bendiner, Marvin R. "Corruption in the World War." *American Mercury* 34 (Feb. 1935): 225– 34.

1844 Bogart, Ernest L. "Economic Organization for War." *American Political Science Review* 14 (Nov. 1920): 587– 606.

1845 Clark, John M. "The Basis of War-Time Collectivism." *American Economic Review* 7 (Dec. 1917): 772– 90.

1846 Crowell, Benedict, and Robert F. Wilson. *The Giant Hand: Our Mobilization and Control of Industry and National Resources, 1917– 1918.* New Haven: Yale University Press, 1921.

1847 Cuff, Robert D. "Organizing for War: Canada and the United States during World War I." In Canadian Historical Association, *Historical Papers, 1969.* Ottawa: Canadian Historical Association, 1969.

1848 ——. "We Band of Brothers—Woodrow Wilson's War Managers." *Canadian Review of American Studies* 5 (Fall 1974): 135– 48.

1849 DeWeerd, Harvey A. "American Industrial Mobilization for War, 1917– 1918." *Ohio Archeological and Historical Quarterly* 49 (July– Sept. 1940): 249– 61.

1850 Fesler, James W. "Areas for Industrial Mobilization, 1917– 1938." *Public Administration Review* 1 (Winter 1941): 149– 66.

1851 Hippelhauser, Richard H., ed. *American Industry in the War: A Report of the War Industries Board* (March 1921). . . . New York: Prentice-Hall, 1941.

1852 Holcombe, A. N. "New Problems of Governmental Efficiency." *American Economic Review* 8 (March 1918): 271– 80.

1853 Leake, James M. "The Conflict Over Coordination." *American Political Science Review* 12 (Aug. 1918): 365– 80.

1854 Moore, Geoffrey T. *Production of Industrial Materials in World Wars I and II.* New York: National Bureau of Economic Research, 1944.

1855 Quinton, A. B., Jr. "War Planning and Industrial Mobilization." *Harvard Business Review* 9 (Oct. 1930): 8– 17.

1856 Rothbard, Murray N. "War Collectivism in World War I." In *A New History of Leviathan,* edited by Murray N. Rothbard and Ronald Radosh. New York: Dutton, 1972.

1857 Soule, George, *Prosperity Decade: From War to Depression, 1917– 1929.* New York: Rinehart, 1947.

1858 Tobin, Harold J., and Percy W. Bidwell. *Mobilizing Civilian America.* New York: Council on Foreign Relations, 1940.

1859 U.S. Congress. House. Select Committee on Expenditures in the War Department. *Hearings on Expenditures in the War Department,* 66th Cong., 1st– 3d Sess., 1919– 1921, 15 vols. [Graham Committee.]

1860 U.S. Congress. Senate. Committee on Military Affairs. Hearings: *Investigation of the War Department,* 65th Cong., 2d Sess., 1918, 8 pts. [Chamberlain Committee.]

1861 U.S. General Staff. War Plans Division. Historical Branch. *Economic Mobilization in the United States for the War of 1917.* Washington, D.C., 1918.

1862 U.S. War Policies Commission. *Hearings before the Commission Appointed under the Authority of Public Resolution no. 98,* 71st Cong., 2d Sess., 1931, H. J. Res. 251, 3 pts.

1863 Van Dorn, Harold A. *Government Owned Corporations.* New York: Knopf, 1926.

1864 Waldman, Seymour. *Death and Profits: A Study of the War Policies Commission.* Reprint. New York: Garland, 1971.

1865 Willoughby, William F. *Government Organization in War-Time and After: A Survey of the Federal Civil Agencies Created for the Prosecution of the War.* New York: Appleton, 1919.

1866 Wright, Chester W., ed. *Economic Problems of War and Its Aftermath.* Reprint. Freeport, New York: Books for Libraries Press, 1972.

Background Studies

1867 Diamond, William. *The Economic Thought of Woodrow Wilson.* Baltimore: Johns Hopkins Press, 1943.

1868 Eddy, Arthur J. *The New Competition. . . .* Chicago: McClurg, 1913.

1869 Haber, Samuel. *Efficiency and Uplift: Scientific Management in the Progressive Era, 1890– 1920.* Chicago: University of Chicago Press, 1964.

1870 "Industrial Preparedness." *Journal of the American Society of Mechanical Engineers* 38 (June 1916): 435– 54.

1871 Sharfman, I. L. "The Trade Association Movement." *American Economic Review* 16 (Mar. 1926), supplement: 203– 18.

1872 Weinstein, James. *The Corporate Ideal in the Liberal State, 1900– 1918.* Boston: Beacon Press, 1968.

1873 Wiebe, Robert H. *Businessmen and Reform: A Study of the Progressive Movement.* Cambridge: Harvard University Press, 1962.

1874 ——. *The Search for Order, 1877– 1920.* New York: Hill & Wang, 1967.

Biographical Studies and Memoirs (Alphabetically by Subject)

1875 Baruch, Bernard M. *Baruch: My Own Story.* New York: Holt, 1957.

1876 ——. *Baruch: The Public Years.* New York: Holt, Rinehart, & Winston, 1960.

1877 Coit, Margaret L. *Mr. Baruch.* Boston: Houghton Mifflin, 1957.

1878 Cuff, Robert D. "Bernard Baruch: Symbol and Myth in Industrial Mobilization." *Business History Review* 43 (Summer 1969): 115– 33.

1879 Hagedorn, Hermann. *Brookings: A Biography.* New York: Macmillan, 1937.

1880 Wildman, Edwin. "Howard Coffin and the War in the Air." *Forum* 59 (Mar. 1918): 257– 68.

1881 Nevins, Allan, and Frank E. Hill. *Ford: Expansion and Challenge, 1915– 1933.* New York: Scribner's, 1957.

1882 Heaton, Herbert. *A Scholar in Action: Edwin F. Gay.* New York: Greenwood Press, 1968.

1883 Crissey, Forrest. *Alexander Legge, 1866– 1933.* . . . Chicago: Alexander Legge Memorial Committee, 1936.

1884 Martin, Franklin H. *The Joy of Living: An Autobiography.* 2 vols. Garden City, New York: Doubleday, Doran, 1933.

1885 Otis, Charles. *Here I Am: A Rambling Account of the Exciting Times of Yesteryear.* Cleveland: Buehler Printcraft, 1951.

1886 Cuff, Robert D. "A 'Dollar-a-Year Man' in Government: George M. Peek and the War Industries Board." *Business History Review* 41 (Winter 1967): 404– 20.

1887 Vauclain, Samuel M., with Earl C. May. *Steaming Up!: The Autobiography of Samuel M. Vauclain.* New York: Brewer & Warren, 1930.

1888 Wehle, Louis B. *Hidden Theads of History: Wilson through Roosevelt.* New York: Macmillan, 1953. [Wehle.]

1889 Hungerford, Edward. *Daniel Willard Rides the Line: The Story of the Great Railroad Man.* New York: Putnam's, 1938.

1890 Cuff, Robert D. "Woodrow Wilson and Business-Government Relations during World War I." *Review of Politics* 31 (July 1969): 385– 407.

Prewar Preparations

1891 Adams, John W. "The Influences Affecting Naval Shipbuilding Legislation, 1910– 1916." *Naval War College Review* 22 (Dec. 1969): 41– 70.

1892 Coffin, Howard E. "The Automobile Engineer and Preparedness." *S.A.E. Bulletin* 10 (July 1916): 461– 74.

1893 Gifford, Walter S. "Realizing Industrial Preparedness: An Inventory of Our Resources." *Scientific American* 114 (June 31, 1916): 576.

1894 Knoeppel, Charles E. *Industrial Preparedness.* New York: Engineering Magazine, 1916.

1895 ———. "Industrial Preparedness and American Business." *Efficiency Society Journal* 5 (Sept. 1916): 454– 60.

1896 Rappaport, Armin. *The Navy League of the United States.* Detroit: Wayne State University Press, 1962.

1897 Robins, Thomas. "America's Industrial Organization for National Defense." *Scientific American* 115 (July 8, 1916): 40, 48– 49.

1898 Scott, Lloyd N. *Naval Consulting Board of the United States.* Washington, D.C.: G.P.O., 1920.

1899 Wright, C. W. "American Economic Preparations for War, 1914– 1917 and 1939– 1941." *Canadian Journal of Economics and Political Science* 8 (May 1942): 157– 75.

English Models for the United States (See also VII, B/Comparison Studies [The War and Other Societies])

1900 Baker, Charles W. *Government Control and Operation of Industry in Great Britain and the United States during the World War.* New York: Oxford University Press, 1921.

1901 Carver, Thomas N. *Government Control of the Liquor Business in Great Britain and the United States.* New York: Oxford University Press, 1919.

1902 Gray, Howard L. *War Time Control of Industry: The Experience of England.* New York: Macmillan, 1918.

1903 Walter, Henriette R. "Output and Hours: A Summary of the English Experience." *Survey* 38 (Apr. 21, 1917): 51– 53.

Mobilization Agencies: The War Industries Board and Others

1904 Beaver, David R. "Newton D. Baker and the Genesis of the War Industries Board, 1917– 1918." *Journal of American History* 52 (June 1965): 43– 58.

1905 Breen, William J. "The Council of National Defense: Industrial and Social Mobilization in the United States (1916–1920)." Ph.D. dissertation, Duke University, 1968.

1906 Clarkson, Grosvenor B. *Industrial America in the World War: The Strategy behind the Line, 1917–1918.* Boston: Houghton Mifflin, 1923.

1907 Cuff, Robert D. "Business, Government and the War Industries Board." Ph.D. dissertation, Princeton University, 1966.

1908 ———. "Business, the State, and World War I: The American Experience." In *War and Society in North America.* . . , edited by J. L. Granatstein and R. D. Cuff. Toronto: Nelson, 1971.

1909 ———. *The War Industries Board: Business-Government Relations during World War I.* Baltimore: Johns Hopkins Press, 1973.

1910 Hitchcock, Curtice N. "The War Industries Board: Its Development, Organization and Functions." *Journal of Political Economy* 26 (June 1918): 545–66.

1911 Kester, Randall B. "The War Industries Board, 1917–1918: A Study in Industrial Mobilization." *American Political Science Review* 34 (Aug. 1940): 655–84.

1912 Martin, Franklin H. *Digest of the Proceedings of the Council of National Defense during the World War: Prepared in Narrative Form.* Washington, D.C.: G.P.O., 1934.

1913 Ohl, John K. "General Hugh S. Johnson and the War Industries Board." *Military Review* 55 (May 1975): 35–48.

1914 ———. "The Navy, the War Industries Board, and the Industrial Mobilization for War." *Military Affairs* 40 (Feb. 1976): 17–25.

1915 Peoples, John M. "The Genesis of the War Industries Board." Ph.D. dissertation, University of California, 1942.

1916 Tyson, James L. "The War Industries Board, 1918." *Fortune* 22 (Sept. 1940), supplement.

1917 U.S. Congress. Senate. Special Committee to Investigate the Munitions Industry. *Munitions Industry: Digest of the Proceedings of the Council of National Defense during the World War,* by Franklin Martin, 73d Cong., 2d Sess., 1934, doc. no. 193.

1918 ———. *Munitions Industry: Final Report of the Chairman of the United States War Industries Board to the President of the United States, February 1919,* 74th Cong., 1st Sess., 1935, Senate Committee print no. 3.

1919 U.S. Council of National Defense. *First (–Fourth) Report of the Council of National Defense.* 4 vols. Washington, D.C.: G.P.O., 1917–1920.

1920 ———. *Munitions Industry.* Minutes of the Advisory Commission of the Council of National Defense (Dec. 1916–Feb. 1921). Washington, D.C.: G.P.O., 1936.

1921 ———. Advisory Commission. *Munitions Industry: Minutes of the Advisory Commission of the Council of National Defense (Dec. 6, 1916–Aug. 5, 1918) and Minutes of the Munitions Standards Board.* Washington, D.C.: G.P.O., 1936.

1922 U.S. Council of National Defense. General Munitions Board. *Munitions Industry: Minutes of the General Munitions Board from April 4 to August 9, 1917.* Washington, D.C.: G.P.O., 1936.

1923 U.S. War Industries Board. *American Industry in the War: A Report of the War Industries Board* (March 1921), by Bernard M. Baruch, edited by Richard H. Hippelheuser. New York: Prentice-Hall, 1941. [See also no. 1851.]

1924 ———. *Members of the War Industries Board Organization.* . . . Washington, D.C.: G.P.O., 1919.

1925 ———. . . . *Munitions Industry: Minutes of the War Industries Board from August 1, 1917 to December 19, 1918.* Washington, D.C.: G.P.O., 1935.

Military Procurement

1926 "The Aircraft Production Board." *Proceedings of the Academy of Political Science* 7 (Feb. 1918): 104–14.

1927 Beaver, Daniel R. "George W. Goethals and the P. S. and T." In *Some Pathways in Twentieth Century History,* edited by Daniel R. Beaver. Detroit: Wayne State University Press, 1969.

1927a ———. "The Problem of American Military Supply, 1890–1920." In *War, Business, and American Society: Historical Perspectives on the Military-Industrial Complex.* Edited by Benjamin F. Cooling. Port Washington, New York: Kennikat Press, 1977.

1928 Crowell, Benedict, and Robert F. Wilson. *The Armies of Industry . . . Our Nation's Manufacture of Munitions for a World in Arms, 1917–1918.* New Haven: Yale University Press, 1921.

1929 Engelbrecht, Helmuth C., and Frank C. Hanighen. *Merchants of Death: A Study of the International Armament Industry.* New York: Dodd, Mead, 1934.

1929a Ferrell, Henry C., Jr. "Regional Rivalries, Congress, and MIC: The Norfolk and Charleston Navy Yards, 1913–20." In *War, Business, and American Society: Historical Perspectives on the Military-Industrial Complex.*

Edited by Benjamin F. Cooling. Port Washington, New York: Kennikat Press, 1977.

1930 U.S. Congress, House. Committee on Naval Affairs. *Hearings . . . on Estimates Submitted by the Secretary of the Navy. 1918*, 65th Cong., 2d Sess., 1918.

1931 U.S. Congress. House. Select Committee on Expenditures in the War Department. *Expenditures in the War Department-Aviation . . . Report*, 66th Cong., 2d Sess., 1920, House Rpt. 637.

1932 U.S. War Department. *American Munitions 1917– 1918: Report of Benedict Crowell, the Assistant Secretary of War, Director of Munitions.* Washington, D.C.: G.P.O., 1919.

Business-Government Relations in Economic Mobilization

1933 Crowell, John F. *Government War Contracts.* New York: Oxford University Press, 1920.

1934 Cuff, Robert D. "Newton D. Baker, Frank A. Scott, and 'The American Reinforcement in the World War,' " *Military Affairs* 34 (Feb. 1970): 11– 13.

1935 Koistinen, Paul A. C. "The 'Industrial-Military Complex' in Historical Perspective: The InterWar Years." *Journal of American History* 56 (Mar. 1970): 819– 39.

1936 ———. "The 'Industrial-Military Complex' in Historical Perspective: World War I." *Business History Review* 41 (Winter 1967): 378– 403.

The System of Business Self-Regulation

1937 Cuff, Robert D. "The Dollar-a-Year Men of the Great War." *Princeton University Library Chronicle* 30 (Autumn 1968): 10– 24.

1938 ———. "Herbert Hoover, The Ideology of Voluntarism and War Organization during the Great War." *Journal of American History* 64 (Sept. 1977): 358– 72.

1939 Davis, G. Cullom. "The Transformation of the Federal Trade Commission, 1914– 1929." *Mississippi Valley Historical Review* 49 (Dec. 1962): 437– 55.

1940 Galambos, Louis. *Competition and Cooperation: The Emergence of a National Trade Association.* Baltimore: Johns Hopkins Press, 1966.

1941 Himmelberg, Robert F. "Business, Antitrust Policy, and the Industial Board of the Department of Commerce, 1919." *Business History Review* 42 (Spring 1968): 1– 23.

1942 ———. "The War Industries Board and the Antitrust Question in November 1918." *Journal of American History* 52 (June 1965): 59–74.

1943 Howenstine, E. Jay, Jr. "Business Proposals for a Controlled Market after World War I." *Southwestern Social Science Quarterly* 24 (Mar. 1944): 289–302.

1944 Molnor, T. T. "National Defense and Anti-trust Laws" (1917–1952). *Georgia Bar Journal* 14 (May 1952): 401–09.

1945 Reagan, Michael D. "Serving Two Masters: Problems in the Employment of Dollar-a-Year and without Compensation Personnel." Ph.D. dissertation, Princeton University, 1959.

1946 Rosenberg, James M. "The Sherman Act and the War." *Columbia Law Review* 18 (Feb. 1918): 137–46.

1947 Schaffer, Ronald. "Business: The New Capitalism." *Mankind* 5 (Feb. 1977): 30–32.

1948 Urofsky, Melvin I. *Big Steel and the Wilson Administration: A Study in Business-Government Relations.* Columbus: Ohio State University Press, 1969.

1949 ———. "Josephus Daniels and the Armor Trust." *North Carolina Historical Review* 45 (July 1968): 237–63.

War Finance

1950 Adams, T. S. "Principles of Excess Profit Taxation." *Annals of the American Academy of Political and Social Science* 75 (Jan. 1918): 147–58.

1951 American Economic Association. Committee on War Finance. "Report of the Committee on War Finance of the American Economic Association." N.p., 1918.

1952 Anderson, Frank F. "Fundamental Factors in War Finance." *Journal of Political Economy* 25 (Nov. 1917): 857–87.

1953 Blakey, Roy G. "The War Revenue Act of 1917." *American Economic Review* 7 (Dec. 1917): 791–815.

1954 ———, and Gladys C. Blakey. "The Revenue Act of 1918." *American Economic Review* 9 (June 1919): 213–43.

1955 Bogart, Ernest L. *War Costs and Their Financing: A Study of the Financing of the War and the After-war Problems of Debt and Taxation.* New York: Appleton, 1921.

1956 Carver, Thomas N. *War Thrift.* New York: Oxford University Press, 1919.

1957   Dennis, Roger L. "War Savings Stamp Campaign in South Dakota for the Year 1918." *South Dakota Historical Collections* 10 (1921): 269–78.

1958   Fisher, Irving. "How the Public Should Pay for the War." *The Annals* 78 (July 1918): 112–17.

1959   Gilbert, Charles. *American Financing of World War I.* Westport, Connecticut: Greenwood, 1970.

1960   Greenough, Walter S. . . . *The War Purse of Indiana: The Five Liberty Loans and War Savings and Thrift Campaigns in Indiana during the World War.* Indianapolis: Indiana Historical Commission, 1922.

1961   Hillje, John W. "New York Progressives and the War Revenue Act of 1917." *New York History* 53 (Oct. 1972): 437–59.

1962   Hokanson, Nels M. "The Foreign Language Division of the Chicago Liberty Loan Campaign." *Journal of the Illinois State Historical Society* 67 (Sept. 1974): 429–39.

1963   Hollander, Jacob H. *War Borrowing: A Study of Treasury Certificates of Indebtedness of the United States.* New York: Macmillan, 1919.

1964   Holmes, George E. *Federal Income Tax, War Profits and Excess-Profits Taxes: Including Stamp Taxes, Capital Stock Tax, Tax on Employment of Child Labor, Tax on Undistributed Profits.* Chicago: Callaghan, 1919.

1965   Ingle, H. Larry. "The Dangers of Reaction: Repeal of the Revenue Act of 1918." *North Carolina Historical Review* 44 (Jan. 1967): 72–88.

1966   Lindbergh, Charles A. *Your Country at War and What Happens to You after a War.* Philadelphia: Dorrance, 1934.

1967   Miller, A. C. "War Finance and Inflation." *Annals of the American Academy of Political and Social Science* 75 (Jan. 1918): 113–34.

1968   Noyes, Alexander D. *The War Period of American Finance, 1908–1925.* New York: Putnam's, 1926.

1969   Patten, S. N. "Liquidation Taxes." *Annals of the American Academy of Political and Social Science* 75 (Jan. 1918): 165–81.

1970   ———. "Problems of War Finance." *Yale Review* 7 (Oct. 1917): 73–89.

1971   Patterson, E. M. "Some Tendencies in the Federal Reserve System." *The Annals* 78 (July 1918): 118–29.

1972   Schiff, Mortimer L. "War Time Borrowing by the Government." *Annals of the American Academy of Political and Social Science* 75 (Jan. 1918): 38–51.

1973   Seligman, Edwin R. A. "Loans versus Taxes in War Finance." *Annals of the American Academy of Political and Social Science* 75 (Jan. 1918): 52– 82.

1974   Stephenson, Gilbert T. "The War Savings Campaign in 1918." *North Carolina Historical Review* 1 (Jan. 1924): 26– 34.

1975   Vanderlip, Frank A. "Financing with War Savings Certificates." *Annals of the American Academy of Political and Social Science* 75 (Jan. 1918): 31– 37.

1976   Viner, Jacob. "Who Paid for the War?" *Journal of Political Economy* 28 (Jan. 1920): 46– 76.

1977   Whitney, Nathaniel R. *The Sale of War Bonds in Iowa.* Iowa City: State Historical Society, 1923.

1978   Willoughby, Woodbury. *The Capital Issues Committee and War Finance Corporation.* Baltimore: Johns Hopkins Press, 1934.

1979   Zoller, J. F. "A Criticism of the War Revenue Act of 1917." *Annals of the American Academy of Political and Social Science* 75 (Jan. 1918): 182– 90.

Price Regulation

1980   Adams, George P., Jr. *Wartime Price Control.* Washington, D.C.: American Council on Public Affairs, 1942.

1981   Anderson, Benjamin M., Jr. "Value and Price Theory in Relation to Price-Fixing and War Finance." *American Economic Review* 8 (Mar. 1918): 239– 56.

1982   Bartley, Joseph C. *A Study of Price Control by the United States Food Administration.* Gettysburg, Pennsylvania: Gettysburg Compiler Printing Co., 1922.

1983   Berglund, Abraham. "Price Fixing in the Iron and Steel Industry." *Quarterly Journal of Economics* 32 (Aug. 1918): 597– 620.

1984   Cuff, Robert D., and Melvin I. Urofsky. "The Steel Industry and Price-fixing during World War I." *Business History Review* 44 (Autumn 1970): 291– 306.

1985   Davies, Joseph E. "Price Control." *Annals of the American Academy of Political and Social Science* 74 (Nov. 1917): 288– 93.

1986   Friedman, Milton. "Price, Income, and Monetary Changes in Three Wartime Periods." *American Economic Review* 42:2 (May 1952): 612– 25.

1987 Haney, Lewis H. "Price-Fixing in the United States During the War." *Political Science Quarterly* 34 (Mar. 1919): 104– 26; (June 1919): 262– 89; (Sept. 1919): 434– 53.

1988 Hardy, Charles O. *Wartime Control of Prices.* Washington, D.C.: Brookings Institution, 1940.

1989 Lauck, William Jett. *Cost of Living and the War: An Analysis of Recent Changes.* Cleveland: Doyle & Waltz, 1918.

1990 Litman, Simon. *Prices and Price Control in Great Britain and the United States during the World War.* New York: Oxford University Press, 1920.

1991 Mitchell, Wesley C. . . . *History of Prices during the War.* Washington, D.C.: G.P.O., 1919.

1992 ——. "Prices and Reconstruction." *American Economic Review* 10 (Mar. 1920), supplement: 129– 56.

1993 Morse, Lewis K. "The Price Fixing of Copper." *Quarterly Journal of Economics* 33 (Nov. 1918): 71– 106.

1994 National Industrial Conference Board. "Changes in the Cost of Living, July 1914– March 1923." Research Rpt., no. 60. New York: National Industrial Conference Board, 1923.

1995 Patten, Simon N. "The Fallacy of Price Bidding." *The Annals* 78 (July 1918): 129– 43.

1996 Stein, Herbert. *Government Price Policy in the United States during the World War.* Williamstown, Massachusetts: Williams College, 1939.

1997 Taussig, Frank W. "Price Fixing as Seen by a Price-Fixer." *Quarterly Journal of Economics* 33 (Feb. 1919): 205– 41.

1998 U.S. Federal Trade Commission. *World War Activities of the Federal Trade Commission, 1917– 1918.* A memorandum by Henry Miller, July 15, 1940. Washington, D.C.: Federal Trade Commission, 1940(?).

1999 Van Hise, Charles R. "The Necessity for Government Regulation of Prices in War Time." *Annals of the American Academy of Political and Social Science* 74 (Nov. 1917): 224– 35.

War Profits

2000 Meyer, Eugene, Jr. *War Profiteering: Some Practical Aspects of its Control.* Washington, D.C., 1917.

2001 U.S. Federal Trade Commission. *Report of the Federal Trade Commission on War-time Costs and Profits of Southern Pine Lumber Companies.* Washington, D.C.: G.P.O., 1922.

2002 ———. *Report on War-Time Profits and Costs of the Steel Industry.* Washington, D.C.: G.P.O., 1925.

International Trade

2003 Culbertson, William S. *Commercial Policy in War Time and After. . . .* New York: Appleton, 1919.

2004 Kaufman, Burton I. *Efficiency and Expansion: Foreign Trade Organization in the Wilson Administration, 1913–1921.* Westport, Connecticut: Greenwood, 1974.

2005 ———. "Wilson's 'War Bureaucracy' and Foreign Trade Expansion, 1917–1921." *Prologue* 6 (Spring 1974): 19–31.

2006 Parrini, Carl P. *Heir to Empire: United States Economic Diplomacy, 1916–1923.* Pittsburgh: University of Pittsburgh Press, 1969.

2007 Safford, Jeffrey. "Experiment in Containment: The United States Steel Embargo and Japan, 1917–1918." *Pacific Historical Review* 39 (Nov. 1970): 439–51.

2008 Scheiber, Harry N. "World War I as Entrepreneurial Opportunity: Willard Straight and the American International Corporation." *Political Science Quarterly* 84 (Sept. 1969): 486–511.

Transportation

2009 Crennan, C. H., and W. E. Warrington, comps. "Documents and Statistics Pertinent to Current Railroad Problems." *Annals of the American Academy of Political and Social Science* 76 (Mar. 1918): 272–304.

2010 Cunningham, William J. *American Railroads: Government Controls and Reconstruction Policies.* Chicago: A. W. Shaw, 1922.

2011 ———. "The Railroads under Government Operation: I, The Period to the Close of 1918." *Quarterly Journal of Economics* 35 (Feb. 1921): 288–340.

2012 ———. "The Railroads under Government Operation: II, From January 1, 1919 to March 1, 1920." *Quarterly Journal of Economics* 36 (Nov. 1921): 30–71.

2013 Dixon, Frank H. "Federal Operation of Railroads during the War." *Quarterly Journal of Economics* 33 (Aug. 1919): 577–631.

2014 ———. *Railroads and Government: Their Relations in the United States, 1910–1921*. New York: Scribner's, 1922.

2015 ———, and Julius H. Parmalee. *War Administration of the Railways in the United States and Great Britain*. New York: Oxford University Press, 1918.

2016 Dunn, Samuel O. "The Railways in Peace and War." *Yale Review* 7 (Jan. 1918): 362–81.

2017 Godfrey, Aaron A. *Government Operation of the Railroads: Its Necessity, Success, and Consequences, 1918–1920*. Austin: Jenkins Publishing, 1974.

2018 Hessen, Robert. "Charles Schwab and the Shipbuilding Crisis of 1918." *Pennsylvania History* 38 (Oct. 1971): 389–99.

2019 Hines, Walker D. *War History of American Railroads*. New Haven: Yale University Press, 1928.

2020 Hurley, Edward N. *The Bridge to France*. Philadelphia: Lippincott, 1927.

2021 Hutchins, John G. B. "The Effects of the Civil War and the Two World Wars on American Transportation." *American Economics Review* 42:2 (May 1952): 626–38.

2022 Kerr, K. Austin. *American Railroad Politics, 1914–1920: Rates, Wages and Efficiency*. Pittsburgh: University of Pittsburgh Press, 1968.

2023 ———. "Decisions for Federal Control: Wilson, McAdoo, and the Railroads, 1917." *Journal of American History* 54 (Dec. 1967): 550–60.

2024 Kolko, Gabriel. *Railroads and Regulation, 1877–1916*. Princeton: Princeton University Press, 1965.

2025 Mattox, W. C. *Building the Emergency Fleet: A Historical Narrative of the Problems and Achievements of the United States Shipping Board Emergency Fleet Corporation*. Cleveland: Penton Publishing Co., 1920.

2026 Parmalee, Julius H. "Physical Needs of the Railways under Government Control." *Annals of the American Academy of Political and Social Science* 76 (Mar. 1918): 42–58.

2027 Rae, John B. *The American Automobile*. Chicago: University of Chicago Press, 1965. [Ch. 5, "War and Readjustment."]

2028 Safford, Jeffrey J. "Edward Hurley and American Shipping Policy: An Elaboration on Wilsonian Diplomacy, 1918–1919." *Historian* 35 (Aug. 1973): 568–86.

2029 Salter, James A. *Allied Shipping Control.* Oxford: Clarendon Press, 1921.

2030 Smith, Darrell H., and P. V. Betters. *The United States Shipping Board.* Washington, D.C.: Brookings Institution, 1931.

2031 Smith, Joseph R. *Influence of the Great War upon Shipping.* New York: Oxford University Press, 1919.

2032 Stevens, Raymond B. "Problems before the Shipping Board." *Proceedings of the Academy of Political Science* 7 (Feb. 1918): 93–99.

2033 Sullivan, Mark. *Wake Up America!* New York: Macmillan, 1918.

2034 Thelen, Max. "Federal Control of Railroads in War Time." *Annals of the American Academy of Political and Social Science* 76 (Mar. 1918): 14–24.

2035 Thorne, Clifford. "Government Operation of American Railroads." *Annals of the American Academy of Political and Social Science* 76 (Mar. 1918): 84–110.

2036 Thurston, William N. "Management-Leadership in the United States Shipping Board, 1917–1918." *American Neptune* 32 (July 1972): 155–70.

2037 U.S. Congress. Senate. Committee on Commerce. Hearings: *United States Shipping Board Emergency Fleet Corporation,* 65th Cong., 2d Sess., 1918.

2038 Webb, William J. "The United States Wooden Steamship Program during World War I." *American Neptune* 35 (Oct. 1975): 275–88.

Energy

2039 Bickelhaupt, W. G. "South Dakota Fuel Administration." *South Dakota Historical Collections* 10 (1921): 279–88.

2040 Garfield, Harry A. "The Task of the Fuel Administration." *Proceedings of the Academy of Political Science* 7 (Feb. 1918): 50–54.

2041 Keller, Charles. "Electric Power during the World War." *Military Engineer* 17 (Nov.-Dec. 1925): 462–68.

2042 ——. *The Power Situation during the War.* Washington, D.C.: G.P.O., 1921.

2043 "The North Carolina Fuel Administration." *North Carolina Historical Review* 1 (Apr. 1924): 138–75.

2044 O'Brien, Dennis J. "The Oil Crisis and the Foreign Policy of the Wilson Administration, 1917– 1921." Ph.D. dissertation, University of Missouri, 1974.

2045 Smith, George O., ed. *The Strategy of Minerals: A Study of the Mineral Factor in the World Position of America in War and in Peace.* New York: Appleton, 1919.

2046 U.S. Congress. Senate. Committee on Manufactures. Hearings before the Subcommittee on Manufactures: *Shortage of Coal,* 65th Cong., 2d Sess., 1918.

2047 U.S. Engineer Department. *The Power Situation during the War,* by Colonel Charles Keller, Corps of Engineers. Washington, D.C.: G.P.O., 1921.

2048 U.S. Fuel Administration. *Final Report of the United States Fuel Administrator, 1917– 1919,* by H. A. Garfield. Washington, D.C.: G.P.O., 1921.

2049 Williamson, Harold F.; Ralph L. Andreano; Arnold R. Daum; and Gilbert C. Klose. "The American Petroleum Industry in World War I." Ch. 8 of *The American Petroleum Industry: The Age of Energy, 1899– 1959.* Evanston, Illinois: Northwestern University Press, 1963.

Agricultural Products and Processing

2050 Bernhardt, Joshua. "Government Control of Sugar during the War." *Quarterly Journal of Economics* 33 (Aug. 1919): 672– 713.

2051 ———. *Government Control of the Sugar Industry in the United States: An Account of the Work of the United States Food Administration and the United States Sugar Equalization Board, Inc.* New York: Macmillan, 1920.

2052 Cooke, Jay. "The Work of the Federal Food Administration." *The Annals* 78 (July 1918): 175– 84.

2053 Dewey, John. "Enlistment for the Farm." 2d ed. New York: Columbia University Division of Intelligence and Publicity, 1917.

2054 Dickson, Maxcy R. *The Food Front in World War I.* Washington, D.C.: American Council on Public Affairs, 1944.

2055 Eldred, Wilfred. "The Wheat and Flour Trade under Food Administration Control: 1917– 1918." *Quarterly Journal of Economics* 33 (Nov. 1918): 1– 70.

2056 Guerrier, Edith. *We Pledge Allegiance: A Librarian's Intimate Story of the United States Food Administration.* Stanford: Stanford University Press, 1941.

2057 Hall, Tom G. "Wilson and the Food Crisis: Agricultural Price Control during World War I." *Agricultural History* 47 (Jan. 1973): 25–46.

2058 Herreid, Charles N. "The Federal Food Administration in South Dakota during the World War." *South Dakota Historical Collections* 10 (1921): 295–314.

2059 Hibbard, Benjamin H. *Effects of the Great War upon Agriculture in the United States and Great Britain.* New York: Oxford University Press, 1919.

2060 Hidy, Ralph W.; Frank E. Hill; and Allan Nevins. *Timber and Men: The Weyerhauser Story.* New York: Macmillan, 1963. [Ch. 18 "An Industry at War."]

2061 Kellogg, Vernon. "The Food Problem." In *The New World of Science,* edited by Robert M. Yerkes. Freeport, New York: Books for Libraries Press, 1969.

2062 McCain, George N. *War Rations for Pennsylvanians: The Story of the Operations of the Federal Food Administration in Pennsylvania. . . .* Philadelphia: John C. Winston, 1920.

2063 Merritt, Albert N. *War Time Control of Distribution of Foods: A Short History of the Distribution Division of the United States Food Administration.* New York: Macmillan, 1920.

2064 Mullendore, William C. *History of the United States Food Administration, 1917–1919.* Stanford: Stanford University Press, 1941.

2065 Pack, Charles L. *The War Garden Victorious.* Philadelphia: Lippincott, 1919.

2066 Pinchot, Gifford. "Essentials to a Food Program for Next Year." *The Annals* 78 (July 1918): 156–63.

2067 Pollock, Ivan L. . . . *The Food Administration in Iowa.* 2 vols. Iowa City: State Historical Society, 1923.

2068 Smith, George W. "New Mexico's Wartime Food Problems, 1917–1918: A Case Study in Emergency Administration." *New Mexico Historical Review* 18 (Oct. 1943): 349–85; 19 (Jan. 1944): 1–54.

2069 Surface, Frank M. *American Pork Production in the World War.* Chicago: A. W. Shaw, 1926.

2070 ———. *The Grain Trade during the World War: Being a History of the Food Administration Grain Corporation and the United States Grain Corporation.* New York: Macmillan, 1928.

2071 ———. *The Stabilization of the Price of Wheat during the War and Its Effect upon the Returns to the Producer.* Washington, D.C.: U.S. Grain Corporation, 1925.

2072 ———, and R. L. Bland. *American Food in the World War and Reconstruction Period.* Stanford: Stanford University Press, 1931.

2073 Taylor, Alonzo E. "International and National Food Control." *The Annals* 78 (July 1918): 149– 56.

2074 Weld, L. D. H. "The Livestock and Meat Situation." *The Annals* 78 (July 1918): 168– 75.

2075 Winters, Donald L. "The Hoover-Wallace Controversy during World War I." *Annals of Iowa,* 3d ser. 39 (Spring 1969): 586– 97.

Statistics

2076 Clark, John M. *The Costs of the World War to the American People.* Reprint. New York: A. M. Kelley, 1970.

2077 Kuznets, Simon S. *National Product in Wartime.* New York: National Bureau of Economic Research, 1945.

F/Regulation of Public Attitudes

General

2078 Allen, Frank H. "Government Influence on News in the United States during the World War." Ph.D. dissertation, University of Illinois, 1934.

2079 Ellul, Jacques. *Propaganda: The Formation of Men's Attitudes.* Translated by K. Kellen and J. Lerner. New York: Knopf, 1965.

2080 Irion, Frederick C. *Public Opinion and Propaganda.* New York: Thomas Y. Crowell, 1950.

2081 Kelsey, Carl. Foreward to "Mobilizing America's Resources for the War." *The Annals* 78 (July 1918): vii– x.

2082 Lasswell, Harold D. *Propaganda: Technique in the World War.* New York: P. Smith, 1938.

2083 Read, James M. *Atrocity Propaganda, 1914– 1919.* New Haven: Yale University Press, 1941.

2084 Schaffer, Ronald. "Censorship: Hear No Evil, Speak No Evil." *Mankind* 5 (Feb. 1977): 27– 30.

Biographies and Memoirs (Alphabetically by Subject)

2085 Creel, George. *Rebel at Large: Recollections of Fifty Crowded Years.* New York: Putnam's, 1947.

2086 Fleming, Thomas. "George Creel: Forgotten Genius." *Army* 22 (Mar. 1972): 43– 48.

2087 Nelles, Walter. *A Liberal in Wartime: The Education of Albert De Silver.* New York: Norton, 1940.

2088 Milner, Lucille. *The Education of an American Liberal: An Autobiography.* New York: Horizon Press, 1954.

2089 Goldman, Eric F. "Woodrow Wilson and the Test of War." In *Woodrow Wilson and the World of Today,* edited by Arthur P. Dudden. Philadelphia: University of Pennsylvania Press, 1957.

Federal Information Programs

2090 Altschul, Charles. *German Militarism and Its German Critics.* Washington, D.C.: Committee on Public Information, 1918.

2091 Baker, Newton D. *Frontiers of Freedom.* New York: Doran, 1918.

2092 Buffington, Joseph. *Friendly Words to the Foreign Born.* New York: Committee on Public Information, 1918.

2093 Call, Arthur D., comp. *The War for Peace.* Washington, D.C.: Committee on Public Information, 1918.

2094 Creel, George. *How We Advertized America.* New York: Harper, 1920.

2095 ———. "Public Opinion in War Time." *The Annals* 78 (July 1918): 185– 94.

2096 ———. *The War, the World and Wilson.* New York: Harper, 1920.

2097 Dickson, Maxcy R. "The Food Administration-Educator." *Agricultural History* 16 (Apr. 1942): 91– 96.

2098 Flagg, James M. *Roses and Buckshot.* New York: Putnam's, 1946.

2099 Graham, Jeanne. "The Four Minute Men: Volunteers for Propaganda." *Southern Speech Journal* 32:1 (1966): 49– 57.

2100 Greene, Evarts B. *American Interest in Popular Government Abroad.* Washington, D.C.: Committee on Public Information, 1917.

2101 Hazen, Charles D. *The Government of Germany.* Washington, D.C.: G.P.O., 1917.

2102 Johnson, Donald. "Wilson, Burleson, and Censorship in the First World War." *Journal of Southern History* 28 (Feb. 1962): 46–58.

2103 Johnston, Winifred. *Memo on the Movies: War Propaganda, 1914–1939.* Norman, Oklahoma: Cooperative Books, 1939.

2104 Lansing, Robert, and Louis F. Post. *A War of Self-defense.* Washington, D.C.: G.P.O., 1917.

2105 Larson, Cedric, and Mock, James R. "The Lost Files of the Creel Committee of 1917–1919." *Public Opinion Quarterly* 3 (Jan. 1939): 5–29.

2106 McLaughlin, Andrew C. *The Great War: From Spectator to Participant.* Washington, D.C.: G.P.O., 1917.

2107 Mock, James R. "The Creel Committee in Latin America." *Hispanic-American Historical Review* 22 (May 1942): 262–79.

2108 ———, and Cedric Larson. *Words That Won the War: The Story of the Committee on Public Information.* Princeton: Princeton University Press, 1939.

2109 Munro, Dana G.; George C. Sellery; and August C. Krey; eds. *German War Practices.* Washington, D.C.: Committee on Public Information, 1918.

2110 Nicholas, Wayne A. "Crossroads Oratory: A Study of the Four Minute Men of World War I." Ph.D. dissertation, Columbia University, 1953.

2111 Notestein, Wallace, and Elmer E. Stoll, comps. *Conquest and Kultur: Aims of the Germans in Their Own Words.* Washington, D.C.: Committee on Public Information, 1918.

2112 Oukrop, Carol. "The Four Minute Men Became National Network during World War I." *Journalism Quarterly* 52 (Winter 1975): 632–37.

2113 Paxson, Frederic L.; Edward S. Corwin; and Samuel B. Harding. *War Cyclopedia: A Handbook for Ready Reference on the Great War.* Washington, D.C.: Committee on Public Information, 1918.

2114 Pennell, Joseph. *Joseph Pennell's Liberty Loan Poster.* Philadelphia: Lippincott, 1918.

2115 Rickards, Maurice, ed. *Posters of the First World War.* New York: Walker, 1968.

2116 Scott, George W., and James W. Garner. *The German War Code Contrasted with the War Manuals of the United States, Great Britain, and France.* Washington, D.C.: Committee on Public Information, 1919.

2117   Sherman, Stuart P. . . . *American and Allied Ideals: An Appeal to Those Who Are Neither Hot Nor Cold.* Washington, D.C.: G.P.O., 1918.

2118   Snell, John L. "Wilsonian Rhetoric Goes to War." *Historian* 14 (Spring 1952): 191– 208.

2119   Sperry, E. E., and Willis M. West. *German Pilots and Intrigues in the United States during the Period of Our Neutrality.* Washington, D.C.: Committee on Public Information, 1918.

2120   Tatlock, John S. P. *Why America Fights Germany* (Cantonment edition). Washington, D.C.: Committee on Public Information, 1918.

2121   U.S. Committee on Public Information. *American Loyalty by Citizens of German Descent.* Washington, D.C.: G.P.O., 1917.

2122   ———. *The Battle Line of Democracy: Prose and Poetry of the World War.* Washington, D.C.: G.P.O., 1917.

2123   ———. *The Creel Report: Complete Report of the Chairman of the Committee on Public Information 1917, 1918, 1919.* Reprint. New York: Da Capo Press, 1972.

2124   ———. *The German Whisper.* Washington, D.C.: G.P.O., 1918.

2125   ———. *Germany's Confession: The Lichnowsky Memorandum.* Washington, D.C.: G.P.O., 1918.

2126   ———. *The German-Bolshevik Conspiracy.* Washington, D.C.: G.P.O., 1918.

2127   ———. *"How the War Came to America."* Washington, D.C.: G.P.O., 1917.

2128   ———. *The Kaiserite in America: One Hundred and One German Lies.* Washington, D.C.: G.P.O., 1918(?).

2129   ———. *National Service Handbook.* Washington, D.C.: G.P.O., 1917.

2130   ———. *War Work of Women in Colleges.* . . . Washington, D.C.: G.P.O., 1918.

2131   U.S. War Department. *Home Reading Course for Citizen Soldiers.* Washington, D.C.: G.P.O., 1917.

2132   Walcott, Frederic C. *The Prussian System.* Washington, D.C.: Committee on Public Information, 1918.

2133   Zook, George F. *America at War: A Series of Illustrated Lectures on American War Activities.* 9 vols. Washington, D.C.: Committee on Public Information, 1918.

Federal Government and Civil Liberties

2134 Auerbach, Jerold S. "Woodrow Wilson's 'Prediction' to Frank Cobb: Words Historians Should Doubt Ever Got Spoken." *Journal of American History* 54 (Dec. 1967): 608– 17.

2135 Braeman, John. "World War I and the Crisis of American Liberty." *American Quarterly* 16 (Spring 1964): 104– 12.

2136 Caygill, Harry W. "Press Censorship in War Time." *Infantry Journal* 42 (July– Aug. 1935): 344– 50; (Sept.– Oct. 1935): 441– 46.

2137 Chafee, Zechariah, Jr. *Free Speech in the United States.* Cambridge: Harvard University Press, 1964.

2138 Gutfeld, Arnon. "The Ves Hall Case, Judge Bourquin, and the Sedition Act of 1918." *Pacific Historical Review* 37 (May. 1968): 163– 78.

2139 Hilton, O. A. "Freedom of the Press in Wartime, 1917– 1919." *Southwestern Historical Quarterly* 28 (Mar. 1948): 346– 61.

2140 Hough, Emerson. *The Web.* Chicago: Reilly & Lee, 1919.

2141 Jensen, Joan M. *The Price of Vigilance.* Chicago: Rand McNally, 1968.

2142 Johnson, Donald. "Wilson, Burleson, and Censorship in the First World War." *Journal of Southern History* 28 (Feb. 1962): 46– 58.

2143 Milham, Chester R. "A History of National Espionage Legislation and Its Operation in the United States during the World War." Ph.D. dissertation, University of Southern California, 1938.

2144 Mock, James R. *Censorship, 1917.* Princeton: Princeton University Press, 1941.

2145 Murphy, Paul L. *The Meaning of Freedom of Speech: First Amendment Freedoms from Wilson to FDR.* Westport, Connecticut: Greenwood, 1972.

2146 O'Brian, John Lord. "New Encroachments on Individual Freedom." *Harvard Law Review* 66 (Nov. 1952): 1– 27.

2147 Peterson, Horace C., and Gilbert C. Fite. *Opponents of War, 1917– 1918.* Madison: University of Wisconsin Press, 1957.

2148 Preston, William Jr. *Aliens and Dissenters: Federal Suppression of Radicals, 1903– 1933.* Cambridge: Harvard University Press, 1963.

2149 Scheiber, Harry N. "What Wilson Said to Cobb in 1917: Another View of Plausibility." *Wisconsin Magazine of History* 52 (Summer 1969): 344– 47.

2150 ———. *The Wilson Administration and Civil Liberties, 1917–1921.* Ithaca, New York: Cornell University Press, 1960.

2151 Sprague, Lloyd D. "The Suppression of Dissent during the Civil War and World War I." Ph.D. dissertation, Syracuse University, 1959.

2152 Swisher, Carl B. "Civil Liberties in War Time." *Political Science Quarterly* 55 (Sept. 1940): 321–47.

State and Local Regulation of Public Opinion (See also VII, D/State and Local Studies)

2153 Doyle, Henry G. "Shall History Repeat Itself?: The Fate of Foreign Language Study If Another War Comes." *School and Society* 50 (Aug. 12, 1939): 196–201.

2154 Hickey, Donald R. "The Prager Affair: A Study in Wartime Hysteria." *Journal of the Illinois State Historical Society* 62 (Summer 1969): 117–34.

2155 Hilton, Ora A. "The Minnesota Commission of Public Safety in World War I, 1917–1919." Stillwater: Oklahoma Agricultural and Mechanical College, 1951.

2156 Iowa. State Council of Defense. *The Alleged "Reign of Terror," the Non-Partisan League, the Expulsion of Mr. Pierce, Full Proceedings of the Council of Defense Upon . . . How Best to Win the War.* Des Moines (?), 1918.

2157 Jenson, Carol E. "Agrarian Pioneer in Civil Liberties: The Nonpartisan League in Minnesota during World War I." Ph.D. dissertation, University of Minnesota, 1968.

2158 Lovin, Hugh T. "World War Vigilantes in Idaho, 1917–1918." *Idaho Yesterdays* 18 (Fall 1974): 2–11.

2159 Roff, Willis H. "Coercion and Freedom in a War Situation: A Critical Analysis of Minnesota Culture during World War I." Ph.D. dissertation, University of Minnesota, 1957.

The Civil Liberties Movement

2160 Auerbach, Jerold S. "The Patrician as Libertarian: Zechariah Chafee, Jr. and Freedom of Speech." *New England Quarterly* 42 (Dec. 1969): 511–31.

2161 Johnson, Donald. *Challenge to American Freedoms: World War I and the Rise of the American Civil Liberties Union.* Lexington: University of Kentucky Press, 1963.

2162   Prude, Jonathan. "Portrait of a Civil Libertarian: The Faith and Fear of Zechariah Chafee, Jr." *Journal of American History* 60 (Dec. 1973): 633–56.

G/Pacifism and Antimilitarism

2163   Addams, Jane. *Peace and Bread in Time of War.* New York: Macmillan, 1922.

2164   ———; Emily G. Balch; and Alice Hamilton. *Women at the Hague: The International Congress of Women and Its Results.* New York: Macmillan, 1915.

2165   Brock, Peter. *Twentieth-century Pacifism.* New York: Van Nostrand Reinhold, 1970.

2166   Brommel, Bernard J. "The Pacifist Speechmaking of Eugene V. Debs." *Quarterly Journal of Speech* 52 (Apr. 1966): 146–54.

2167   Buck, Philo M., Jr. "Pacifism in the Middle West." *Nation* 104 (May 17, 1917): 595–97.

2168   Chatfield, Charles. *For Peace and Justice: Pacifism in America, 1914–1941.* Knoxville: University of Tennessee Press, 1971.

2169   ———. "World War I and the Liberal Pacifist in the United States." *American Historical Review* 75 (Dec. 1970): 1920–37.

2170   Conway, Jill. "The Woman's Peace Party and the First World War." In *War and Society in North America,* edited by J. L. Granatstein and R. D. Cuff. Toronto: Nelson, 1971.

2171   Cook, Blanche W. "Woodrow Wilson and the Antimilitarists, 1914–1917." Ph.D. dissertation, Johns Hopkins University, 1970.

2172   Curti, Merle E. *Peace or War: The American Struggle, 1636–1936.* New York: Norton, 1936.

2173   Degen, Mary L. *The History of the Woman's Peace Party.* Baltimore: Johns Hopkins Press, 1939.

2174   Duram, James C. "In Defense of Conscience: Norman Thomas as an Exponent of Christian Pacifism during World War I." *Journal of Presbyterian History* 52 (Spring 1974): 19–32.

2175   Garlid, George W. "The Antiwar Dilemma of the Farmer-Labor Party." *Minnesota History* 40 (Winter 1967): 365–74.

2176   Gray, Harold S. *Character "Bad": The Story of a Conscientious Objector, as Told in the Letters of Harold Studley Gray.* Edited by Kenneth I. Brown. New York: Harper, 1934.

2177   Hartzler, J. S. *Mennonites in the World War: Or Nonresistance under Test.* Scottdale, Pennsylvania: Mennonite Publishing House, 1922.

2178   Herman, Sondra R. *Eleven Against War: Studies in American Internationalist Thought, 1898–1921.* Stanford: Hoover Institution Press, 1969.

2179   Hershey, Burnet. *The Odyssey of Henry Ford and the Great Peace Ship.* New York: Taplinger, 1967.

2180   Holbo, Paul S. "The Vote against War: A Study of Motivations." Ph.D. dissertation, University of Chicago, 1961.

2181   Hull, William I. *Preparedness: The American versus the Military Programme.* New York: Revell, 1919.

2182   Lochner, Louis P. *Always the Unexpected.* New York: Macmillan, 1956.

2183   Marchand, C. Roland. *The American Peace Movement and Social Reform, 1898–1918.* Princeton: Princeton University Press, 1973.

2184   May, Mark A. "The Psychological Examination of Conscientious Objectors." *American Journal of Psychology* 31 (Apr. 1920): 152–65.

2185   Meyer, Ernest L. *"Hey! Yellowbacks!" The War Diary of a Conscientious Objector.* New York: John Day, 1930.

2186   Moore, William H. "Prisoners in the Promised Land: The Molokans in World War I." *Journal of Arizona History* 14 (Winter 1973): 281–302.

2187   Stucky, Gregory J. "Fighting against War: Mennonite *Vorwaerts* from 1914–1919." *Kansas Historical Quarterly* 38 (Summer 1972): 169–86.

2188   Teichroew, Allan. "World War I and the Mennonite Migration to Canada to Avoid the Draft." *Mennonite Quarterly Review* 45 (July 1971): 219–49.

2189   Thomas, Norman. *The Conscientious Objector in America.* New York: Huebsch, 1923.

2190   ——. *Is Conscience a Crime?* New York: Vanguard, 1927.

2191   Thompson, Ralph. "Henry Ford's Great Adventure." *American Mercury* 36 (Sept. 1935): 60–66.

2192   U.S. War Department. *Statement Concerning the Treatment of Conscientious Objectors in the Army.* Washington, D.C.: G.P.O., 1919.

2193   Waldner, Jakob. "An Account: Diary of a Conscientious Objector in World War I." Edited by Theron Schlabach, translated by Ilse Reist and Elizabeth Bender. *Mennonite Quarterly Review* 48 (Jan. 1974): 73–111.

2194 Willis, James F. "The Cleburne County Draft War." *Arkansas Historical Quarterly* 26 (Spring 1967): 24– 39.

2195 Wreszin, Michael. *Oswald Garrison Villard: Pacifist at War.* Bloomington: Indiana University Press, 1965.

H/Ethnic Groups and Nativism in Wartime

2196 Blum, John M. "Nativism, Anti-Radicalism, and the Foreign Scare, 1917– 1920." *Midwest Journal* 3 (1950– 1951): 46– 53.

2197 Child, Clifton J. *The German-Americans in Politics, 1914– 1917.* Madison: University of Wisconsin Press, 1939.

2198 Cuddy, Edward. "Pro-Germanism and American Catholicism, 1914– 1917." *Catholic Historical Review* 54 (Oct. 1968): 427– 54.

2199 DeWitt, Howard A. *Images of Ethnic and Radical Violence in California Politics, 1917– 1930: A Survey.* San Francisco: R and E Research Associates, 1975.

2200 Dorsett, Lyle W. "The Ordeal of Colorado's Germans during World War I." *Colorado Magazine* 51 (Fall 1974): 277– 93.

2201 Egan, Maurice F., and John B. Kennedy. *Knights of Columbus in Peace and War.* 2 vols. New Haven: Knights of Columbus, 1920.

2202 Eldredge, H. Wentworth. "Enemy Aliens: New Haven Germans during the World War." In *Studies in the Science of Society: Presented to Albert Galloway Keller,* edited by George P. Murdick. New Haven: Yale University Press, 1937.

2203 Hachey, Thomas E. "British War Propaganda and American Catholics, 1918." *Catholic Historical Review* 61 (Jan. 1973): 48– 66.

2204 Hartmann, Edward G. *The Movement to Americanize the Immigrant.* New York: Columbia University Press, 1948.

2205 Higham, John. *Strangers in the Land: Patterns of American Nativism 1860– 1925.* New York: Atheneum, 1965.

2206 Kahn, Otto H. *Right Above Race.* New York: Century, 1918.

2207 Keller, Phyllis. "German-America and the First World War." Ph.D. dissertation, University of Pennsylvania, 1969.

2208 Luebke, Frederick C. *Bonds of Loyalty: German-Americans and World War I.* DeKalb: Northern Illinois University Press, 1974.

2209 ———. "Superpatriotism in World War I: The Experience of a Lutheran Pastor." *Concordia Historical Institute Quarterly* 41 (Feb. 1968): 3– 11.

2210   Manning, Clarence A. "The Ukrainians and the United States in World War I." *Ukrainian Quarterly* 13 (Dec. 1957): 346– 57.

2211   Moore, Wallace H. "German-Language Instruction during the War—the Conflict Concerning the German Language and German Propaganda in the Public Secondary Schools of the United States, 1917– 1919." *American-German Review* 5:4 (1939): 14– 15.

2212   Nelson, Clifford L. *German-American Political Behavior in Nebraska and Wisconsin, 1916– 1920.* Lincoln: University of Nebraska, 1972.

2213   Nohl, Frederick. "The Lutheran Church-Missouri Synod Reacts to United States Anti-Germanism during World War I." *Concordia Historical Institute Quarterly* 35 (July 1962): 49– 66.

2214   O'Connor, Richard. *The German-Americans: An Informal History.* Boston: Little, Brown, 1968.

2215   Polishook, Sheila S. "The American Federation of Labor, Zionism, and the First World War." *American Jewish Historical Quarterly* 65 (Mar. 1976): 228– 44.

2216   Rappaport, Joseph. "Jewish Immigrants and World War I: A Study of American Yiddish Press Reactions." Ph.D. dissertation, Columbia University, 1950.

2217   Stephenson, George M. "The Attitude of Swedish-Americans toward the World War." *Mississippi Valley Historical Association Proceedings* 10, pt. 1 (1920): 79– 94.

2218   Taylor, Graham. "Enforcing English by Proclamation." *Survey* 40 (July 6, 1918): 394.

2219   U.S. Department of the Interior. Bureau of Education. *Americanization as a War Measure: Report of a Conference . . . Apr. 3, 1918.* Bulletin no. 18. Washington, D.C.: 1918.

2220   Waldenrath, Alexander. "The German Language Newspress in Pennsylvania during World War I." *Pennsylvania History* 42 (Jan. 1975): 25– 41.

2221   White, Bruce. "The American Military and the Melting Pot in World War I." In *War and Society in North America,* edited by J. L. Granatstein and R. D. Cuff. Toronto: Nelson, 1971.

2222   Wittke, Carl F. *German-Americans and the World War (with Special Emphasis on Ohio's German Language Press).* Columbus: Ohio State Archeological and Historical Society, 1936.

2223 Wolkerstorfer, Marianne K. "Nativism in Minnesota in World War I: A Comparative Study of Brown, Ramsey, and Stearns Counties, 1914–1918." Ph.D. dissertation, University of Minnesota, 1973.

I/The War and American Workers

General

2224 Bing, Alexander. *War-time Strikes and Their Adjustment.* New York: Dutton, 1921.

2225 Fickle, James E. "Management Looks at the Labor Problem: The Southern Pine Industry during World War I and the Postwar Era." *Journal of Southern History* 40 (Feb. 1974): 61– 76.

2226 Gompers, Samuel. *American Labor and the War.* New York: Doran, 1919.

2227 ———. "American Labor's Position in Peace or in War." *American Federationist* 24 (Apr. 1917): 269– 84.

2228 ———. "Justice and Democracy: The Handmaids of Preparedness." *American Federationist* 23 (Mar. 1916): 173– 80.

2229 ———. *Seventy Years of Life and Labor: An Autobiography.* 2 vols. New York: Dutton, 1925.

2230 Lovejoy, Owen R. *Safeguarding Childhood in Peace and War.* New York: National Child Labor Committee, 1917.

2231 Mandel, Bernard. *Samuel Gompers: A Biography.* Yellow Springs, Ohio: Antioch Press, 1963.

2232 National Industrial Conference Board. "Changes in Wages during and since the War, September 1914– March 1920." Research Rpt., no. 31. New York: National Industrial Conference Board, 1920.

2233 ———. "Strikes in American Industry in Wartime: April 6 to October 6, 1917." Research Rpt., no. 3. Boston: National Industrial Conference Board, 1918.

2234 ———. *Wages and Hours in American Industry, July 1914– July, 1921.* New York: Century, 1922.

2235 ———. "Wartime Employment of Women in the Metal Trades." Research Rpt., no. 8. Boston: National Industrial Conference Board, 1918.

2236 Shapiro, Stanley. "The Great War and Reform: Liberals and Labor, 1917– 1919." *Labor History* 12 (Summer 1971): 323– 44.

2237 Smith, John S. "Organized Labor and Government in the Wilson Era, 1913–1921: Some Conclusions." *Labor History* 3 (Fall 1962): 265–86.

2238 Steuben, John. *Labor in Wartime*. New York: International Publishers, 1940.

2239 Sullivan, J. W. "The Maintenance of Labor Standards." *The Annals* 78 (July 1918): 90–96.

2240 Tead, Ordway. "The American Labor Situation in Wartime." *Century* 95 (Jan. 1918): 354–59.

2241 Wilson, William B. "The Efficiency of Labor." *The Annals* 78 (July 1918): 66–74.

2242 Woehlke, Walter V. *Union Labor in Peace and War*. San Franscisco: Sunset Publishing House, 1918.

The Federal Government and Organized Labor

2243 Bernhardt, Joshua. *The Railroad Labor Board: Its History, Activities and Organization*. Baltimore: Johns Hopkins Press, 1923.

2244 Blackman, John L., Jr. "Navy Policy toward the Labor Relations of Its War Contractors." *Military Affairs* 18 (Winter 1954): 176–87; 19 (Spring 1955): 21–31.

2245 Carter, W. S. "Effect of Federal Control on Railway Labor." *Proceedings of the Academy of Political Science* 8:2 (1920): 64–76.

2246 Commons, John R., et al. *History of Labor in the United States*. 10 vols. New York: Macmillan, 1918–1935.

2247 Connor, Valerie J. "The National War Labor Board, 1918–1919." Ph.D. dissertation, University of Virginia, 1974.

2248 [Drury, Horace B.] *Marine and Dock Labor: Work, Wages, and Industrial Relations during the Period of the War: Report of the Director of Marine and Dock Industrial Relations Division, United States Shipping Board*. Washington, D.C.: G.P.O., 1919.

2249 Dubofsky, Melvyn. "Organized Labor in New York City and the First World War, 1914–1918." *New York History* 42 (Oct. 1961): 380–400.

2250 Feiss, Richard A. "Stimulating Labor Efficiency in War Time." *The Annals* 78 (July 1918): 106–11.

2251 Frankfurter, Felix. "The Conservation of the New Federal Standards." *Survey* 41 (Dec. 7, 1918): 291–93.

2252 ———. "New Labor Ideas Taught by the War." In *Reconstructing America,* edited by Edwin Wildmar. Boston: Page, 1919.

2253 Grubbs, Frank L., Jr. "Council and Alliance Labor Propaganda: 1917– 1919." *Labor History* 7 (Spring 1966): 156– 72.

2254 Hotchkiss, Willard E., and Henry R. Seager. *History of the Shipbuilding Labor Adjustment Board, 1917 to 1919.* Washington, D.C.: G.P.O., 1921.

2255 Hyman, Harold M. *Soldiers and Spruce: Origins of the Loyal Legion of Loggers and Lumbermen.* Los Angeles: University of California Institute of Industrial Relations, 1963.

2256 Jones, Dallas L. "The Wilson Administration and Organized Labor, 1912– 1919." Ph.D. dissertation, Cornell University, 1954.

2257 Krivy, Leonard P. "American Organized Labor and the First World War, 1917– 1918: A History of Labor Problems and the Development of a Government War Labor Program." Ph.D. dissertation, New York University, 1965.

2258 Macy, V. Everit. "Labor Adjustment under War Conditions." *Proceedings of the Academy of Political Science* 7 (Feb. 1918): 129– 35.

2259 ———. "Labor Policies that Will Win the War." *The Annals* 78 (July 1918): 74– 80.

2260 Marshall, L. C. "The War Labor Program and Its Administration." *Journal of Political Economy* 26 (May 1918): 425– 60.

2261 Radosh, Ronald. *American Labor and United States Foreign Policy.* New York: Random House, 1969.

2262 Smith, John S. "Organized Labor and Government in the Wilson Era, 1913– 1921: Some Conclusions." *Labor History* 3 (Fall 1962): 265– 86.

2263 Tyler, Robert L. "The United States Government as Union Organizer: The Loyal Legion of Loggers and Lumbermen." *Mississippi Valley Historical Review* 47 (Dec. 1960): 434– 51.

2264 U.S. Bureau of Labor Statistics. *National War Labor Board: A History of Its Formation and Activities.* Washington, D.C.: G.P.O., 1922.

2265 U.S. War Department. *A Report of the Activities of the War Department in the Field of Industrial Relations during the War, Sept. 15, 1919.* Washington, D.C.: G.P.O., 1919.

2266 United States Spruce Production Corporation. *History of Spruce Production Division, United States Army and United States Spruce Production*

Corporation. Portland, Oregon: Press of Kilhan Stationery & Printing Co., 1920(?).

2267 Watkins, Gordon S. *Labor Problems and Labor Administration in the United States during the World War.* 2 vols. Urbana: University of Illinois, 1920.

2268 Wehle, Louis B. "The Adjustment of Labor Disputes Incident to Production for War in the United States." *Quarterly Journal of Economics* 32 (Nov. 1917): 122– 41.

2269 ———. "War Labor Policies and Their Outcome in Peace." *Quarterly Journal of Economics* 33 (Feb. 1919): 321– 43.

Socialism and Radicalism

2270 Basset, Michael. "The American Socialist Party and the War 1917– 1918." *Australian Journal of Politics and History* 11 (Dec. 1965): 277– 91.

2271 Bindler, Norman. "American Socialism and the First World War." Ph.D. dissertation, New York University, 1970.

2272 Brazier, Richard. "The Mass I.W.W. Trial of 1918: A Retrospect." *Labor History* 7 (Spring 1966): 178– 92.

2273 Brissenden, Paul F. *The I.W.W.: A Study of American Syndicalism.* New York: Columbia University Press, 1920.

2274 Cantor, Milton. "The Radical Confrontation with Foreign Policy: War and Revolution, 1914– 1920." In *Dissent: Explorations in the History of American Radicalism,* edited by Alfred F. Young. De Kalb: University of Illinois, 1968.

2275 Dubofsky, Melvyn. *We Shall Be All: A History of the Industrial Workers of the World.* Chicago: Quadrangle Books, 1969.

2276 Folk, Richard A. "Socialist Party of Ohio—War and Free Speech." *Ohio History* 78 (Spring 1969): 104– 15, 152– 54.

2277 Gambs, John S. *The Decline of the I.W.W.* New York: Columbia University Press, 1932.

2278 Giffin, Frederick C. *Six Who Protested: Radical Opposition to the First World War.* Port Washington, New York: Kennikat Press, 1977.

2279 Ginger, Ray. *The Bending Cross: A Biography of Eugene Victor Debs.* New Brunswick: Rutgers University Press, 1949.

2280 Goldman, Emma. "Preparedness: The Road to Universal Slaughter." *Mother Earth* 10 (Dec. 1915): 331– 38.

2281   Hendrickson, Kenneth E., Jr. "Pro-War Socialists: The Social Democratic League and the Ill-fated Drive for Industrial Democracy in America, 1917– 1920." *Labor History* 11 (Summer 1970): 304– 22.

2282   ——. "The Socialists of Reading, Pennsylvania—A Question of Loyalty." *Pennsylvania History* 36 (Oct. 1969): 430– 50.

2283   Kallen, Horace H. "A Programme for Pacifists." *Dial* 62 (May 3, 1917): 377– 79.

2284   Karsner, David. *Debs Goes to Prison*. New York: I. K. Davis, 1919.

2285   Koppes, Clayton R. "The Kansas Trial of the I.W.W., 1917– 1919." *Labor History* 16 (Summer 1975): 338– 58.

2286   Lindquist, John H. "The Jerome Deportation of 1917." *Arizona and the West* 11 (Autumn 1969): 233– 46.

2287   Miller, Sally M. "Socialist Party Decline and World War I: Bibliography and Interpretation." *Science and Society* 34 (Winter 1970): 398– 411.

2288   Nearing, Scott. *The Great Madness: A Victory for the American Plutocracy*. New York: Rand School of Social Science, 1917.

2289   ——. *The Trial of Scott Nearing and the American Socialist Society. . . .* New York: Rand School of Social Science, 1919.

2290   Oneal, James. "The Socialists in the War." *American Mercury* 10 (Apr. 1927): 418– 26.

2291   O'Neill, William L., ed. *Echoes of Revolt: The Masses, 1911– 1917.* Chicago: Quadrangle Books, 1966.

2292   Reitman, Ben L. "Why You Shouldn't Go to War—Refuse to Kill or Be Killed." *Mother Earth* 12 (Apr. 1917): 41– 44.

2293   Renshaw, Patrick. "The I.W.W. and the Red Scare, 1917– 1924." *Journal of Contemporary History* 3 (Oct. 1968): 63– 72.

2294   Shannon, David. *The Socialist Party of America: A History*. New York: Macmillan, 1955.

2295   Shepperson, Wilbur S. "Socialist Pacifism in the American West during World War I: A Case Study." *Historian* 29 (Aug. 1967): 619– 33.

2296   Taft, Philip. "The Federal Trials of the I.W.W." *Labor History* 3 (Winter 1962): 57– 91.

2297   ——. "The I.W.W. in the Grain Belt." *Labor History* 1 (Winter 1960): 53– 67.

2298   Trachtenberg, Alexander, ed. *The American Socialists and the War: A Documentary History of the Attitude of the Socialist Party toward War and Militarism since the Outbreak of the Great War.* New York: Rand School of Social Science, 1917.

2299   Weinstein, James. "Anti-War Sentiment and the Socialist Party, 1917–1918." *Political Science Quarterly* 74 (June 1959): 215–39.

2300   ———. *The Decline of Socialism in America, 1912–1925.* New York: Monthly Review Press, 1967.

2301   Whitfield, Stephen J. *Scott Nearing: Apostle of American Radicalism.* New York: Columbia University Press, 1974.

J/The War and American Race Relations

General

2302   Blumenthal, Henry. "Woodrow Wilson and the Race Question." *Journal of Negro History* 48 (Jan. 1963): 1–21.

2303   Clark, Kenneth B. "Morale of the Negro on the Home Front: World Wars I and II." *Journal of Negro Education* 12 (Summer 1943): 417–28.

2304   Cronon, E. David. *Black Moses: The Story of Marcus Garvey and the Universal Negro Improvement Association.* Madison: University of Wisconsin Press, 1969.

2305   Du Bois, W. E. B. "An Essay toward a History of the Black Man in the Great War." *Crisis* 18 (June 1919): 63–87.

2306   ———. "Opinion." *Crisis* 18 (May 1919): 7–14.

2307   Ferguson, George O. "The Intelligence of Negroes at Camp Lee, Virginia." *School and Society* 9 (June 14, 1919): 721–26.

2308   Finney, John D. "A Study of Negro Labor during and after World War I." Ph.D. dissertation, Georgetown University, 1967.

2309   Franklin, Vincent P. "The Philadelphia Race Riot of 1918." *Pennsylvania Magazine of History and Biography* 99 (July 1975): 336–50.

2310   Haynes, George E. "The Effect of War Conditions on Negro Labor." *Proceedings of the Academy of Political Science* 8 (Feb. 1919): 165–78.

2311   Henri, Florette. *Black Migration: Movement North, 1900–1920.* Garden City, New York: Anchor Doubleday, 1975.

2312   Higgs, Robert. "The Boll Weevil, the Cotton Economy, and Black Migration, 1910–1930." *Agricultural History* 50 (Apr. 1976): 335–50.

2313   Hilts, Helen M. "Hampton Training and War Service." *Southern Workman* 47 (July 1918): 335–44.

2314   Hunton, Addie W., and Kathryn M. Johnson. *Two Colored Women with the American Expeditionary Forces.* Reprint. New York: AMS Press, 1971.

2315   Jones, Lester M. "The Editorial Policy of the Negro Newspapers of 1917–1918 as Compared with That of 1941–1942." *Journal of Negro History* 29 (Jan. 1944): 24–31.

2316   Kellogg, Charles F. *NAACP: A History of the National Association for the Advancement of Colored People.* Baltimore: Johns Hopkins Press, 1967.

2317   Kennedy, Louis V. *The Negro Peasant Turns Cityward: Effects of Recent Migrations to Northern Cities.* New York: Columbia University Press, 1930.

2318   Miller, Carroll L. "The Negro and Volunteer War Agencies." *Journal of Negro Education* 12 (Summer 1943): 438–51.

2319   Miller, Kelly. *History of the World War for Human Rights.* Washington, D.C.: Austin Jenkins, 1919.

2320   Moton, Robert R. *Finding a Way Out: An Autobiography.* Garden City, New York: Doubleday, Page, 1920.

2321   Osofsky, Gilbert. *Harlem: The Making of a Ghetto: Negro New York, 1890–1930.* New York: Harper, 1968.

2322   Palmer, Dewey H. "Moving North: Negro Migration during World War I." *Phylon* 28 (Spring 1967): 52–62.

2323   Reid, Ira De A. "A Critical Summary: The Negro on the Home Front in World Wars I and II." *Journal of Negro Education* 12 (Summer 1943): 511–20.

2324   Rudwick, Elliott M. *Race Riot at East St. Louis, July 2, 1917.* Carbondale: Southern Illinois University Press, 1964.

2325   Scheiber, Jane L., and Harry N. Scheiber. "The Wilson Administration and the Wartime Mobilization of Black Americans, 1917–1918." *Labor History* 10 (Summer 1969): 433–58.

2326   Scheiner, Seth M. *Negro Mecca: A History of the Negro in New York City, 1865–1920.* New York: New York University Press, 1965.

2327 Scott, Emmett J. *Negro Migration during the War*. New York: Oxford University Press, 1920.

2328 ———. "The Participation of Negroes in World War I: An Introductory Statement." *Journal of Negro Education* 12 (Summer 1943): 288– 97.

2329 ———. *Scott's Official History of the American Negro in the World War*. Chicago: Homewood Press, 1919.

2330 Spear, Allan H. *Black Chicago: The Making of a Negro Ghetto, 1890– 1920*. Chicago: University of Chicago Press, 1967.

2331 Spingarn, Arthur. "The War and Venereal Disease among Negroes." *Social Hygiene* 4 (July 1918): 333– 46.

2332 Sweeney, W. Allison. *History of the American Negro in the Great World War*. New York: Johnson Reprint Corp., 1970.

2333 Tuttle, William M., Jr. *Race Riot: Chicago in the Red Summer of 1919*. New York: Atheneum, 1970.

2334 ———. "Views of a Negro during 'The Red Summer' of 1919 — A Document." *Journal of Negro History* 51 (July 1966): 209– 18.

2335 U.S. Department of Labor. Division of Negro Economics. *The Negro at Work during the World War and Reconstruction*. Washington, D.C.: G.P.O., 1921.

2336 ———. *Negro Migration in 1916– 1917*. Washington, D.C.: G.P.O., 1919.

2337 Weiss, Nancy J. "The Negro and the New Freedom: Fighting Wilsonian Segregation." *Political Science Quarterly* 84 (Mar. 1969): 61– 79.

2338 Williams, Charles H. "Negro Y.M.C.A. Secretaries Overseas." *Southern Workman* 47 (Jan. 1918): 9– 16.

Black Servicemen (See also unit histories)

2339 Barbeau, Arthur E., and Florette Henri. *The Unknown Soldiers: Black American Troops in World War I*. Philadelphia: Temple University Press, 1974.

2340 Clement, Rufus E. "Problems of Demobilization and Rehabilitation of the Negro Soldier after World Wars I and II." *Journal of Negro Education* 12 (Summer 1943): 533– 42.

2341 Davis, J. P. "The Negro in the Armed Forces of America." In *The American Negro Reference Book*, edited by J. P. Davis. Englewood Cliffs, New Jersey: Prentice-Hall, 1960.

2342 Du Bois, W. E. B., ed. "Documents of the War." *Crisis* 18 (May 1919): 16– 19.

2343 ——. "The Negro Soldier in Service Abroad during the First World War." *Journal of Negro Education* 12 (Summer 1943): 324– 34.

2344 Fletcher, Marvin E. *The Black Soldier and Officer in the United States Army, 1891– 1917.* Columbia: University of Missouri Press, 1974.

2345 Hastie, William H. "Negro Officers in Two World Wars." *Journal of Negro Education* 12 (Summer 1943): 316– 23.

2346 Haynes, Robert V. "The Houston Mutiny and Riot of 1917." *Southwestern Historical Quarterly* 76 (Apr. 1973): 418– 39.

2347 Henri, Florette, and Richard Stillman. *Bitter Victory: A History of Black Soldiers in World War I.* Garden City, New York: Doubleday, 1970.

2348 Jamieson, J. A., et al. *Complete History of the Colored Soldiers in the World War.* New York: Barnett & Churchill, 1919.

2349 Johnson, Campbell C. "The Mobilization of Negro Manpower for the Armed Forces." *Journal of Negro Education* 12 (Summer 1943): 298– 306.

2350 Lee, Ulysses G. *The Employment of Negro Troops.* Washington, D.C.: Department of the Army, Office of the Chief of Military History, 1966.

2351 Long, Howard H. "The Negro Soldier in the Army of the United States." *Journal of Negro Education* 12 (Summer 1943): 307– 15.

2352 Moorland, Jesse E. "The Y.M.C.A. with Colored Troops." *Southern Workman* 48 (Apr. 1919): 171– 75.

2353 Schuler, Edgar A. "The Houston Race Riot, 1917." *Journal of Negro History* 29 (July 1944): 300– 338.

2354 Seward, Walter E. *Negroes Call to the Colors and Soldiers Camp-Life Poems.* Athens, Georgia: Knox Institute Press, 1919.

2355 U.S. Army War College. *Colored Soldiers in the U.S. Army.* Washington, D.C.: G.P.O., 1942.

2356 U.S. Department of State. *Colored Soldiers in the French Army.* Washington, D.C.: G.P.O., 1919.

2357 War Camp Community Service. *War Camp Community Service and the Negro Soldier.* N.p., 1920(?).

2358 Williams, Charles H. *Sidelights on Negro Soldiers.* Boston: Brimmer, 1923.

K/American Women in the War

2359	American Legion. Auxiliary. Indiana. *Indiana Women in the World War.* Indianapolis, 1938.

2360	Austin, Mary. "Food Conservation and the Women." *Unpopular Review* 9 (Apr. 1918): 373–84.

2361	[Blair, Emily N.] *The Woman's Committee, United States Council of National Defense: An Interpretive Report, April 21, 1917 to February 27, 1919.* Washington, D.C.: G.P.O., 1920.

2362	Blatch, Harriot S. *Mobilizing Woman-power.* New York: Woman's Press, 1918.

2363	Bowen, Mrs. Joseph T. "The War Work of the Women of Illinois." *Illinois State Historical Society Journal* 12 (Oct. 1919): 317–29.

2364	Clark, B. A. "The Women's Land Army of America." *House Beautiful* 44 (Oct. 1918): 254–56.

2365	Clarke, Ida C. *American Women and the World War.* New York: Appleton, 1918.

2366	Cohen, Michaele. "Women: The Ambiguous Emancipation." *Mankind* 5 (Feb. 1977): 24–27.

2367	Dessez, Eunice C. *The First Enlisted Women, 1917–1918.* Philadelphia: Dorrance, 1955.

2368	Flexner, Eleanor. *Century of Struggle: The Woman's Rights Movement in the United States.* Cambridge: Harvard University Press, 1975.

2369	Gildersleeve, V. C. "Women Farm Workers." *New Republic* 12 (Sept. 1, 1917): 132–34.

2370	Gilman, Charlotte P. "The Housekeeper and the Food Problem." *Annals of the American Academy of Political and Social Science* 74 (Nov. 1917): 123–31.

2371	Goldman, Eric. "Progress—By Moderation and Agitation." *New York Times Magazine* (June 18, 1961): 5, 10–12.

2372	Greenwald, Maurine W. "Women Workers and World War I: The American Railroad Industry, A Case Study." *Journal of Social History* 9 (Winter 1975): 154–77.

2373	Hancock, Joy B. *Lady in the Navy: A Personal Reminiscence.* Annapolis: U.S. Naval Institute, 1972.

2374 Hewitt, Linda L. *Women Marines in World War I.* Washington, D.C.: U.S. Marine Corps, History and Museums Division Headquarters, 1974.

2375 Hitchcock, Nevada D. "The Mobilization of Women." *The Annals* 78 (July 1918): 24–31.

2376 Indiana. State Council of Defense. Woman's Section. *Report of the Woman's Section of the Indiana State Council of Defense: From October, 1917 to April, 1919.* Indianapolis: W. B. Burford, 1919.

2377 James, Bessie R. *For God, for Country, for Home: The National League for Woman's Service, a Story of the First National Organization of American Women Mobilized for War Service.* New York: Putnam's, 1920.

2378 Knoeppel, Charles E. *Women in Industry.* New York: C. E. Knoeppel, 1918(?).

2379 [McDougall, Grace.] *A Nurse at War.* New York: McBride, 1917.

2380 McGovern, James R. "The American Woman's Pre-World War I Freedom in Manners and Morals." *Journal of American History* 55 (Sept. 1968): 315–33.

2381 Malan, Nancy E. "How Ya Gonna Keep 'Em Down?: Women and World War I." *Journal of the National Archives* 5 (Winter 1973): 208–39.

2382 Schaffer, Ronald. "Jeannette Rankin: Progressive-Isolationist." Ph.D. dissertation, Princeton University, 1959.

2383 Smith, Annie S. *As Others See Her: An Englishwoman's Impressions of the American Woman in War Time.* Boston: Houghton Mifflin, 1919.

2384 *Those War Women: By One of Them.* New York: Coward-McCann, 1929.

2385 U.S. Women's Bureau. *The New Position of Women in American Industry.* Women's Bureau Bulletin no. 12. Washington, D.C.: G.P.O., 1920.

2386 Van Kleeck, Mary. "Women's Invasion of Industry and Changes in Protective Standards." *Proceedings of the Academy of Political Science* 8:2 (1920): 5–12.

2387 Van Rensselaer, Mrs. Coffin. "The National League for Woman's Service." *The Annals* 79 (Sept. 1918): 275–82.

2388 Wait, Clara H. "Report of the War Work of the Daughters of the American Revolution of Michigan from April 1915 to April 1919." *Michigan History* 4 (Jan. 1920): 193–242.

L/The War and Social Reform

General

2389 Goldman, Eric F. *Rendezvous with Destiny*. New York: Knopf, 1953.

2390 Hirschfeld, Charles. "Nationalist Progressivism and World War I." *Mid-America* 45 (July 1963): 139– 56.

2391 Lathrop, Julia. "The Children's Bureau in Wartime." *North American Review* 206 (Nov. 1917): 734– 46.

2392 Shapiro, Stanley. "The Twilight of Reform: Advanced Progressives after the Armistice." *Historian* 33 (May 1971): 349– 64.

2393 Stearns, Harold E. *Liberalism in America: Its Origins, Its Temporary Collapse, Its Future*. New York: Boni & Liveright, 1919.

2394 Thompson, J. A. "American Progressive Publicists and the First World War, 1914– 1917." *Journal of American History* 58 (Sept. 1971): 364– 83.

2395 Thornburn, Neil. "A Progressive and the First World War: Frederic C. Howe." *Mid-America* 51 (Apr. 1969): 108– 18.

2396 Trattner, Walter I. "Progressivism and World War I: A Reappraisal." *Mid-America* 44 (July 1962): 131– 45.

Relief and Welfare Programs

2397 Byington, Margaret F. "The Scope and Organization of the Department of Civilian Relief." *The Annals* 79 (Sept. 1918): 88– 96.

2398 Davis, Allen F. "Welfare Reform and World War I." *American Quarterly* 19 (Fall 1967): 516– 33.

2399 Douglas, Paul H. "The War Risk Insurance Act." *Journal of Political Economy* 26 (May 1918): 461– 83.

2400 Fullbrook, Earl S. *The Red Cross in Iowa*. 2 vols. Iowa City: State Historical Society, 1922.

2401 Glenn, Mary W. "Purpose and Methods of a Home Service Section." *The Annals* 79 (Sept. 1918): 97– 105.

2402 Hansen, Marcus L. *Welfare Campaigns in Iowa*. Iowa City: State Historical Society, 1921.

2403 Lathrop, Julia C. "Provisions for the Care of the Families and Dependents of Soldiers and Sailors." *Proceedings of the Academy of Political Science* 7 (Feb. 1918): 140– 51.

2404 Lindsay, Samuel M. "Purpose and Scope of War Risk Insurance." *The Annals* 79 (Sept. 1918): 52– 68.

2405 Love, Thomas B. "The Social Significance of War Risk Insurance." *The Annals* 79 (Sept. 1918): 46– 51.

2406 [National Jewish Welfare Board.] *The Jewish Welfare Board: A Final Report of War Emergency Activities.* New York, 1920.

2407 Penrose, Laura E. *My Monograph: War Relief Work in Old Louisiana.* New York: Himebaugh & Browne, 1919.

2408 Persons, W. Frank. "The Soldiers' and Sailors' Families." *Annals of the American Academy of Political and Social Science* 77 (May 1918): 171– 84.

2409 Simkhovitch, Mary K. "Settlement War Program." *Survey* 38 (May 5, 1917): 111– 12.

2410 Watts, Phyllis A. "Casework above the Poverty Line: The Influence of Home Service in World War I on Social Work." *Social Service Review* 38 (Sept. 1964): 303– 15.

2411 Wolfe, S. H. "Eight Months of War Risk Insurance Work." *The Annals* 79 (Sept. 1918): 68– 79.

Government Regulation of Sex (See Also V, Q/U.S. Military Personnel, Recreation and Morale of Servicemen; Military Medicine)

2412 Additon, Henrietta S. "Work among Delinquent Women and Girls." *The Annals* 79 (Sept. 1918): 152– 60.

2413 Allen, Edward F., and Raymond B. Fosdick. *Keeping Our Fighters Fit for War and After.* New York: Century, 1918.

2414 Anderson, George J. "Making the Camps Safe for the Army." *The Annals* 79 (Sept. 1918): 143– 51.

2415 Ayres, Harrol B. "Democracy at Work: San Antonio Being Reborn." *Social Hygiene* 4 (Apr. 1918): 211– 17.

2416 Baker, Newton D. "Invisible Armor." *Survey* 39 (Nov. 17, 1917): 159– 60.

2417 Baldwin, Fred G. "The Invisible Armor." *American Quarterly* 16 (Fall 1964): 432– 44.

2418 Clarke, Walter. "The Promotion of Social Hygiene in War Time." *The Annals* 79 (Sept. 1918): 178– 89.

2419 Falconer, Martha P. "The Segregation of Delinquent Women and Girls as a War Problem." *The Annals* 79 (Sept. 1918): 160– 67.

2420　Fosdick, Raymond B. *Chronicle of a Generation: An Autobiography.* New York: Harper, 1958.

2421　———. "The Commission on Training Camp Activities." *Proceedings of the Academy of Political Science* 7 (Feb. 1918): 163–70.

2422　———. "The War and Navy Departments' Commissions on Training Camp Activities." *The Annals* 79 (Sept. 1918): 130–42.

2423　Gulick, Luther H. *Morals and Morale.* New York: Association Press, 1919.

2424　Hocking, W. E. "Personal Problems of the Soldier." *Yale Review* 7 (July 1918): 712–26.

2425　Johnson, Bascom J. "Eliminating Vice from Camp Cities." *The Annals* 78 (July 1918): 60–64.

2426　———. "Next Steps." *Social Hygiene* 4 (Jan. 1918): 9–23.

2427　Lane, W. D. "Girls and Khaki." *Survey* 39 (Dec. 1, 1917): 236–40.

2428　Maurer, Maurer. "The Court-Martialing of Camp Followers, World War I." *American Journal of Legal History* 9 (July 1965): 203–15.

2429　Seymour, Gertrude. "Venereal Disease Abroad." *Survey* 39 (Dec. 29, 1917): 227–32.

2430　Smythe, Donald. "Venereal Disease: The A.E.F.'s Experience." *Prologue* 9 (Summer 1977): 65–74.

2431　Snow, William F. "Social Hygiene and the War." *Social Hygiene* 3 (July 1917): 417–50.

2432　U.S. Commission on Training Camp Activities (War Department). *Committee on Protective Work for Girls.* Washington, D.C., 1917(?).

2433　———. *Next Steps: A Program of Activities against Prostitution and Venereal Diseases for Communities Which Have Closed Their 'Red Light' Districts.* Washington, D.C., 1918.

2434　Walker, George. *Venereal Disease in the American Expeditionary Forces.* Baltimore: Medical Standard Book Co., 1922.

2435　Zinsser, William H. "Working with Men Outside the Camps." *The Annals* 79 (Sept. 1918): 194–203.

Public Housing Programs

2436　Childs, Richard S. "The Government's Model Villages." *Survey* 41 (Feb. 1, 1919): 584–92.

2437 [Colean, Miles L.] *Housing for Defense.* . . . New York: Twentieth Century Fund, 1940.

2438 Hammel, Victor F. *Construction and Operation of a Shell Loading Plant and the Town of Amatol, New Jersey, for the United States Government, Ordnance Department, U.S. Army.* New York: Atlantic Loading Company, 1918.

2439 Hitchcock, Curtice N. "The War Housing Program and Its Future." *Journal of Political Economy* 27 (Apr. 1919): 241– 79.

2440 Lubove, Roy. "Homes and 'A Few Well-Placed Fruit Trees': An Object Lesson in Federal Housing." *Social Research* 27 (Jan. 1961): 469– 86.

2441 National Housing Association. *A Symposium on War Housing.* New York: National Housing Association, 1918.

2442 United States Housing Corporation. *Report of the United States Housing Corporation: December 3, 1918.* Washington, D.C.: G.P.O., 1919.

2443 ———. *War Emergency Construction (Housing War Workers): Report of the United States Housing Corporation.* 2 vols. Washington, D.C.: G.P.O., 1920.

2444 Veiller, Lawrence. "The Housing of the Mobilized Population." *The Annals* 78 (July 1918): 19– 24.

2445 Whitaker, Charles H., et al. *The Housing Problem in War and Peace.* Washington, D.C.: Journal of the American Institute of Architects, 1918.

Prohibition

2446 Rogers, Lindsay. "The War and Liquor Restriction in the United States." *Contemporary Review* 112 (Oct. 1917): 393– 402.

2447 Sinclair, Andrew. *Era of Excess: A Social History of the Prohibition Movement.* New York: Harper & Row, 1964.

2448 Timberlake, J. H. *Prohibition and the Progressive Movement, 1900– 1920.* Cambridge: Harvard University Press, 1963.

M/Effects of the War on Manners and Morals (See also VII, K/American Women in the War and VII, L/Government Regulation of Sex)

2449 May, Henry F. *The End of American Innocence: A Study of the First Years of Our Own Time, 1912– 1917.* New York: Knopf, 1959.

2450 Robinson, Victor, ed. *Morals in Wartime.* New York: Publishers Foundation, 1943.

2451 Tannenbaum, Frank. "The Moral Devastation of War." *Dial* 66 (Apr. 5, 1919): 333– 36.

2452 Taylor, J. N. "The Social Status of the Sailor." *Social Hygiene* 4 (Apr. 1918): 157– 78.

N/The War and Sports and Recreation

2453 Lewis, Guy. "World War I and the Emergence of Sport for the Masses." *Maryland Historian* 4 (Fall 1973): 109– 22.

O/The War and Religion

2454 Abrams, Ray H. *Preachers Present Arms: A Study of the War-time Attitudes and Activities of the Churches and Clergy in the United States, 1914– 1918.* New York: Round Table Press, 1933.

2455 Committee on the War and the Religious Outlook. *Religion among American Men: As Revealed by a Study of Conditions in the Army.* New York: Association Press, 1920.

2456 Edwards, Martha L. "Ohio's Religious Organizations and the War." *Ohio Archeological and Historical Quarterly* 28 (Apr. 1919): 207– 24.

2457 Graebner, Alan. "World War I and Lutheran Union." *Concordia Historical Institute Quarterly* 41 (May 1968): 51– 64.

2458 Hicks, Granville. "The Parsons and the War." *American Mercury* 10 (Feb. 1927): 129– 42.

2459 Johnson, Neil M. "The Patriotism and Anti-Prussianism of the Lutheran Church — Missouri Synod 1914– 1918." *Concordia Historical Institute Quarterly* 39 (Oct. 1966): 99– 118.

2460 Jorgensen, Daniel P. *The Service of Chaplains to Army Air Units, 1917– 1946.* Washington, D.C., 1961.

2461 Land, Gary. "The Perils of Prophesying: Seventh-day Adventists Interpret World War One." *Adventist Heritage* 1 (Jan. 1974): 28– 33, 55– 56.

2462 Levinger, Lee J. *A Jewish Chaplain in France.* New York: Macmillan, 1922.

2463 Lynch, Frederick H. *The Christian in Wartime.* New York: Revell, 1917.

2464 McMahan, Russel R. "The Protestant Churches during World War I: The Home Front." Ph.D. dissertation, St. Louis University, 1968.

2465 Mathews, Shailer. *Patriotism and Religion.* New York: Macmillan, 1918.

2466 Moellering, Ralph L. "Some Lutheran Reactions to War and Pacifism, 1917– 1941." *Concordia Historical Institute Quarterly* 41 (Aug. 1968): 121– 30.

2467 Morgan, David T. "The Revivalist as Patriot: Billy Sunday and World War I." *Journal of Presbyterian History* 51 (Summer 1973): 199– 215.

2468 Piper, Paul F. "The American Churches in World War I." *Journal of the American Academy of Religion* 38 (June 1970): 147– 55.

2469 Procko, Bohdan P. "American Ukrainian Catholic Church: Humanitarian and Patriotic Activities, World War I." *Ukrainian Quarterly* 23 (Summer 1967): 161– 69.

2470 Rugh, Charles E. "Religious Education as a Means of National Preparedness." *NEA Addresses and Proceedings* 55 (1917): 107– 11.

2471 Scheidt, David L. "Some Effects of World War I on the General Synod and General Council." *Concordia Historical Institute Quarterly* 43 (May 1970): 83– 93.

2472 Stearns, Gustav. *From Army Corps and Battle Fields.* Minneapolis: Augsburg Publishing, 1919.

2473 Stephens, D. Owen. *With Quakers in France.* London: C. W. Daniel, 1921.

2474 Stewart, George J., and H. B. Wright. *The Practice of Friendship: Studies in Personal Evangelism with Men of the United States Army and Navy in American Training Camps.* New York: Association Press, 1918.

2475 Summerbell, Carlyle. *A Preacher Goes to War: The True Story of a Chaplain in France during the World War.* Norwood, Massachusetts: Ambrose Press, 1936.

2476 Thompson, Joseph J. "The Knights of Columbus in the War and After." *Illinois Catholic Historical Review* 3 (Jan. 1921): 268– 83.

2477 [Waring, George J.] *United States Catholic Chaplains in the World War.* New York: Ordinariate, Army and Navy Chaplains, 1924.

2478 Wilcox, Francis M. *Seventh-Day Adventists in Time of War.* Washington, D.C.: Review & Herald Publishing Association, 1936.

2479 Yale University Divinity School. *Religion and the War: By Members of the School of Religion, Yale University.* Edited by E. Hershey Sneath. New Haven: Yale University Press, 1918.

P/Journalism in World War I

2480 Cobb, Frank I. *Cobb of "The World": A Leader in Liberalism.* Compiled by John L. Heaton. New York: Dutton, 1924.

2481 Crozier, Emmet. *American Reporters on the Western Front, 1914– 1918.* New York: Oxford University Press, 1959.

2482 Knightley, Phillip. *The First Casualty: From the Crimea to Vietnam: The War Correspondent as Hero, Propagandist, and Myth Maker.* New York: Harcourt Brace Jovanovich, 1975.

2483 Mathews, Joseph J. *Reporting the Wars.* Minneapolis: University of Minnesota Press, 1957.

2484 Shepherd, William G. *Confessions of a War Correspondent.* New York: Harper, 1917.

2485 Villard, Oswald G. *Fighting Years: Memoirs of a Liberal Editor.* New York: Harcourt, Brace, 1939.

Q/The War and the Visual Arts

Works about the Visual Arts in Wartime

2486 Howell, Edgar M. "An Artist Goes to War: Harvey Dunn and the A.E.F. War Art Program." *Smithsonian Journal of History* 2 (Winter 1967– 1968): 45–56.

2487 Isenberg, Michael T. "World War I Film Comedies and American Society: The Concern with Authoritarianism." *Film and History* 5 (Sept. 1975): 7–15, 21.

2488 Soderbergh, Peter A. " 'Aux Armes!' The Rise of the Hollywood War Film, 1916–1930." *South Atlantic Quarterly* 65 (Autumn 1966): 509–22.

Works by American Artists

2489 Bailey, Vernon H. *Drawings and Lithographs of War Work in America.* New York: A. H. Hahlo, 1917.

2490 Butler, Alban B., Jr. *Training for the Trenches: A Book of Humorous Cartoons on a Serious Subject.* New York: Palmer, 1917.

2491 Day, Kirkland. *Camion Cartoons.* Boston: Marshall Jones, 1919.

2492 Pennell, Joseph. *Joseph Pennell's Pictures of War Work in America.* Philadelphia: Lippincott, 1918.

R/The War and Literature

Works about Wartime Writers

2493 Aldridge, John W. *After the Lost Generation: A Critical Study of the Writers of Two Wars.* New York: McGraw-Hill, 1951.

2494 Aveilhe, Art. "Literature: No Heroes among Us." *Mankind* 5 (Feb. 1977): 34–35.

2495 Bowerman, George F. "The Spirit of the War Literature: Prose." *American Library Association Bulletin* 12 (Sept. 1918): 60–72.

2496 Connor, James R. "Pen and Sword: World War I Novels in America, 1916–1941." Ph.D. dissertation, University of Winconsin, 1961.

2497 Cooperman, Stanley. *World War I and the American Novel.* Baltimore: Johns Hopkins Press, 1967.

2498 Cowley, Malcolm. "Après La Guerre Finie." *Horizon* 10 (Winter 1968): 112–19.

2499 ———. *Exile's Return: A Literary Odyssey of the 1920's.* New York: Viking, 1951.

2500 Critoph, Gerald E. "The American Literary Reaction to World War I." Ph.D. dissertation, University of Pennsylvania, 1957.

2501 Feigenbaum, Laurence H. "War as Viewed by the Postwar Novelists of World Wars I and II." Ph.D. dissertation, New York University, 1950.

2502 Fenton, Charles A. "American Ambulance Drivers in France and Italy, 1914–1918." *American Quarterly* 3 (Winter 1951): 326–43.

2503 ———. "A Literary Fracture of World War I." *American Quarterly* 12 (Summer 1960): 119–32.

2504 Hart, J. A. "American Poetry of the First World War: A Survey and Checklist." Ph.D. dissertation, Duke University, 1964.

2505 Joyner, Charles W. "John Dos Passos and World War I: The Literary Use of Historical Experience." Ed.D. dissertation, University of South Carolina, 1965.

2506 Mizener, Arthur. *The Far Side of Paradise: A Biography of F. Scott Fitzgerald.* 2d ed. Boston: Houghton Mifflin, 1965.

2507 Turnbull, Andrew. *Scott Fitzgerald.* New York: Scribner's, 1962.

2508 Winterich, John T., ed. *Mademoiselle from Armentières.* Mount Vernon, New York: Peter Pauper Press, 1953.

2509 Wolle, Francis. "Novels of Two World Wars." *Western Humanities Review* 5 (Summer 1951): 279– 96.

War Prose

2510 Adams, Samuel H. *Common Cause: A Novel of the War in America.* Boston: Houghton Mifflin, 1919.

2511 Allen, Hervey. *It Was Like This: Two Stories of the Great War.* New York: Farrar & Rinehart, 1940.

2512 Anderson, Maxwell, and Laurence Stallings. "What Price Glory?" In their *Three American Plays.* New York: Harcourt, Brace, 1926.

2513 Andrews, Mary R. S. *Her Country.* New York: Scribner's, 1918.

2514 ——. *Joy in the Morning.* New York: Scribner's, 1919.

2515 Bailey, Temple. *The Tin Soldier.* Philadelphia: Penn Publishing, 1918.

2516 Barretto, Larry. *Horses in the Sky.* New York: John Day, 1929.

2517 Binns, Archie. *The Laurels Are Cut Down.* New York: Reynal & Hitchcock, 1937.

2518 Boyd, Thomas A. *Through the Wheat.* New York: Scribner's, 1926.

2519 [Campbell, William E. M.] *Company K,* by William March, pseud. New York: Smith & Haas, 1933.

2520 Cather, Willa S. *One of Ours.* New York: Knopf, 1922.

2521 Cobb, Humphrey. *Paths of Glory.* New York: Viking, 1935.

2522 Dos Passos, John R. *First Encounter.* New York: Philosophical Library, 1945.

2523 ——. *1919.* New York: Harcourt, Brace, 1932.

2524 ——. *Three Soldiers.* New York: Doran, 1921.

2525 Dunbar, Ruth. *The Swallow.* New York: Boni & Liveright, 1919.

2526 Empey, Arthur G. *Tales from a Dugout.* New York: Century, 1918.

2527 Faulkner, William. *Soldiers' Pay.* New York: Boni & Liveright, 1926.

2528 Fisher, Dorothy Canfield. *The Day of Glory.* New York: Holt, 1919.

2529 ——. *Home Fires in France.* New York: Holt, 1918.

2530 Harrison, Charles Y. *Generals Die in Bed.* New York: Morrow, 1930.

2531 Hemingway, Ernest. *A Farewell to Arms.* New York: Scribner's, 1929.

2532 Heth, Edward H. *Told with a Drum.* Boston: Houghton Mifflin, 1937.

2533 Kelly, Thomas H. *What Outfit Buddy?* New York: Harper, 1920.

2534 Lazo, Hector T. *Taps: A Novel of War and Peace.* Boston: B. Humphries, 1934.

2535 Lee, Mary. *"It's a Great War!"* Boston: Houghton Mifflin, 1929.

2536 Mack, Charles E. *Two Black Crows in the A.E.F.* Indianapolis: Bobbs-Merrill, 1928.

2537 Miller, Warren H. *Sea Fighters: Navy Yarns of the Great War.* New York: Macmillan, 1920.

2538 Nason, Leonard. *Sergeant Eadie.* Garden City: Doubleday, Doran, 1928.

2539 Nordhoff, Charles, and James N. Hall. *Falcons of France: A Tale of Youth and the Air.* Boston: Little, Brown, 1929.

2540 Oppenheim, E. Phillips. *The Pawn's Count.* New York: Burt, 1920.

2541 Paul, Elliot. *Impromptu: A Novel in Four Movements.* New York: Knopf, 1924.

2542 Scanlon, William. *God Have Mercy on Us.* Boston: Houghton Mifflin, 1929.

2543 Sinclair, Upton. *Jimmie Higgins.* New York: Boni & Liveright, 1919.

2544 Stallings, Laurence. *Plumes.* New York: Harcourt, Brace, 1924.

2545 The Stars and Stripes. *Squads Write. . . .* Edited by John T. Winterich. New York: Harper, 1931.

2546 Stevens, James. *Mattock.* New York: Knopf, 1927.

2547 Train, Arthur. *Earthquake.* New York: Scribner's, 1918.

2548 Trumbo, Dalton. *Johnny Got His Gun.* Philadelphia: Lippincott, 1939.

2549   Tucker, William J. *Not All Ashes.* Dallas: Southwest Press, 1941.

2550   Wharton, Edith. *The Marne.* New York: Appleton, 1918.

2551   ——. *A Son at the Front.* New York: Scribner's, 1923.

2552   Whiting, John D. *S.O.S.: A Story of the World War at Sea.* Indianapolis: Bobbs-Merrill, 1928.

2553   Witwer, Harry C. *From Baseball to Boches.* Boston: Small, Maynard, 1918.

War Poetry and Song Lyrics

2554   Appleton, Everard J. *With the Colors: Songs of the American Service.* Cincinnati: Stewart & Kidd, 1917.

2555   Baldridge, Cyrus L., and Hilman R. Bankhage. *"I Was There!" with the Yanks on the Western Front.* New York: Putnam's, 1919.

2556   Braley, Berton. *In Camp and Trench: Songs of the Fighting Forces.* New York: Doran, 1918.

2557   Brooks, Leon D. *The Ballads of a Doughboy.* New York: J. R. Anderson, 1919.

2558   ——. *The Ballads of a Rookie: Essex 1—No. 117.* New York: J. R. Anderson, 1917.

2559   Camp, Frank B. *American Soldier Ballads.* Los Angeles: G. Rice & Sons, 1917.

2560   ——. *Rhymes in Khaki.* Boston: Cornhill, 1918.

2561   Campbell, Gus W., and J. B. Livingstone, comps. *Buddies: A Collection of World War Poems "Written by Our Buddies for Our Buddies."* De Kalb, Illinois: Barb City Book Co., 1930.

2562   Christian, W. E. *Rhymes of the Rookies: Sunny Side of Soldier Service.* New York: Dodd, Mead, 1917.

2563   Clarke, George H., ed. *A Treasury of War Poetry: British and American Poems of the World War, 1914—1919.* Boston: Houghton Mifflin, 1917.

2564   Cushing, Joseph R. *Doughboy Ditties.* Philadelphia: Hoeflich, 1927.

2565   Ellershaw, Edward. *Some War Songs.* Jacksonville, Florida: Arnold Printing Co., 1917.

2566   Gibbons, Herbert A., comp. *Songs from the Trenches: The Soul of the A.E.F.* New York: Harper, 1918.

2567 Guest, Edgar A. *Over Here.* Chicago: Reilly & Britton, 1918.

2568 Howe, Mark A. De Wolfe. *The Known Soldier and Other Reminders of the War Decade.* Boston: McGrath-Sherrill Press, 1924.

2569 Leahy, Francis T. *The Godlike Hour: World War Poems and Other Verses.* New York: Loughlin Press, 1918.

2570 Niles, John J. *Singing Soldiers.* Detroit: Singing Tree Press, 1968.

2571 ———; Douglas S. Moore; and A. A. Wallgren. *The Songs My Mother Never Taught Me.* . . . New York: Macaulay, 1929.

2572 Robinson, Corinne. *Service and Sacrifice Poems.* New York: Scribner's, 1919.

2573 Roosevelt, Theodore, Jr., and Grantland Rice, comps. *Taps: Selected Poems of the Great War.* Garden City, New York: Doubleday, Doran, 1932.

2574 Sanger, William C. *War Poems.* New York: Putnam's, 1924.

2575 Smylie, Adolphe E. *The Marines and Other War Verse.* New York: Knickerbocker, 1919.

2576 The Stars and Stripes. *Squads Write.* . . . Edited by John T. Winterich. New York: Harper, 1931.

2577 ———. *Yanks.* New York: Putnam's, 1919.

2578 Stokes, Will. *Songs of the Services: Army, Navy and Marine Corps.* New York: Stokes, 1919.

2579 Van Dyke, Henry. *The Red Flower: Poems Written in War-time.* New York: Scribner's, 1917.

2580 Wallrich, William J., ed. *Air Force Airs: Songs and Ballads of the United States Air Force, World War I through Korea.* New York: Duell, Sloan & Pearce, 1957.

2581 Wilder, Amos N. *Battle-Retrospect and Other Poems.* New Haven: Yale University Press, 1923.

2582 Williams, Oscar. *The War Poets: An Anthology of the War Poetry of the 20th Century.* New York: John Day, 1945.

2583 Wyeth, John A. B. *This Man's Army: A War in Fifty-odd Sonnets.* New York: H. Vinal, 1928.

2584 Yale Review. *War Poems From the Yale Review.* New Haven: Yale University Press, 1918.

2585 Young Men's Christian Associations. Bureau of Libraries and Periodicals. *Popular Songs of the A.E.F.* Paris: F. Salabert, 1918.

War Humor

2586 Lardner, Ring W. *Treat 'em Rough: Letters from Jack the Kaiser Killer.* Indianapolis: Bobbs-Merrill, 1918.

2587 Majors, C. L., comp. *World War Jokes.* Ramer, Tennessee, 1930.

2588 Streeter, Edward. *"As You Were, Bill!"* New York: Stokes, 1920.

2589 ——. *"Dere Mable"* —*Love Letters of a Rookie.* New York: Stokes, 1918.

2590 ——. *"Same Old Bill, eh Mable!"* New York: Stokes, 1919.

2591 ——. *"That's Me All Over, Mable."* New York: Stokes, 1919.

2592 Summers, Florence E. *Dere Bill: Mable's Love Letters to Her Rookie.* New York: Stokes, 1919.

S/Education in Wartime

2593 Ackerman, J. H. "The Normal School as an Agency for Teaching Patriotism." *NEA Addresses and Proceedings* 55 (1917): 57–62.

2594 Amherst College (Amherst, Massachusetts). *The Amherst Memorial Volume, A Record of the Contribution Made by Amherst College and Amherst Men in the World War, 1914–1918.* Edited by Claude M. Fuess. Amherst, Massachusetts: Amherst College, 1926.

2595 Aydelotte, Frank W. *Final Report of the War Issues Course of the Students' Army Training Corps.* Washington, D.C.: War Department Committee on Education and Special Training, 1919.

2596 Benson, Albert E., ed. *Saint Mark's School in the War against Germany.* Norwood, Massachusetts, 1920.

2597 Birdzell, Luther E. "North Dakota's Contribution of Men." *Quarterly Journal* (University of North Dakota) 10 (Oct. 1919): 3–16.

2598 Bolton, Frederick E. "Maintenance of Standards in All Schools as a Necessary Element of Preparedness." *NEA Addresses and Proceedings* 55 (1917): 82–88.

2599 Boston College (Boston, Massachusetts). *Boston College in the World War, 1917–1918.* Chestnut Hill, Massachusetts: Boston College, 1924(?).

2600 Boston High School of Commerce (Boston, Massachusetts). *The Boston High School of Commerce in the World War.* Norwood, Massachusetts: Plimpton Press, 1921.

2601   California. State Board of Education. *All for America: What California Schools Can Do in the Present Crisis.* Sacramento: State Printing Office, 1917.

2602   Capen, Samuel P. "The Effect of the World War, 1914–1918, on American Colleges and Universities." *Educational Record* 21 (Jan. 1940): 40–48.

2603   Clark, Eugene F., ed. *War Record of Dartmouth College, 1917–1918.* Hanover: Dartmouth College, 1922.

2604   Cornell University. *Military Records of Cornell University in the World War.* Ithaca, New York: Cornell University, 1930.

2605   Cross, Arthur L. "The University of Michigan and the Training of Her Students for the War." *Michigan History* 4 (Jan. 1920): 115–40.

2606   Dean, Arthur D. *Our Schools in War Time and After.* Boston: Ginn, 1918.

2607   Ellis, Horace, and Ellis U. Graff, eds. *War Service Text-book for Indiana High Schools.* Indianapolis: Indiana State Council of Defense, 1918.

2608   Fahey, Sara H. "How the Public School Can Foster the American Ideal of Patriotism." *NEA Addresses and Proceedings* 55 (July 7–14, 1917): 48–57.

2609   Fuess, Claude M., ed. *Phillips Academy, Andover, in the Great War.* New Haven: Yale University Press, 1919.

2610   Greenlaw, Edwin A., ed. *Builders of Democracy: The Service, Told in Song and Story of Those Who Gave Us Freedom; the New Crisis and How It Must Be Met; and the Greater Freedom That Is to Come.* Chicago: Scott, Foresman, 1918. [Part of a school history series.]

2611   Groce, H. Emilie. *Landsdowne School and the World War.* Philadelphia: Central Press Co., 1919.

2612   Hamlin, Charles H. *Educators Present Arms: The Use of the Schools and Colleges as Agents of War Propaganda, 1914–1918.* Zebulon, North Carolina: Record Publishing, 1939.

2613   Harding, Samuel B. *The Study of the Great War: A Topical Outline.* New York: Committee on Public Information, 1918.

2614   Hart, Albert B., ed. *America at War: A Handbook of Patriotic Education References.* New York: Doran, 1918.

2615   Haynes, Rowland. "The Colleges in the Preparedness Program, 1917–1918 and 1940." *Educational Record* 21 (Oct. 1940): 489–96.

2616 Howe, Mark A. de Wolfe. *Memoirs of the Harvard Dead in the War against Germany.* Cambridge: Harvard University Press, 1920–1924.

2617 Illinois, University of. *War Publications and Reports of the War Committee of the University of Illinois, 1917–1919.* Urbana: University of Illinois, 1923.

2618 Kerr, William J. "Education and the World War." *NEA Addresses and Proceedings* 55 (1917): 111–19.

2619 Kolbe, Parke R. *The Colleges in War-times and After: A Contemporary Account of the Effect of the War upon Higher Education in America.* New York: Appleton, 1919.

2620 Massachusetts Agricultural College. *Massachusetts Agricultural College in the War.* Amherst: Massachusetts Agricultural College, 1921.

2621 Mead, Frederick S., ed. *Harvard's Military Record in the World War.* Boston: Harvard Alumni Association, 1921.

2622 Nettleton, George H. *Yale in the World War.* 2 vols. New Haven: Yale University Press, 1925.

2623 Palmer, Jean M. "The Impact of World War I on Louisiana's Schools and Community Life." *Louisiana History* 7 (Fall 1966): 323–32.

2624 Patton, John S. *The University of Virginia in the World War.* Charlottesville(?), 1927(?).

2625 Princeton University. *Princeton in the World War.* Princeton: Princeton University, Office of the Secretary, 1932.

2626 ———. Department of History and Politics. *The World Peril: America's Interest in the War.* Princeton: Princeton University Press, 1917.

2627 Ruckman, John H., ed. *Technology's War Record: An Interpretation of the Contribution Made by the Massachusetts Institute of Technology in the Great War, 1914–1919.* Cambridge, Massachusetts: Murray Printing, 1920.

2628 St. Lawrence University. *St. Lawrence University in the World War: A Memorial.* Canton, New York: St. Lawrence University, 1931.

2629 Siebert, Wilbur H. *History of the Ohio State University.* Vol. 4: *The University in the Great War.* Pt. I: *Wartime on Campus.* Columbus: Ohio State University Press, 1934.

2630 Summerscales, William. *Affirmation and Dissent: Columbia's Response to the Crisis of World War I.* New York: Teacher's College Press, 1970.

2631   Thwing, Charles F. *The American Colleges and Universities in the Great War, 1914– 1919: A History.* New York: Macmillan, 1920.

2632   Todd, Lewis P. *Wartime Relations of the Federal Government and the Public Schools, 1917– 1918.* New York: Columbia University Teachers College, 1945.

2633   Van Hise, Charles R. "War Measures of Higher Educational Institutions." *NEA Addresses and Proceedings* 55 (1917): 293– 96.

2634   Williams College (Williamstown, Massachusetts). *Williams College in the World War.* Edited by Frederic T. Wood. Williamstown, Massachusetts: President and Trustees of Williams College, 1926.

2635   Wisconsin, University of. *War Book of the University of Wisconsin Papers on the Causes and Issues of the War by Members of the Faculty.* Madison: University of Wisconsin, 1918.

2636   Zimmerman, Norman A. "A Triumph for Orthodoxy: The University of Wisconsin during World War I." Ph.D. dissertation, University of Minnesota, 1971.

T/War and American Intellectuals

General

2637   Bourne, Randolph S. *War and The Intellectuals: Essays, 1915– 1919.* Edited by Carl Resek. New York: Harper & Row, 1964.

2638   ——. *The World of Randolph Bourne: An Anthology.* Edited by Lillian Schlissel. New York: Dutton, 1965.

2639   Curti, Merle E. "The American Scholar in Three Wars." *Journal of the History of Ideas* 3 (June 1942): 241– 64.

2640   Cywar, Alan. "John Dewey in World War I: Patriotism and International Progressivism." *American Quarterly* 21 (Fall 1969): 578– 94.

2641   ——. "John Dewey: Toward Domestic Reconstruction, 1915– 1920." *Journal of the History of Ideas* 30 (July– Sept. 1969): 385– 400.

2642   Dewey, John. "Universal Service as Education." *New Republic* 6 (Apr. 22, 1916): 309– 11; (Apr. 29, 1916): 334– 35.

2643   Eulau, Heinz. "Wilsonian Idealist: Walter Lippmann Goes to War." *Antioch Review* 14 (Mar. 1954): 87– 108.

2644   Forcey, Charles. *The Crossroads of Liberalism: Croly, Weyl, Lippmann, and the Progressive Era, 1900– 1925.* New York: Oxford University Press, 1961.

2645 Grattan, C. Hartley. "The Historians Cut Loose." *American Mercury* 11 (Aug. 1927): 414–30.

2646 Gruber, Carol S. *Mars and Minerva: World War I and the Uses of the Higher Learning in America.* Baton Rouge: Louisiana State University Press, 1976.

2647 Hirschfeld, Charles. "Nationalist Progressivism and World War I." *Mid-America* 45 (July 1963): 139–56.

2648 Kaplan, Sidney. "Social Engineers as Saviors: Effects of World War I on Some American Liberals." *Journal of the History of Ideas* 17 (June 1956): 347–69.

2649 Knoles, George H. "American Intellectuals and World War I." *Pacific Northwest Quarterly* 59 (Oct. 1968): 203–15.

2650 Lasch, Christopher. *The New Radicalism in America, 1889–1963: The Intellectual as a Social Type.* New York: Knopf, 1965.

2651 May, Henry F. *The End of American Innocence: A Study of the First Years of Our Own Time, 1912–1917.* New York: Knopf, 1959.

2652 Nicholas, William E., III. "Academic Dissent in World War I, 1917–1918." Ph.D. dissertation, Tulane University, 1970.

2653 ———. "World War I and Academic Dissent in Texas." *Arizona and the West* 14 (Autumn 1972): 215–30.

2654 Perry, Ralph B. *The Free Man and the Soldier: Essays on the Reconciliation of Liberty and Discipline.* New York: Scribner's, 1916.

2655 ———. *The Present Conflict of Ideals: A Study of the Philosophical Background of the World War.* New York: Longmans, Green, 1918.

2656 Simms, L. Moody, Jr. "World War I and the American Intellectual." *Social Science* 45 (June 1970): 157–62.

2657 Winterrle, John. "John Dewey and the First World War: A Study in Pragmatic Acquiescence." *North Dakota Quarterly* 35 (Winter 1967): 15–28.

The Historical Profession in the War

2658 Blakey, George T. *Historians on the Homefront: American Propagandists for the Great War.* Lexington: University Press of Kentucky, 1970.

2659 Josephson, Harold. "History for Victory: The National Board for Historical Service." *Mid-America* 52 (July 1970): 205–24.

2660   Kennedy, Thomas C. "Charles A. Beard in Midpassage." *Historian* 30 (Feb. 1968): 179– 98.

2661   Mereness, Newton D., ed. "American Historical Activities during the World War." *Annual Report of the American Historical Association for the Year 1919.* Washington, D.C.: G.P.O., 1923, 1: 139– 293.

2662   National Board for Historical Service. *War Readings.* New York: Scribner's, 1918.

2663   Snyder, Phil L. "Carl Becker and the Great War: A Crisis for a Humane Intelligence." *Western Political Quarterly* 9 (Mar. 1956): 1– 10.

2664   Wilkes, James D. "Van Tyne: The Professor and the Hun!" *Michigan History* 55 (Fall 1971): 183– 204.

U/Science in Wartime America (See also V, S/Technology and Weapons)

2665   Ames, Joseph S. "Science at the Front." *Atlantic Monthly* 121 (Jan. 1918): 90– 100.

2666   Angell, James R. "The National Research Council." In *The New World of Science*, edited by Robert M. Yerkes. Freeport, New York: Books for Libraries Press, 1969.

2667   Camfield, Thomas M. "Psychologists at War: The History of American Psychology and the First World War." Ph.D. dissertation, University of Texas, 1969.

2668   ———. " 'Will to Win'—The U.S. Army Troop Morale Program of World War I." *Military Affairs* 41 (Oct. 1977): 125– 28.

2669   Cohen, I. Bernard. "American Physicists at War: From the First World War to 1942." *American Journal of Physics* 13 (Oct. 1945): 337– 46.

2670   Compton, K. T. "Edison's Laboratory in Wartime." *Science* 75 (Jan. 15, 1932): 70– 71.

2671   Dupree, A. Hunter. *Science in the Federal Government: A History of Policies and Activities to 1940.* Cambridge: Harvard University Press, 1957.

2672   Fleming, Winston. "Testing the Brains of Our Naval Fighters." *Illustrated World* 29 (Aug. 1918): 897– 900.

2673   Hale, George E. "The Possibilities of Cooperation in Research." In *The New World of Science*, edited by Robert M. Yerkes. Freeport, New York: Books for Libraries Press, 1969.

2674 ———. "War Services of the National Research Council." In *The New World of Science,* edited by Robert M. Yerkes. Freeport, New York: Books for Libraries Press, 1969.

2675 Howe, Harrison E. "Optical Glass for War Needs." In *The New World of Science,* edited by Robert M. Yerkes. Freeport, New York: Books for Libraries Press, 1969.

2676 Howe, Henry M. "Contributions of Metallurgy to Victory." In *The New World of Science,* edited by Robert M. Yerkes. Freeport, New York: Books for Libraries Press, 1969.

2677 Ives, Herbert E. "War-time Photography." In *The New World of Science,* edited by Robert M. Yerkes. Freeport, New York: Books for Libraries Press, 1969.

2678 Johnson, Douglas W. "Contributions of Geography." In *The New World of Science,* edited by Robert M. Yerkes. Freeport, New York: Books for Libraries Press, 1969.

2679 ———. "Contributions of Geology." In *The New World of Science,* edited by Robert M. Yerkes. Freeport, New York: Books for Libraries Press, 1969.

2680 Jones, Daniel P. "The Role of Chemists in Research on War Gases in the United States during World War I." Ph.D. dissertation, University of Wisconsin, 1969.

2681 Kevles, Daniel J. "Federal Legislation for Engineering Experiment Stations: The Episode of World War I." *Technology and Culture* 12 (Apr. 1971): 182–89.

2682 ———. "George Ellery Hale, the First World War, and the Advancement of Science in America." *Isis* 59 (Winter 1968): 427–37.

2683 ———. " 'Into Hostile Political Camps': The Reorganization of International Science in World War I." *Isis* 62 (Spring 1971): 47–60.

2684 ———. "Testing the Army's Intelligence: Psychologists and the Military in World War I." *Journal of American History* 55 (Dec. 1968): 565–81.

2685 Millikan, Robert A. *Autobiography.* Englewood Cliffs, New Jersey: Prentice-Hall, 1950.

2686 ———. "Contributions of Physical Science." In *The New World of Science,* edited by Robert M. Yerkes. Freeport, New York: Books for Libraries Press, 1969.

2687 ———. "Some Scientific Aspects of the Meteorological Work of the United States Army." In *The New World of Science,* edited by Robert M. Yerkes. Freeport, New York: Books for Libraries Press, 1969.

2688 Munro, Charles E. "The Production of Explosives." In *The New World of Science,* edited by Robert M. Yerkes. Freeport, New York: Books for Libraries Press, 1969.

2689 Pursell, Carroll W., Jr. "Science and Government Agencies." In *Science and Society in the United States,* edited by David D. Van Tassel and Michael G. Hall. Homewood, Illinois: Dorsey, 1966.

2690 Spring, Joel H. "Psychologists and the War: The Meaning of Intelligence in the Alpha and Beta Tests." *History of Education Quarterly* 12 (Spring 1972): 3–15.

2691 Stevens, Neil E. "American Botany and the Great War." *Science* 48 (Aug. 23, 1918): 177–79.

2692 Talbot, Henry P. "Chemistry at the Front." *Atlantic Monthly* 122 (Aug. 1918): 265–74.

2693 ———. "Chemistry behind the Front." *Atlantic Monthly* 122 (Nov. 1918): 651–63.

2694 Tobey, Ronald C. *The American Ideology of National Science.* Pittsburgh: University of Pittsburgh Press, 1971.

2695 Wright, Helen. *Explorer of the Universe: A Biography of George Ellery Hale.* New York: Dutton, 1966.

2696 Yerkes, Robert M. "How Psychology Happened into the War." In *The New World of Science,* edited by Robert M. Yerkes. Freeport, New York: Books for Libraries Press, 1969.

2697 ———, ed. *Psychological Examining in the United States Army.* Washington, D.C.: G.P.O., 1921.

2698 ———. "What Psychology Contributed to the War." In *The New World of Science,* edited by Robert M. Yerkes. Freeport, New York: Books for Libraries Press, 1969.

2699 Yoakum, Clarence S., and Robert M. Yerkes. *Army Mental Tests.* New York: Holt, 1931.

V/Civilian Medicine and Public Health

2700 Allen, Frederick L. "The Flu Epidemic of 1918." *Scribner's* 103:1 (1938): 27–30, 74.

2701 Andrews, John B. "National Effectiveness and Health Insurance." *The Annals* 78 (July 1918): 50– 57.

2702 Costello, C. A. "Principal Defects Found in Persons Examined for Service in the United States Navy." *American Journal of Public Health* 7 (May 1917): 489– 92.

2703 Crosby, Alfred W., Jr. *Epidemic and Peace, 1918*. Westport, Connecticut: Greenwood, 1976.

2704 Galishoff, Stuart. "Newark and the Great Influenza Pandemic of 1918." *Bulletin of the History of Medicine* 43 (May– June 1969): 246– 58.

2705 Hanner, John W. "Advances in Surgery during the War." In *The New World of Science*, edited by Robert M. Yerkes. Freeport, New York: Books for Libraries Press, 1969.

2706 Hoehling, Adolph A. *The Great Epidemic*. Boston: Little, Brown, 1961.

2707 Katz, Robert S. "Influenza 1918– 1919: A Study in Mortality." *Bulletin of the History of Medicine* 48 (Fall 1974): 416– 22.

2708 Macmahon, Arthur W. "Health Activities of State Councils of Defense." *The Annals* 79 (Sept. 1918): 239– 45.

2709 Mock, Harry E. "Reclamation of the Disabled from the Industrial Army." *The Annals* 80 (Nov. 1918): 29– 34.

2710 Orr, Harry D. "Examination of Recruits for the Army and the Militia." *American Journal of Public Health* 7 (Mar. 1917): 485– 88.

2711 Paine, Jocelyn. "Health: The Pandemic Catastrophe." *Mankind* 5 (Feb. 1977): 32– 34.

2712 Perry, J. C. "Military Health Dependent on Civil Health." *The Annals* 78 (July 1918): 34– 40.

2713 Pilcher, Lewis S. "The Influence of War Surgery upon Civil Practice." *Annals of Surgery* 69 (June 1919): 565– 74.

2714 Seymour, Gertrude. "Some Aspects of the American Health Movement in War-Time." *Survey* 40 (Apr. 27, 1918): 89– 94.

2715 Tobey, James A. *The National Government and Public Health*. Baltimore: Johns Hopkins Press, 1926.

2716 Vaughn, Victor C. "Preventive Medicine and the War." In *The New World of Science*, edited by Robert M. Yerkes. Freeport, New York: Books for Libraries Press, 1969.

2717 Walsh, Joseph. "Tuberculosis and the War." *The Annals* 80 (Nov. 1918): 23– 28.

2718 Warren, Benjamin S. . . . *War Activities of the United States Public Health Service.* Washington, D.C.: G.P.O., 1919.

W/Domestic Politics

2719 Adler, Selig. "The Congressional Election of 1918." *South Atlantic Quarterly* 36 (Oct. 1937): 447– 65.

2720 Grant, Philip A. "World War I: Wilson and Southern Leadership." *Presidential Studies Quarterly* 6 (Winter– Spring 1976): 44– 49.

2721 La Follette, Belle C., and Fola La Follette. *Robert M. La Follette, June 14, 1885– June 18, 1925.* 2 vols. New York: Macmillan, 1953.

2722 Livermore, Seward W. *Politics Is Adjourned: Woodrow Wilson and the War Congress, 1916– 1918.* Middletown, Connecticut: Wesleyan University Press, 1966.

2723 ——. "The Sectional Issue in the 1918 Elections." *Mississippi Valley Historical Review* 35 (June 1948): 29– 60.

2724 Merritt, Richard L. "Woodrow Wilson and the 'Great and Solemn Referendum,' 1920." *Review of Politics* 27 (Jan. 1965): 78– 104.

2725 Morlan, Robert L. *Political Prairie Fire: The Nonpartisan League, 1915– 1922.* Minneapolis: University of Minnesota Press, 1955.

2726 Newby, Idus A. "States' Rights and Southern Congressmen during World War I." *Phylon* 24 (Spring 1963): 34– 50.

2727 Paxson, Frederic L. "The American War Government, 1917– 1918." *American Historical Review* 26 (Oct. 1920): 54– 76.

2728 Remele, Larry. "The Tragedy of Idealism: The National Nonpartisan League and American Foreign Policy 1917– 1919." *North Dakota Quarterly* 42 (Autumn 1975): 78– 95.

2728a Safford, Jeffrey J. *Wilsonian Maritime Diplomacy, 1913– 1921.* New Brunswick, New Jersey: Rutgers University Press, 1978.

2729 Sellen, Robert W. "Opposition Leaders in Wartime: The Case of Theodore Roosevelt and World War I." *Midwest Quarterly* 9 (Apr. 1968): 225– 42.

2730 Wimer, Kurt. "Woodrow Wilson's Plan for a Vote of Confidence." *Pennsylvania History* 28 (July 1961): 279– 93.

VIII/Peacemaking

A/Wartime U.S. Diplomacy

2731 Fowler, W. B. *British-American Relations, 1917– 1918: The Role of Sir William Wiseman.* Princeton: Princeton University Press, 1969.

2732 Gaffney, Thomas St. J. *Breaking the Silence: England, Ireland, Wilson and the War.* New York: Liveright, 1930.

2733 Hunter, Charles H. "Anglo-American Relations during the Period of American Belligerency, 1917– 1918." Ph.D. dissertation, Stanford University, 1935.

2734 Kernek, Sterling J. "Distractions of Peace during War: The Lloyd George Government's Reactions to Woodrow Wilson, December 1916– November 1918." *Transactions of the American Philosophical Society*, n.s. 65 (Apr. 1975): 3– 117.

2735 May, Ernest R. "American Policy and Japan's Entrance into World War I." *Mississippi Valley Historical Review* 40 (Sept. 1953): 279– 90.

2736 Noer, Thomas J. "The American Government and the Irish Question during World War I." *South Atlantic Quarterly* 72 (Winter 1973): 95– 114.

2736a Parsons, Edward B. *Wilsonian Diplomacy: Allied-American Rivalries in War and Peace.* St. Louis: Forum Press, 1977.

2737 Réquin, Edouard J. *America's Race to Victory.* New York: Stokes, 1919.

2738 Seymour, Charles. *American Diplomacy during the World War.* Baltimore: Johns Hopkins Press, 1934.

2739 Sharp, William G. *The War Memoirs of William Graves Sharp: American Ambassador to France 1914– 1919.* Edited by Washington Dawson. London: Constable, 1931.

2740   Snell, John L. "Wilson's Peace Program and German Socialism, January– March 1918." Mississippi Valley Historical Review 38 (Sept. 1951): 187– 214.

2741   Walworth, Arthur. America's Moment: 1918, American Diplomacy at the End of World War I. New York: Norton, 1976.

2742   Willert, Arthur. The Road to Safety: A Study in Anglo-American Relations. New York: Praeger, 1953.

B/The Peace Settlement

2743   Ambrosius, Lloyd E. "Wilson, Clemenceau and the German Problems at the Paris Peace Conference of 1919." Rocky Mountain Social Science Journal 12 (Apr. 1975): 69– 79.

2744   ———. "Wilson, the Republicans, and the French Security after World War I." Journal of American History 59 (Sept. 1972): 341– 52.

2745   Bailey, Thomas A. Woodrow Wilson and the Lost Peace. Chicago: Quadrangle Books, 1963.

2746   Baker, Ray S. Woodrow Wilson and the World Settlement. 3 vols. Garden City, New York: Doubleday, Page, 1922.

2747   Barany, George. "Wilsonian Central Europe: Lansing's Contribution." Historian 28 (Feb. 1966): 224– 51.

2748   Baruch, Bernard M. The Making of the Reparation and Economic Sections of the Treaty. New York: Harper, 1920.

2749   Binkley, R. C. "Ten Years of Peace Conference History." Journal of Modern History 1 (Dec. 1929): 607– 29.

2750   Birdsall, Paul. "The Second Decade of Peace Conference History." Journal of Modern History 11 (Sept. 1939): 362– 78.

2751   ———. Versailles Twenty Years After. New York: Reynal & Hitchcock, 1941.

2752   Bryson, Thomas A. "Walter George Smith and the Armenian Question at the Paris Peace Conference, 1919." Records of the American Catholic Historical Society of Pennsylvania 81 (Mar. 1970): 3– 26.

2753   Burnett, Philip M. Reparation at the Paris Peace Conference from the Standpoint of the American Delegation. 2 vols. New York: Columbia University Press, 1940.

2754   Clemenceau, Georges. Grandeur and Misery of Victory. New York: Harcourt, Brace, 1930.

2755 Curry, George. "Woodrow Wilson, Jan Smuts, and the Versailles Settlement." *American Historical Review* 66 (July 1961): 968–86.

2756 Ferrell, Robert H. "Woodrow Wilson and Open Diplomacy." In *Issues and Conflicts: Studies in Twentieth Century American Diplomacy,* edited by George L. Anderson. Lawrence: University of Kansas Press, 1959.

2757 Fifield, Russell H. *Woodrow Wilson and the Far East: The Diplomacy of the Shantung Question.* 1952. Reprint. Hamden Connecticut: Archon Books, 1965.

2758 Floto, Inga. *Colonel House in Paris: A Study of American Policy at the Paris Peace Conference 1919.* Aarhus: Universitetsforlaget i Aarhus, Eksp: DBK, 1973.

2759 Gelfand, Lawrence E. *The Inquiry: American Preparations for Peace, 1917–1919.* New Haven: Yale University Press, 1963.

2760 Gerson, Louis L. *Woodrow Wilson and the Rebirth of Poland, 1914–1920: A Study in the Influence on American Policy of Minority Groups of Foreign Origin.* New Haven: Yale University Press, 1953.

2761 Greene, Theodore P., ed. *Wilson at Versailles.* Boston: Heath, 1957.

2762 Hoover, Herbert C. *America's First Crusade.* New York: Scribner's, 1942.

2763 House, Edward M., and Charles Seymour, eds. *What Really Happened at Paris: The Story of the Peace Conference, 1918–1919, by American Delegates.* New York: Scribner's, 1921.

2764 Lansing, Robert. *The Big Four and Others of the Peace Conference.* Boston: Houghton Mifflin, 1921.

2765 ———. *The Peace Negotiations: A Personal Narrative.* Reprint. Port Washington, New York: Kennikat, 1969.

2766 Levin N. Gordon, Jr. *Woodrow Wilson and World Politics: America's Response to War and Revolution.* New York: Oxford University Press, 1968.

2767 Lippmann, Walter. *The Politicial Scene: An Essay on the Victory of 1918.* New York: Holt, 1919.

2768 Lloyd George, David. *Memoirs of the Peace Conference.* 2 vols. New Haven: Yale University Press, 1939.

2769 Logan, Rayford W. *The Senate and the Versailles Mandate System.* Washington, D.C.: Minorities Publishers, 1945.

2770 Martin, Laurence W. *Peace Without Victory: Wilson and the British Liberals.* New Haven: Yale University Press, 1958.

2771 ———. "Woodrow Wilson's Appeals to the People of Europe: British Radical Influence on the President's Strategy." *Political Science Quarterly* 74 (Dec. 1959): 498– 516.

2772 May, Ernest R. *"Lessons" of the Past: The Use and Misuse of History in American Foreign Policy.* New York: Oxford University Press, 1973.

2773 Mayer, Arno J. *Politics and Diplomacy of Peacemaking: Containment and Counterrevolution at Versailles, 1918– 1919.* New York: Knopf, 1967.

2774 ———. *Wilson vs. Lenin: Political Origins of the New Diplomacy, 1917– 1918.* Cleveland: World, 1964.

2775 Miller, David H. *My Diary at the Conference of Paris, with Documents.* 21 vols. New York: Appeal Printing, 1924.

2776 Nelson, Keith L. "What Colonel House Overlooked in the Armistice." *Mid-America* 51 (Apr. 1969): 75– 91.

2777 Nevins, Allan. *Henry White: Thirty Years of American Diplomacy.* New York: Harper, 1930.

2778 Nicolson, Harold. *Peacemaking, 1919.* New York: Harcourt, Brace, 1939.

2779 Nock, Albert J. *The Myth of a Guilty Nation.* New York: Huebsch, 1922.

2780 Prinz, Friedrich. "The USA and the Foundation of Czechoslovakia." *Central Europe Journal* 20:5 (1972): 171– 85.

2781 Rudin, Harry R. *Armistice, 1918.* New Haven: Yale University Press, 1944.

2782 [Seymour, Charles.] *Letters from the Paris Peace Conference.* Edited by Harold B. Whiteman, Jr. New Haven: Yale University Press, 1965.

2783 Seymour, Charles. "The Paris Education of Woodrow Wilson." *Virginia Quarterly Review* 32 (Fall 1956): 578– 94.

2784 ———. "Woodrow Wilson and Self-Determination in the Tyrol." *Virginia Quarterly Review* 38 (Autumn 1962): 567– 87.

2785 Shotwell, James T. *At the Paris Peace Conference.* New York: Macmillan, 1937.

2786 Smith, Gaddis. "The Alaska Panhandle at the Paris Peace Conference, 1919." *International Journal* [Canada] 17 (Winter 1961– 1962): 25– 29.

2787 Startt, James D. "The Uneasy Partnership: Wilson and the Press at Paris." *Mid-America* 52 (Jan. 1970): 55– 69.

2788 ———. "Wilson's Mission to Paris: The Making of a Decision." *Historian* 30 (Aug. 1968): 599– 616.

2789 Temperley, Harold W. V., ed. *A History of the Peace Conference of Paris*. 6 vols. London: Frowde, Hodder, & Stoughton, 1920– 1924.

2790 Thompson, Charles T. *The Peace Conference Day by Day*. New York: Brentano's, 1920.

2791 Thompson, John M. *Russia, Bolshevism and the Versailles Peace*. Princeton: Princeton University Press, 1966.

2792 Tillman, Seth P. *Anglo-American Relations at the Paris Peace Conference of 1919*. Princeton: Princeton University Press, 1961.

2793 Willis, Edward F. "Herbert Hoover and the Blockade of Germany, 1918– 1919." In *Studies in Modern European History in Honor of Franklin Charles Palm*, edited by Frederick J. Cox et al. New York: Bookman Associates, 1956.

2794 Yates, Louis A. R. *The United States and French Security, 1917– 1921: A Study in American Diplomatic History*. New York: Twayne, 1957.

2795 Zivojinović, Dragan R. *America, Italy, and the Birth of Yugoslavia (1917– 1919)*. New York: Columbia University Press, 1973.

2796 ———. "The Vatican, Woodrow Wilson, and the Dissolution of the Hapsburg Monarchy, 1914– 1918." *East European Quarterly* 3 (Mar. 1969): 31– 70.

C/The League of Nations

2797 Ambrosius, Lloyd E. "Wilson's League of Nations." *Maryland Historical Magazine* 65 (Winter 1970): 369– 93.

2798 Bartlett, Ruhl. *The League to Enforce Peace*. Chapel Hill: University of North Carolina Press, 1944.

2799 Boothe, Leon E. "Anglo-American Pro-League Groups Lead Wilson 1915– 1918." *Mid-America* 51 (Apr. 1969): 92– 107.

2800 ———. "Lord Grey, the United States, and the Political Effort for a League of Nations, 1914– 1920." *Maryland Historical Magazine* 65 (Spring 1970): 36– 54.

2801 Dubin, Martin D. "Elihu Root and the Advocacy of a League of Nations, 1914– 1917." *Western Political Quarterly* 19 (Sept. 1966): 439– 55.

2802 Fleming, Denna F. *The United States and the League of Nations 1918– 1920*. New York: Putnam's, 1932.

2803 Grubbs, Frank L., Jr. "Organized Labor and the League to Enforce Peace." *Labor History* 14 (Spring 1973): 247–58.

2804 Helbich, Wolfgang J. "American Liberals in the League of Nations Controversy." *Public Opinion Quarterly* 31 (Winter 1967–1968): 568–96.

2805 Kuehl, Warren F. *Seeking World Order: The United States and World Organization to 1920.* Nashville: Vanderbilt University Press, 1969.

2806 Miller, David Hunter. *The Drafting of the Covenant.* 2 vols. New York: Putnam's, 1928.

2807 Schwabe, Klaus. "Woodrow Wilson and Germany's Membership in the League of Nations, 1918–1919." *Central European History* 8 (Mar. 1975): 3–22.

2808 Startt, James D. "Early Press Reaction to Wilson's League Proposal." *Journalism Quarterly* 39 (Summer 1962): 301–08.

2809 Wimer, Kurt. "Woodrow Wilson's Plan to Enter the League of Nations through an Executive Agreement." *Western Political Quarterly* 11 (Dec. 1958): 800–812.

D/U.S. Rejection of the Treaty of Versailles

2810 Bailey, Thomas A. *Woodrow Wilson and the Great Betrayal.* Chicago: Quadrangle Books, 1963.

2811 Duff, John B. "German-Americans and the Peace, 1918–1920." *American Jewish Historical Quarterly* 59 (June 1970): 424–44.

2812 ———. "The Versailles Treaty and the Irish-Americans." *Journal of American History* 55 (Dec. 1968): 582–98.

2813 Evans, Lawrence. *The United States and the Partition of Turkey, 1914–1924.* Baltimore: Johns Hopkins Press, 1965.

2814 Flannagan, John H., Jr. "The Disillusionment of a Progressive: U.S. Senator David I. Walsh and the League of Nations Issue, 1918–1920." *New England Quarterly* 41 (Dec. 1968): 483–504.

2815 Garraty, John A. *Henry Cabot Lodge: A Biography.* New York: Knopf, 1953.

2816 Grantham, Dewey W., Jr. "The Southern Senators and the League of Nations." *North Carolina Historical Review* 26 (Jan. 1949): 187–205.

2817 Hewes, James E., Jr. "Henry Cabot Lodge and the League of Nations." *Proceedings of the American Philosophical Society* 114 (Aug. 1970): 245–55.

2818 Holt, W. Stull. *Treaties Defeated by the Senate: A Study of the Struggle between President and the Senate Over the Conduct of Foreign Relations.* Baltimore: Johns Hopkins Press, 1933.

2819 Lancaster, James L. "The Protestant Churches and the Fight for Ratification of the Versailles Treaty." *Public Opinion Quarterly* 31 (Winter 1967– 1968): 597– 619.

2820 Lodge, Henry Cabot. *The Senate and the League of Nations.* New York: Scribner's, 1925.

2821 Lower, Richard C. "Hiram Johnson: The Making of an Irreconcilable." *Pacific Historical Review* 41 (Nov. 1972): 505– 26.

2822 Maxwell, Kenneth R. "Irish-Americans and the Fight for Treaty Ratification." *Public Opinion Quarterly* 31 (Winter 1967– 1968): 620– 41.

2823 Meaney, N. K. "The British Empire in the American Rejection of the Treaty of Versailles." *Australian Journal of Politics and History* 9 (Nov. 1963): 213– 34.

2824 Mervin, David. "Henry Cabot Lodge and the League of Nations." *Journal of American Studies* 4 (Feb. 1971): 201– 14.

2825 Murray, Robert K. "How Harding Saved the Versailles Treaty." *American Heritage* 20 (Dec. 1968): 66– 67, 111.

2826 Perkins, Dexter. "Woodrow Wilson's Tour." In *America in Crisis: Fourteen Crucial Episodes in American History,* edited by Daniel Aaron. New York: Knopf, 1952.

2827 Smith, Daniel M. "Lansing and the Wilson Interregnum, 1919– 1920." *Historian* 21 (Feb. 1959): 135– 61.

2828 Stern, Sheldon M. "American Nationalism vs. The League of Nations: The Correspondence of Albert J. Beveridge and Louis A. Coolidge, 1918– 1920." *Indiana Magazine of History* 72 (June 1976): 138– 58.

2829 Stone, Ralph A. *The Irreconcilables: The Fight against the League of Nations.* Lexington: University Press of Kentucky, 1970.

2830 ——. "The Irreconcilables' Alternatives to the League of Nations." *Mid-America* 49 (July 1967): 163– 73.

2831 ——. "Two Illinois Senators among the Irreconcilables." *Mississippi Valley Historical Review* 50 (Dec. 1963): 443– 63.

2832 ——, ed. *Wilson and the League of Nations: Why America's Rejection?* New York: Holt, Rinehart & Winston, 1967.

2833   Vinson, J. Chalmers. *Referendum for Isolation: The Defeat of Article Ten of the League of Nations Covenant.* Athens: University of Georgia Press, 1961.

2834   Wimer, Kurt. "Senator Hitchcock and the League of Nations." *Nebraska History* 44 (Sept. 1963): 189– 204.

IX/Survivals and Precedents

A/General Effects of the War on America

2835 Allen, Frederick L. *Only Yesterday: An Informal History of the 1920's.* New York: Harper, 1931.

2836 Link, Arthur S. "What Happened to the Progressive Movement in the 1920's?" *American Historical Review* 64 (July 1959): 833–51.

B/Demobilization

2837 Crowell, Benedict, and Robert F. Wilson. *Demobilization: Our Industrial and Military Demobilization after the Armistice, 1918–1920.* New Haven: Yale University Press, 1921.

2838 Howenstine, E. Jay, Jr. "Lessons of World War I." *Annals of the American Academy of Political and Social Science* 238 (Mar. 1945): 180–87. [Demobilization of veterans.]

2839 Mock, James R., and Evangeline Thurber. *Report on Demobilization.* Norman: University of Oklahoma Press, 1944.

2840 Paxson, Frederic L. "The Great Demobilization." *American Historical Review* 44 (Jan. 1939): 237–51.

2841 Shaw, Albert. "The Demobilization of Labor in War Industries and in Military Service." *Proceedings of the Academy of Political Science* 8:2 (1920): 127–34.

2842 Small, James L., comp. *Home—and Then What? The Mind of the Doughboy Himself.* New York: Doran, 1920.

2843 Woll, Matthew. "American Labor Readjustment Proposals." *Proceedings of the Academy of Political Science* 8:2 (1920): 47–58.

C/Veterans

General

2844 Dillingham, William P. *Federal Aid to Veterans, 1917–1941.* Gainsville: University of Florida Press, 1952.

2845 Hersey, Harold B. *When the Boys Come Home.* New York: Britton, 1919.

2846 James, Marquis. *A History of the American Legion.* New York: William Green, 1923.

2847 Mayo, Katherine. *Soldiers What Next!* Boston: Houghton Mifflin, 1934.

2848 Reid, Bill G. "Franklin K. Lane's Idea for Veterans' Colonization 1918–1921." *Pacific Historical Review* 33 (Nov. 1964): 447–61.

2849 ———. "Proposals for Soldier Settlement during World War I." *Mid-America* 46 (July 1964): 172–86.

2850 Ward, Stephen R., ed. *The War Generation: Veterans of the First World War.* Port Washington, New York: Kennikat, 1975.

2851 Weber, Gustavus A., and Laurence F. Schmeckebier. *The Veterans Administration: Its History Activities, and Organization.* Washington, D.C.: Brookings Institution, 1934.

2852 Wector, Dixon. *When Johnny Comes Marching Home.* Boston: Houghton Mifflin, 1944.

Rehabilitation

2853 Brackett, Elliott G. "Rehabilitation of Diseased and Injured Soldiers Due to the War." *American Journal of Public Health* 8 (Jan. 1918): 11–13.

2854 Clement, Rufus E. "Problems of Demobilization and Rehabilitation of the Negro Soldier after World Wars I and II." *Journal of Negro Education* 12 (Summer 1943): 533–42.

2855 Devine, Edward T., and Lilian Brandt. *Disabled Soldiers and Sailors Pensions and Training.* New York: Oxford University Press, 1919.

2856 Harris, Garrard. *The Redemption of the Disabled: A Study of Programmes of Rehabilitation of the Disabled.* New York: Appleton, 1919.

2857 Keough, Frederic W. "The Employment of Disabled Service Men." *The Annals* 80 (Nov. 1918): 84–94.

2858 Lakeman, Curtis E. "The After-Care of Our Disabled Soldiers and Sailors." *The Annals* 79 (Sept. 1918): 114–29.

2859 Leigh, Robert D. *Federal Health Administration.* New York: Harper, 1927.

2860 McMurtrie, Douglas C. *The Disabled Soldier.* New York: Macmillan, 1919.

2861 Prosser, Charles A. "A Federal Program for the Vocational Rehabilitation of Disabled Soldiers and Sailors." *The Annals* 80 (Nov. 1918): 117–22.

2862 U.S. Congress. Senate. Committee on Education and Labor. *Hearings . . . Vocational Rehabilitation of Disabled Soldiers and Sailors . . .* (on S.4284 and H.R. 11367 . . . Apr. 30, May 1, May 2, 1918). 65th Cong., 2d Sess., 1918.

2863 U.S. Federal Board for Vocational Education. *Vocational Rehabilitation of Disabled Soldiers and Sailors: A Preliminary Study.* (Feb. 1918). Washington, D.C.: G.P.O., 1918.

D/Reconstruction

2864 Lippincott, Isaac. *Problems of Reconstruction.* New York: Macmillan, 1919.

2865 Simons, Algie M. *The Vision for Which We Fought: A Study in Reconstruction.* New York: Macmillan, 1919.

2866 Wildman, Edwin, ed. *Reconstructing America: Our Next Big Job.* Boston: Page, 1919.

E/The Red Scare

2867 Coben, Stanley. *A. Mitchell Palmer: Politician.* New York: Columbia University Press, 1963.

2868 ———. "A Study in Nativism: The American Red Scare of 1919–1920." *Political Science Quarterly* 79 (Mar. 1964): 52–75.

2869 Cook, Philip L. "Red Scare in Denver." *Colorado Magazine* 43 (Fall 1966): 309–26.

2870 Damon, Allan L. "The Great Red Scare." *American Heritage* 19 (Feb. 1968): 22–27, 75–77.

2871 Jaffe, Julian F. *Crusade against Radicalism: New York during the Red Scare, 1914–1924.* Port Washington, New York: Kennikat, 1972.

2872 Murray, Robert K. *Red Scare: A Study in National Hysteria, 1919–1920.* Minneapolis: University of Minnesota Press, 1955.

2873 Muzik, Edward J. "Victor L. Berger: Congress and the Red Scare." *Wisconsin Magazine of History* 47 (Summer 1964): 309–18.

2874 Vadney, Thomas E. "The Politics of Repression: A Case Study of the Red Scare in New York." *New York History* 49 (Jan. 1968): 56– 75.

F/Economic Consequences: Theory and Practice

2875 Abrahams, Paul P. "American Bankers and the Economic Tactics of Peace: 1919." *Journal of American History* 56 (Dec. 1969): 572– 83.

2876 Anderson, Benjamin M., Jr. *Effects of the War on Money, Credit and Banking in France and the United States*. New York: Oxford University Press, 1919.

2877 Bass, John F., and Harold G. Moulton. *America and the Balance Sheet of Europe*. New York: Ronald Press, 1921.

2878 Blakey, Roy G. "Shifting the War Burden upon the Future." *Annals of the American Academy of Political and Social Science* 75 (Jan. 1918): 90– 104.

2879 Bogart, Ernest L. *Direct and Indirect Costs of the Great World War*. New York: Oxford University Press, 1919.

2880 Clark, John M. *The Costs of the World War to the American People*. New Haven: Yale University Press, 1931.

2881 ———. "The War's Aftermath in America." *Current History* 34 (May 1931): 169– 74.

2882 Dyson, Lowell K. "Was Agricultural Distress in the 1930's a Result of Land Speculating during World War I?: The Case of Iowa." *Annals of Iowa*, 3d ser. 40 (Spring 1971): 577– 84.

2883 Fisher, Irving. "Some Contributions of the War to Our Knowledge of Money and Prices." *American Economic Review* 8 (Mar. 1918), supplement: 257– 58.

2884 Hardy, Charles O. "Adjustments and Maladjustments in the United States after the First World War." *American Economic Review* 32 (Mar. 1942): 24– 30.

2885 Hogan, Michael J. "The United States and the Problem of International Economic Control: American Attitudes toward European Reconstruction, 1918– 1920." *Pacific Historical Review* 44 (Feb. 1975): 84– 103.

2886 Howe, Frederic C. *The Only Possible Peace*. New York: Scribner's, 1919.

2887 Hoyt, Homer. "Standardization and Its Relation to Industrial Concentration." *The Annals* 82 (Mar. 1919): 271– 77.

2888 Ingalls, Walter R. *Wealth and Income of the American People: A Survey of the Economic Consequences of the War.* York, Pennsylvania: G. H. Merlin, 1922.

2889 Janeway, Eliot. "Mobilizing the Economy: Old Errors in a New Crisis." *Yale Review* 40 (Winter 1951): 201–14.

2890 Kaufman, Burton I. "United States Trade and Latin America: The Wilson Years." *Journal of American History* 58 (Sept. 1971): 342–63.

2891 ———. "Wilson's 'War Bureaucracy' and Foreign Trade Expansion, 1917–1921." *Prologue* 6 (Spring 1974): 19–31.

2892 Keynes, John M. *The Economic Consequences of the Peace.* New York: Harcourt, Brace & Howe, 1920.

2893 Marcosson, Isaac F. *The War after the War.* New York: Lane, 1917.

2894 National Bureau of Economic Research. *Income in the United States: Its Amount and Distribution, 1909–1919.* 2 vols. New York: Harcourt, Brace, 1921–1922.

2895 National Industrial Conference Board. *Problems of Industrial Readjustment in the United States.* Boston: National Industrial Conference Board, 1919.

2896 Nelson, Daniel. " 'A Newly Appreciated Art': The Development of Personnel Work at Leeds and Northrup, 1915–1923." *Business History Review* 44 (Winter 1970): 520–35.

2897 Powell, G. Harold. "Regulation of the Perishable Food Industries after the War." *The Annals* 82 (Mar. 1919): 183–88.

2898 Rhodes, Benjamin D. "Reassessing 'Uncle Shylock': The United States and the French War Debt, 1917–1929." *Journal of American History* 55 (Mar. 1969): 787–803.

2899 Ruml, Beardsley. "The Extension of Selective Tests to Industry." *The Annals* 81 (Jan. 1919): 38–46.

2900 Shideler, James H. *Farm Crisis, 1919–1923.* Berkeley: University of California Press, 1957.

2901 Smith, Alexander W. "A Suggested Plan for Permanent Governmental Supervision of Railroad Operation after the War." *Annals of the American Academy of Political and Social Science* 76 (Mar. 1918): 142–56.

2902 Vanderlip, Frank A. *What Happened to Europe?* New York: Macmillan, 1920.

2903   Warburg, Paul M. "Same Phases of Financial Reconstruction." *The Annals* 82 (Mar. 1919): 347– 73.

G/Disillusion and Isolationism

2904   Adler, Selig. "The War Guilt Question and American Disillusionment, 1918– 1928." *Journal of Modern History* 23 (Mar. 1951): 1– 28.

2905   Beard, Charles A. *The Devil Theory of War: An Inquiry into the Nature of History and the Possibility of Keeping Out of War.* New York: Vanguard Press, 1936.

2906   Borchard, Edwin, and William P. Lage. *Neutrality for the United States.* New Haven: Yale University Press, 1937.

2907   Cole, Wayne S. *Senator Gerald P. Nye and American Foreign Relations.* Minneapolis: University of Minnesota Press, 1962.

2908   DeWitt, Howard A. "Hiram Johnson and World War I: A Progressive in Transition." *Southern California Quarterly* 61 (Fall 1974): 295– 305.

2909   Hammett, Hugh B. "Reviewing the Revisionists: America's Entry into World War I." *International Review of History and Political Science* 9 (May 1972): 79– 102.

2910   Turner, John K. *Shall It Be Again?* New York: Huebsch, 1922.

2911   Wiltz, John E. *In Search of Peace: The Senate Munitions Inquiry, 1934– 1936.* Baton Rouge: Louisiana State University Press, 1963.

H/Precedents for the Hoover and Roosevelt Administrations

2912   Howenstine, E. Jay, Jr. "The Industrial Board, Precursor of the N.R.A.: The Price-Reduction Movement after World War I." *Journal of Political Economy* 51 (June 1943): 235– 50.

2913   Leuchtenburg, William E. "The New Deal and the Analogue of War." In *Change and Continuity in Twentieth Century America*, edited by John Braeman, Robert H. Bremner, and Everett Walters. Columbus: Ohio State University Press, 1964.

2914   Nash, Gerald D. "Experiments in Industrial Mobilization: WIB and NRA." *Mid-America* 45 (July 1963): 157– 74.

2915   ———. "Franklin Roosevelt and Labor: The World War I Origins of Early New Deal Policy." *Labor History* 1 (Winter 1960): 39– 52.

2916   ———. "Herbert Hoover and the Origins of the Reconstruction Finance Corporation." *Mississippi Valley Historical Review* 46 (Dec. 1959): 455– 68.

Author Index

Abbey, Edwin A., 964
Abbot, Willis J., 68, 553
Abrahams, Paul P., 2875
Abrams, Ray H., 2454
Acker, John, 1096
Ackerman, Carl W., 697
Ackerman, J. H., 2593
Adams, Briggs K., 965
Adams, Ephraim D., 33
Adams, Donald B., 1153
Adams, George P., Jr., 1980
Adams, James G., 1103
Adams, John W., 1532, 1891
Adams, Samuel H., 2510
Adams, T. S., 1950
Addams, Jane, 2163, 2164
Addison, James T., 1329
Additon, Henrietta S., 2412
Adler, J. O., 1406
Adler, Selig, 153, 2719, 2904
Agard, Walter R., 775
Agnew, James B., 1267
Akers, Herbert H., 1692
Alabama. State Council of Defense, 1711
Albany County (New York). Home Defense
    Committee, 753
Albertine, Connell, 1359
Albertini, Luigi, 52
Albrecht-Carrié, René, 39
Alden, Carroll S., 564
Alden, John D., 565, 566
Aldrich, Mildred, 317
Aldridge, John W., 2493
Alexander, Robert, 1409
Alger, George W., 731

Allard, Dean C., 304, 665
Allen, Edward F., 2413
Allen, Frank H., 2078
Allen, Frederick L., 727, 2700, 2835
Allen, Henry T., 713
Allen, Hervey, 318, 2511
Allen, Howard W., 154
Almond, Nina, 1
Altekruse, G. H., 1464
Altschul, Charles, 2090
Ambrosius, Lloyd E., 2743, 2744, 2797
Ambulance Field Service, 1054
American Battle Monuments Commission,
    260, 1340, 1343, 1347, 1350, 1353,
    1355, 1365, 1369, 1374, 1377, 1379,
    1383, 1388, 1394, 1396, 1399, 1405,
    1410, 1413, 1417, 1419, 1420, 1423,
    1430, 1432, 1435, 1436, 1438.
American Economic Association. Committee
    on War Finance, 1951
American Legion. Auxiliary. Indiana., 2359
American Library Association, 804
Amerine, William H., 1522
Ames, Joseph S., 2665
Amherst College (Amherst, Massachusetts),
    2594
Anderson, Benjamin M., Jr., 1981, 2876
Anderson, Claude H., 1709
Anderson, Frank F., 1952
Anderson, George J., 2414
Anderson, George L., 162
Anderson, Isabel W., 1008
Anderson, J. W., 1229
Anderson, Maxwell, 2512
Andreano, Ralph L., 2049

201

Andrews, Avery D., 296
Andrews, James H., 1185
Andrews, John B., 2701
Andrews, Mary R. S., 2513, 2514
Angell, James R., 2666
Anson, Eldred, 1555
Antrim, Ray P., 263
Appel, H. M., 1264
Appel, Livia, 1770
Appleton, Everard J., 2554
Archibald, Norman, 320
Arizona. State Council of Defense, 1713
Arkansas. State Council of Defense, 1714
Arnold, Henry H., 321
Ashburn, Thomas Q., 1308
Ashe, Elizabeth H., 1009
Ashton, John L., 1137
Asprey, Robert B., 511
Atkinson, Minnie, 1766
Auburn (New York). Mayor's Defense Committee, 1790
Auerbach, Jerold S., 2134, 2160
Austin, Mary, 2360
Aveilhe, Art, 2494
Aydelotte, Frank W., 2595
Ayres, Harrol B., 2415
Ayres, Leonard P., 1079, 1842

Babcock, Conrad S., 512
Bach, Christian A., 1349
Bachman, Walter J., 1215
Bachman, William E., 1299
Bacon, William J., 1219
Bailey, Pearce, 835
Bailey, Temple, 2515
Bailey, Thomas A., 190, 191, 192, 193, 194, 2745, 2810
Bailey, Vernon H., 2489
Bainbridge, William S., 836
Baines, May, 1827
Baker, Charles W., 1900
Baker, George W., 155
Baker, Horace L., 431, 1507
Baker, Leslie S., 1606
Baker, Newton D., 2091, 2416
Baker, Ray S., 96, 2746
Bakewell, Charles M., 1010
Balch, Emily G., 2164
Baldridge, Cyrus L., 2555
Baldridge, Harry A., 305
Baldwin, Fred G., 728, 2417
Baldwin, Hanson W., 40

Baldwin, Marian, 1011
Bancroft, W. D., 837
Bane, Suda L., 567
Bankhage, Hilman R., 2555
Banks, Arthur, 36
Barany, George, 2747
Barbeau, Arthur E., 2339
Barclay, Harold, 838
Barkley, John L., 322
Barnes, Harry Elmer, 53
Barnett, B. J., 513
Barretto, Larry, 2516
Barry, Edward W., 1310
Barth, Clarence G., 1641
Bartimeus [Pseud.] (Ricci, Lewis A. da C.) 568
Bartlett, Ruhl, 2798
Bartley, Joseph C., 1982
Baruch, Bernard M., 1875, 1876, 2748
Bass, Herbert J., 139
Bass, John F., 2877
Basset, Michael, 2270
Battey, George M., Jr., 569
Bauer, William E., 754
Bauer, William T., 1114
Baxter, John S., 272
Bayliss, Gwyn, 2
Beal, Howard W., 839
Beard, Charles A., 2905
Beaver, Daniel R., 3, 85, 1904, 1927, 1927a
Bedford, Massachusetts, 1763
Beer, William, 1753
Belknap, Reginald R., 570
Bell, Herbert C. F., 97
Bell, Sidney, 156
Bellamy, David, 432
Bendiner, Marvin R., 1843
Benson, Albert E., 2596
Benson, Samuel C., 323
Benton, Elbert J., 1813
Benwell, Harry A., 1358
Berglund, Abraham, 1983
Berlin, Ira, 324
Bernet, Milton E., 1630
Bernhardt, Joshua, 2050, 2051, 2243
Bernheim, Bertram M., 325
Bernstorff, Johann A. H. A. graf von, 142
Beston, Henry B., pseud. See Sheahan, Henry B.
Bickelhaupt, W. G., 2039
Biddle, Charles J., 1669

Billington, Monroe, 195
Binder, Raymond S., 1297
Bindler, Norman, 2271
Bing, Alexander, 2224
Bingham, Hiram, 326
Binkley, R. C., 2749
Binns, Archie, 2517
Binswanger, Alvin O., 1323
Birdsall, Paul, 196, 2750, 2751
Birdzell, Luther E., 2597
Birnbaum, Karl E., 197
Bispham, William N., 840
Blackburn, Forrest R., 666
Blackford, Charles M., 327
Blackman, John L., Jr., 2244
Blair, Emily N., 2361
Blakey, George T., 2658
Blakey, Gladys C., 1954
Blakey, Roy G., 1953, 1954, 2878
Bland, R. L., 2072
Blankenhorn, Heber, 961
Blatch, Harriot S., 2362
Blatt, Heiman K., 1737
Bliss, Paul S., 1627
Blodgett, Richard A., 1651
Bloom, Lansing B., 1788
Blum, John M., 95, 98, 2196
Blumenthal, Henry, 2302
Bodfish, Robert W., 1055
Bogart, Ernest L., 1844, 1955, 2879
Bogert, George D., 1339
Bolton, Frederick E., 2598
Bonadio, Felice A., 198
Boothe, Leon E., 2799, 2800
Borchard, Edwin, 199, 2906
Boston College (Boston, Massachusetts), 2599
Boston High School of Commerce (Boston, Massachusetts), 2600
Boughton, Van Tuyl, 1156
Bourne, Randolph S., 2637, 2638
Bowen, A. S., 841
Bowen, Mrs. Joseph T., 2363
Bowerman, George F., 2495
Boyd, Thomas A., 2518
Brackett, Elliott G., 842, 2853
Bradden, William S., 1592
Bradford, J. S., 1185
Bradley, Amy O., 1012, 1056
Bradley, H. C., 837
Bradley, John, 681
Braeman, John, 2135, 2913

Braley, Berton, 2556
Brandt, Lilian, 2855
Brantner, Cecil F., 1575
Brazier, Richard, 2272
Breckel, H. F., 571
Breckinridge, Henry, 732
Breen, William J., 1807, 1905
Bremner, Robert H., 2913
Brewster, D. L. S., 514
Briand, Paul L., Jr., 621
Bridges, Lamar W., 200
Brissenden, Paul F., 2273
Brock, Peter, 2165
Brommel, Bernard J., 2166
Brooks, Alden, 966, 967
Brooks, Edward H., 253
Brooks, Leon D., 2557, 2558
Brophy, Leo P., 903
Broun, Heywood, 482, 483
Brown, Charles R., 604
Brown, Earl S., 1742
Brown, Herbert C., 1176
Brown, Lee D., 533
Brown, Mabel W., 4
Brown, Sevellon, 905
Brown, William, 1440
Brunet, Meade, 1178
Bruno, Henry A., 968
Bruntz, George G., 962
Bryan, Julien H., 1057
Bryson, Thomas A., 2752
Buchanan, A. Russell, 201
Buck, Beaumont B., 328
Buck, Philo M., Jr., 2167
Buck, Solon J., 1770
Bucklew, Leslie L., 1266
Buckley, Harold, 1652
Buehrig, Edward H., 140, 178, 179
Buell, Charles T., 484
Buffington, Joseph, 2092
Bullard, Robert L., 311, 329, 485
Bullitt, William C., 100
Bundy, McGeorge, 127
Bundy, Omar, 1341
Buranelli, Prosper, 572
Burdick, Charles B., 202
Burdick, Joel W., 330
Burgess, George K., 906
Burnett, Philip M., 2753
Burrage, Thomas J., 843
Burton, Allan, 1150
Burton, Harold H., 1586

Buswell, Leslie, 1058
Butler, Alban B., Jr., 1336, 2490
Butters, Henry A., 969
Butts, Edmund L., 1452
Byington, Margaret F., 2397

Cabell, Julian M., 1118
Cadwallader, William, 1517
Cain, J. M., 1415
California. Adjutant General's Office, 755
California. State Board of Education, 2601
Call, Arthur D., 2093
Cameron, John S., 718
Camfield, Thomas M., 2667, 2668
Camp, Charles W., 1289
Camp, Frank B., 2559, 2560
Campbell, Gus W., 2561
Campbell, Peyton R., 433
Campbell, William E. M., 2519
Canright, Eldon J., 1276
Cantor, Milton, 2274
Capen, Samuel P., 2602
Carney, Robert B., 573
Carter, Robert L., 1393
Carter, Russell G., 1239
Carter, W. S., 2245
Carter, William A., 331
Carver, Leland M., 1647
Carver, Thomas N., 1901, 1956
Casari, Robert B., 5
Casey, Robert J., 1265
Cather, Willa S., 2520
Catlin, Albertus W., 515
Caygill, Harry W., 1448, 2136
Chafee, Zechariah, Jr., 2137
Chaffee, Everitte St. J., 1248
Chamberlain, W. P., 845
Chambers, John W., 756
Chambrum, Jacques A. de P., Comte de, 995
Chandler, Walter, 1218
Chapin, Harold, 970
Chapin, William A. R., 971
Chapman, Victor, 1670
Chaskel, Walter, 1085
Chastaine, Ben H., 1395, 1446
Chatfield, Charles, 2168, 2169
Chatterton, Edward K., 574
Cheseldine, Raymond M., 1521
Chicago, University of. Graduate School of
  Business, 878
Child, Clifton J., 203, 2197
Childs, Richard S., 2436

Christian, Royal A., 332
Christian, W. E., 2562
Christman, Franklin W., 1794
Chubb, Robert W., 1315
Church, James R., 846
Churchill, Allen, 1696
Churchill, Marlborough, 944
Churchill, Mary, 434
Churchill, Winston L. S., 41, 333, 667
Cianflone, Frank A., 907
Clapp, Edwin J., 204
Clapp, Frederick M., 1640
Clark, B. A., 2364
Clark, Coleman T., 435
Clark, Eugene F., 2603
Clark, Glenn W., 1060
Clark, John M., 1845, 2076, 2880, 2881
Clark, Kenneth B., 2303
Clark, Salter S., Jr., 435
Clark, Walter, Jr., 1808
Clark, William B., 641
Clarke, George H., 2563
Clarke, Ida C., 2365
Clarke, Walter, 2418
Clarke, William F., 1367
Clarkson, Grosvenor B., 1906
Claudy, Carl H., 879
Clay, H. K., 1274
Clemenceau, Georges, 2754
Clement, Don L., 1175
Clement, Rufus E., 2340, 2854
Cleveland (Ohio). Mayor's Advisory War
  Committee, 1814
Clifford, Edmund L., 1822
Clifford, John G., 733, 734
Clover, Greayer, 334
Clymer, George, 1106
Cobb, Frank I., 2480
Cobb, Humphrey, 2521
Cobb, Irvin S., 335
Coben, Stanley, 2867, 2868
Cochrane, I. L., 1411
Cochrane, Raymond C., 904
Codman, Charles R., 336
Coffin, Howard E., 1892
Coffin, Louis, 1272
Coffman, Edward M., 257, 290, 297, 649,
  650, 651
Cohen, Harry, 1789
Cohen, I. Bernard, 2669
Cohen, Michaele, 2366
Cohen, Warren I., 133, 141

Coit, Margaret L., 1877
Colby, Elbridge, 516, 821, 1360
Cole, Ralph D., 1397
Cole, Robert B., 1458
Cole, Wayne S., 2907
Colean, Miles L., 2437
Coletta, Paola E., 143
Collins, Francis A., 1142
Collins, Louis L., 1284
Colonna, Benjamin A., 1545
Columbia County, New York. Home Defense Committee, 1792
Colyer, Charles M., 1305
Comandini, Adele, 463
Combs, Josiah H., 1117
Commission Internationale pour l'Enseignement de l'Histoire, 6
Committee on the War and the Religious Outlook, 2455
Commons, John R., 2246
Compton, K. T., 2670
Cone, Anthony D., 1235
Connecticut. State Council of Defense, 1716
Conner, Virginia, 337
Connolly, James B., 575
Connor, James R., 2496
Connor, Valerie J., 2247
Considine, Agnes T., 1214
Constable, T. J., 315
Conway, Coleman B., 1501
Conway, Jill, 2170
Coogan, John W., 179a
Cook, Blanche W., 2171
Cook, George C., 338
Cook, Philip L., 2869
Cooke, Jay, 2052
Coolidge, Hamilton, 1649
Cooling, Benjamin F., 1927a, 1929a
Cooper, Alice E., 1115
Cooper, E. H., 1362
Cooper, George W., 1491
Cooper, John M., Jr., 54, 157, 205
Cooperman, Stanley, 2497
Cope, Harley F., 576
Coplin, W. M. L., 1116
Cornell, Corwin S., 847
Cornell University, 2604
Corning, Walter D., 339, 1510
Cortelyou, K. M. Escott, 1231
Corwin, Edward S., 2113
Costello, C. A., 2702
Costrell, Edwin, 1755

Cottman, George S., 1740
Coulter, C. S., 945
Coupal, James F., 844
Cowie, J. S., 577
Cowing, Kemper F., 436
Cowley, Malcolm, 2498, 2499
Cox, Frederick J., 2793
Cox, Ora E., 1736
Coyle, Edward R., 1061
Craighill, Edley, 340
Cram, Ralph W., 1747
Cramer, Clarence H., 86
Crane, A. G., 848
Crawford, Charles, 1333
Crawford, Gilbert H., 1200
Creel, George, 2085, 2094, 2095, 2096
Crennan, C. H., 2009
Crighton, John C., 206, 1777
Crissey, Forrest, 1883
Critoph, Gerald E., 2500
Croly, Herbert, 716
Cronon, E. David, 128, 2304
Crosby, Alfred W., Jr. 2703
Crosby, Wilson G., 1646
Crosley, Harry G., 437
Cross, Arthur L., 2605
Crowder, Enoch H., 757
Crowe, James R., 438
Crowell, Benedict, 880, 1846, 1928, 2837
Crowell, John F., 1933
Crowell, Thomas I., Jr., 1300
Crozier, Emmet, 2481
Crozier, William, 908
Crum, Earl L., 1626
Crump, Irving, 777
Cuddy, Edward, 2198
Cuff, Robert D., 1847, 1848, 1878, 1886, 1890, 1907, 1908, 1909, 1934, 1937, 1938, 1984
Culbertson, William S., 2003
cummings, e. e., 341
Cummins, Cedric C., 1735
Cunningham, William J., 2010, 2011, 2012
Currey, Josiah S., 1727
Curry, George, 2755
Curry, Roy W., 158
Curti, Merle, 144, 2172, 2639
Curtiss, Elmer H., 342
Curtis, Theodore J., 1694
Cushing, Harvey W., 849
Cushing, John T., 1830
Cushing, Joseph R., 2564

Cutchins, John A., 343, 1375
Cutler, Frederick M., 1132
Cywar, Alan, 2640, 2641

Daley, Edith, 1715
Damon, Allan L., 2870
Danforth, Florence W., 1757
Daniels, Jonathan, 1267
Daniels, Josephus, 69, 128, 264, 554
Darnall, J. R., 850
Daughters of the American Revolution. North Carolina. Craighead-Dunlap Chapter, Wadesboro, 1809
Daum, Arnold R., 2049
Davenport, G. H., 851
Davies, A. H., 1165
Davies, Joseph E., 1985
Davis, Allen F., 2398
Davis, Arthur K., 439, 758, 1497, 1831, 1832
Davis, Chester W., 1622
Davis, Delbert M., 1089
Davis, Forrest, 159
Davis, G. Cullom, 1939
Davis, Gerald H., 207, 208
Davis, J. P., 2341
Davis, Paul M., 1274
Davis, Robert M., 1179
Davison, Henry P., 1013
Dawes, Charles G., 344, 881
Day, Clifford L., 1227
Day, Kirkland, 2491
Dean, Arthur D., 2606
Dearing, Vinton A., 440
De Castlebled, Maurice, 486
Deckard, Percy E., 1593
Decker, Joe F., 759
Degen, Mary L., 2173
DeLong, Thomas F., 1095
Dennis, Roger L., 1957
Depew, Albert N., 972
Derby, Richard, 852
Dessez, Eunice C., 2367
Dethlefs, Louis C., 1599
DeVarila, Osborne, 1223
Devine, Edward T., 2855
Devlin, Patrick, 180
DeVore, Ronald M., 909
DeWeerd, Harvey A., 70, 910, 1849
Dewey, John, 2053, 2642
DeWitt, Howard A., 2199, 2908
Dexter, Mary, 1062
Diamond, William, 160, 1867

Dickinson, John, 760
Dickman, Joseph T., 1346
Dickson, Maxcy R., 2054, 2097
Dienst, Charles F., 1576
Dignan, Don K., 209
Dillingham, William P., 2844
District of Columbia. Council of Defense, 1718
Dixon, Frank H., 2013, 2014, 2015
Dodd, William E., 91
Dollen, Charles, 6a
Dooly, William G., Jr., 911
Dornbusch, Charles E., 7, 8
Dorr, Rheta C., 345
Dorsett, Lyle W., 2200
Dos Passos, John R., 71, 2522, 2523, 2524
Douglas, Paul H., 2399
Doyle, Henry G., 2153
Drew, Mrs. Sidney, 1671
Drew, Sidney R., 1671
Drury, Horace B., 2248
Duane, James T., 1470
Dubin, Martin D., 2801
Dobofsky, Melvyn, 2249, 2275
Du Bois, W. E. B., 2305, 2306, 2342, 2343
Duff, James L., 1230
Duff, John B., 2811, 2812
Duffy, Francis P., 1518
Dulles, Foster R., 1014
Dunbar, Ruth, 2525
Duncan, Robert C., 912
Duncan-Clark, Samuel J., 265
Dundas, Wendell A., 1621
Dunham, Edward K., 853
Dunn, Samuel O., 2016
Dunphy, Edward P., 1798
Dupree, A. Hunter, 2671
DuPuy, Charles M., 346
Dupuy, Richard Ernest, 210, 698, 1133
Duram, James C., 2174
Durr, Ernest, 761
Dyer, George P., 882
Dyke, Harold D., 1542
Dyson, Lowell K., 2882

Earle, Edward M., 161
Earle, Ralph, 778
Eberlin, Barnard, 1458, 1544
Eddy, Arthur J., 1868
Eddy, George Sherwood, 1015
Edmonds, F. S., 814
Edmonds, Sir James E., 996

Edwards, Evan A., 1515
Edwards, Frederick T., 441
Edwards, H. W., 652
Edwards, Martha L., 2456
Edwards, Richard A., 347
Edwards, Walter A., 622
Egan, Maurice F., 2201
Eilers, Tom D., 1746
Elcock, Charles, 1185
Elder, Bowman, 1139
Eldred, Wilfred, 2055
Eldredge, H. Wentworth, 2202
Ellershaw, Edward, 2565
Ellington, W. B., 1168
Ellinwood, Ralph E., 719
Elliott, Paul B., 422
Ellis, Allan B., 1613
Ellis, Horace, 2607
Ellis, Olin O., 735
Ellul, Jacques, 2079
Ely, Dinsmore, 443
Emmett, Chris, 1582
Emmons, Roger M., 1695
Empey, Arthur G., 348, 779, 2526
Englebrecht, Helmuth C., 1929
Engineers Club of Trenton, 1186
English, George H., Jr., 1428
Epstein, Fritz T., 162
Erskine, Hazel, 211
Esposito, Vincent J., 38
Esslinger, Dean R., 212
Eulau, Heinz, 2643
Evans, Frank E., 444, 581, 919
Evans, James W., 805
Evans, Lawrence, 2813
Evarts, Jeremiah M., 517, 1447

Fahey, Sara H., 2608
Falconer, Martha P., 2419
Falk, Karen, 1837
Falls, Cyril B., 9, 42
Farnam, Ruth, 1016
Farrell, Thomas F., 518, 1148
Farrow, Edward S., 913
Faulkner, William, 2527
Fay, Sidney B., 55
Feigenbaum, Laurence H., 2501
Feiss, Richard A., 2250
Feldman, Gerald D., 1699
Felice, C. P., 605, 606
Fell, Edgar T., 1354
Fels, Daniel M., 1513
Fenton, Charles A., 1063, 2502, 2503

Ferguson, George O., 2307
Ferrell, Henry C., Jr., 1929a
Ferrell, Robert H., 2756
Fesler, James W., 1850
Fickle, James E., 2225
Field, Francis L., 1293
Fifield, Russell H., 163, 2757
Fike, Claude E., 682, 683
Filene, Peter G., 684
Finnegan, John P., 736, 737
Finney, John D., 2308
Finney, Robert T., 781
Fischer, Fritz, 56, 57
Fisher, Dorothy Canfield, 2528, 2529
Fisher, Irving, 1958, 2883
Fiske, Harold C., 1143
Fiske, Proctor M., 1574
Fite, Gilbert C., 2147
Fitzhugh, Robert S., 1084
Flagg, James M., 2098
Flammer, Philip M., 1672, 1673, 1674
Flannagan, John H., Jr., 2814
Fleming, Denna F., 58, 181, 2802
Fleming, Thomas J., 519, 2086
Fleming, Winston, 2672
Fletcher, A. L., 1262
Fletcher, Marvin E., 2344
Flexner, Eleanor, 2368
Florez, C. de, 1064
Floto, Inga, 2758
Floyd, Frank T., 1203
Flynn, R. M., 1534
Foch, Ferdinand, 997
Folk, Richard A., 2276
Folliard, Edward T., 99
Forbes, Jerome R., 1313
Forcey, Charles, 2644
Ford, Bert, 1361
Ford, Joseph H., 854, 863
Ford, Torrey, 445
Foreman, Edward R., 1801
47th Coast Artillery Regiment, 1131
Fosdick, Raymond B., 2413, 2420, 2421, 2422
Foster, A. T., 1647
Foster, H. Schuyler, Jr., 213
Foster, Pell W., 1232
Fowler, W. B., 2731
Fox, Edward L., 782, 783, 784
Frank, Sam H., 623
Frankfurter, Felix, 2251, 2252
Franklin, Vincent P., 2309
Fraser, Bruce, 1716a

Fraser, Edward, 833
Frazer, Elizabeth, 1017
Fredericks, Pierce G., 72, 258
Freidel, Frank B., 93, 266
French, William F., 578
Fretwell, Frank M., 1456
Freud, Sigmund, 100
Frey, Royal D., 624, 625
Freidman, Milton, 1986
Fries, Amos A., 914
Frost, Meigs O., 425
Frothingham, Thomas G., 182, 259, 555, 668
Fry, M. G., 214
Fuess, Claude M., 1762, 2609
Fullbrook, Earl S., 2400
Fuller, Hurley E., 1533
Fuller, Joseph V., 215
Fuller, Ruth W., 349
Fulton, Garland, 915
Furer, Julius A., 916
Furr, Arthur, 1439

Gaffney, Thomas St. J., 2732
Gaines, Ruth L., 1018, 1019, 1020
Galambos, Louis, 1940
Galishoff, Stuart, 2704
Gallagher, Bernard J., 973
Galloway, Blanche, 806
Gambs, John S., 2277
Gansser, Emil B., 1503, 1504
Garey, E. B., 735
Garfield, Harry A., 2040, 2048
Garlid, George W., 2175
Garlock, Glenn R., 1381
Garner, James W., 2116
Garraty, John A., 101, 2815
Garren, William J., 1167
Geisinger, Joseph F., 1119
Gelfand, Lawrence E., 2759
Genet, Edmond C. C., 1675
Genthe, Charles V., 11
George, Albert E., 1362
George, Alexander L., 102
George, Herbert, 1320
George, Juliette L., 102
Gerard, James W., 145, 146
Gerhart, Harry S., 1236
Gerson, Louis L., 2760
Gibbons, Floyd P., 520
Gibbons, Herbert A., 2566
Gibson, Preston, 1066
Gide, Charles, 1700

Giehrl, Hermann Von, 998, 999
Giffin, Frederick C., 2278
Gifford, Walter S., 1893
Gilbert, Charles, 1959
Gilbert, Eugene, 1370
Gilbert, Martin, 37
Gilbert, W. F., 1167
Gildersleeve, V. C., 2369
Gilman, Charlotte P., 2370
Gilmore, William E., 1277
Ginger, Ray, 2279
Girard, Jolyan P., 714
Gleaves, Albert, 807, 883
Glenn, Mary W., 2401
Glidden, William B., 720
Glock, Carl E., 1554
Goddard, Benjamin, 1828
Godfrey, Aaron, A., 2017
Goldberg, A., 607
Goldhurst, Richard, 298
Goldman, Emma, 2280
Goldman, Eric F., 2089, 2371, 2389
Gompers, Samuel, 2226, 2227, 2228, 2229
Gorrell, Edgar S., 608, 626
Gosnell, H. A., 1080
Gow, Kenneth, 446
Gowenlock, Thomas R., 946
Grace, James L., 1134
Graebner, Alan, 2457
Graff, Ellis U., 2607
Graham, Jeanne, 2099
Graham, Milton P., 1088
Graham, Otis L., Jr., 73
Granatstein, J. L., 1908
Grant, Philip A., 2720
Grant, Robert M., 627
Grantham, Dewey W., Jr., 2816
Grattan, C. Hartley, 183, 2645
Graves, William S., 699
Gray, Andrew, 1067
Gray, Edwyn A., 642
Gray, Harold S., 2176
Gray, Howard L., 1902
Grayson, Cary T., 103
Green, Constance M., 917
Greene, Evarts B., 2100
Greene, Francis V., 487
Greene, Fred, 164
Greene, Theodore P., 2761
Greene, Warwick, 447
Greenlaw, Edwin A., 2610
Greenough, Walter S., 1960
Greenwald, Maurine W., 2372

Greer, Thomas H., **941, 942**
Gregory, Ross, **147, 184, 216**
Grenville, John A. S., **132, 165**
Grey, Charles G., **628**
Grider, John M., **350, 448**
Grissinger, Jay W., **855**
Groce, H. Emilie, **2611**
Grof, William S., **1589**
Grubbs, Frank L., Jr., **2253, 2803**
Gruber, Carol S., **2646**
Guerrier, Edith, **2056**
Guest, Edgar A., **2567**
Guichard, Louis, **579**
Guins, George C., **685**
Gulberg, Martin G., **449**
Gulick, Luther H., **2423**
Gurney, Gene, **629**
Gutfeld, Arnon, **2138**
Guttersen, Granville, **450**

Haber, Samuel, **1869**
Hachey, Thomas E., **2203**
Hagedorn, Hermann, **738, 739, 1879**
Hagood, Johnson, **884**
Haight, Walter L., **1841**
Hale, Frederick A., **59**
Hale, George E., **2673, 2674**
Hale, Louise C., **839**
Hale, Richard W., **447**
Haley, P. Edward, **166**
Hall, Bert, **351, 1676**
Hall, Clifford J., **1823**
Hall, Henry N., **1349**
Hall, James N., **974, 1677, 2539**
Hall, Norman S., **288**
Hall, Tom G., **2057**
Hall, William R., **953**
Halliday, Ernest M., **700**
Halsey, Francis W., **43**
Halsey, William F., **352**
Hamilton, Alice, **2164**
Hamilton, Craig, **353**
Hamlin, Charles H., **2612**
Hammel, Victor F., **2438**
Hammett, Hugh B., **2909**
Hammond, Paul Y., **653**
Hancock, Joy B., **2373**
Hancock County, Indiana. Council of Defense, **1738**
Haney, Lewis H., **1987**
Hanighen, Frank C., **1929**
Hankey, Sir Maurice P. A., **669**
Hanner, John W., **2705**

Hansen, Harold C., **1480**
Hansen, Marcus L., **1743, 2402**
Hanson, Joseph M., **1826**
Harbord, James G., **451, 488, 489, 490, 521**
Harding, Gardner L., **805**
Harding, Samuel B., **2113, 2613**
Hardy, Charles O., **1988, 2884**
Harlow, Rex F., **1220**
Harmon, Ernest N., **1124, 1125**
Harris, Frederick, **1021**
Harris, Garrard, **2856**
Harrison, Carter H., **1022**
Harrison, Charles Y., **2530**
Harrison, Emmett De V., **1805**
Hart, Albert B., **2614**
Hart, Hastings H., **1712, 1824, 1836**
Hart, J. A., **2504**
Hart, Percival G., **1655**
Hart, Walter C., **1568**
Hartmann, Edward G., **2204**
Hartney, Harold E., **1665**
Hartzler, J. S., **2177**
Haslett, Elmer, **354**
Hass, Paul A., **476**
Hastie, William H., **2345**
Haswell, William S., **1207**
Haterius, Carl E., **1511**
Haviland, Jean, **918**
Havlin, Arthur C., **1602**
Hay, Donald D., **1389**
Hayes, Casey, **1228**
Hayes, Ralph A., **279**
Haynes, George E., **2310**
Haynes, Robert V., **2346**
Haynes, Rowland, **2615**
Hayworth, Clarence V., **1739**
Hazen, Charles D., **2101**
Heath, N. B., **1580**
Heaton, Herbert, **1882**
Heaton, John L., **2480**
Hecht, George J., **267**
Helbich, Wolfgang J., **2804**
Hemenway, Frederic V., **1345**
Hemingway, Ernest, **2531**
Henderson, Alice P., **1433**
Henderson, Robert G., **1160**
Hendrick, Burton J., **148, 563**
Hendrickson, Kenneth E., Jr., **2281, 2282**
Hennessy, Juliette A., **1679**
Henney, Fred K., **1750**
Henri, Florette, **2311, 2339, 2347**
Henry, Merton G., **730**

Herman, Sondra R., 2178
Herr, Charles R., 1560
Herreid, Charles N., 2058
Herrick, Sherlock A., 1306
Herring, George C., Jr., 740
Herring, Pendleton, 20
Herring, Ray De W., 355
Hersey, Harold B., 2845
Hershey, Burnet, 2179
Herwig, Holger H., 643
Herzog, Stanley J., 1253, 1254
Hess, Dudley, 1216
Hessen, Robert, 2018
Heth, Edward H., 2532
Hewes, James E., Jr., 2817
Hewitt, Linda L., 2374
Heywood, Chester D., 1594
Hibbard, Benjamin H., 2059
Hickey, Donald R., 2154
Hicks, Granville, 2458
Hicks, William P., Jr., 1091
Hidy, Ralph W., 2060
Higgs, Robert, 2312
Higham, John, 2205
Higham, Robin, 3
Hill, Frank E., 1881
Hill, Howard, 1322
Hill, Jim Dan, 802
Hilliard, Jack B., 12
Hillje, John W., 1961
Hills, Ratcliffe M., 1473
Hilton, Ora A., 1816, 2139, 2155
Hilts, Helen M., 2313
Himmelberg, Robert F., 1941, 1942
Hines, Walker D., 2019
Hinman, Jesse R., 1172
Hippelheuser, Richard H., 1851, 1923
Hirschfeld, Charles, 2390, 2647
Hirst, David W., 217
Hirst, Francis W., 1701
Historical Board of the 315th Infantry, 1552
Historical Records Survey, 1754
History Committee, 79th Division Association, 1416
Hitchcock, Curtice N., 1910, 2439
Hitchcock, Nevada D., 2375
Hitz, Benjamin D., 1113
Hixson, Merrel E., 1210
Hocking, W. E., 2424
Hodges, Leroy, 1833
Hoehling, Adolph A., 218, 491, 556, 2706
Hoehling, Mary, 218
Hoffman, Conrad, 721
Hoffman, Harry A., 452

Hoffman, Robert C., 1492
Hogan, Martin J., 1519
Hogan, Michael J., 2885
Hokanson, Nels M., 1962
Holbo, Paul S., 2180
Holbrook, Franklin F., 1770, 1776
Holcombe, A. N., 1852
Holden, Frank, 356
Hollander, Jacob H., 1963
Holley, I. B., Jr., 654, 943
Hollingsworth, Roy D., 1629
Holmes, Frederick L., 1838
Holmes, George E., 1964
Holmes, Robert D., 357, 975
Holt, W. Stull, 2818
Hoover, Herbert C., 104, 122, 123, 129, 2762
Hoppin, Laura B., 856
Hopkins, Johns, 522
Hopper, Bruce C., 630
Horne, Charles F., 249
Hornik, Anna, 1717
Horowitz, David, 712
Hotchkiss, Willard E., 2254
Hough, Emerson, 2140
House, Edward M., 130, 2763
Houston, D. F., 124
Howard, James M., 1288
Howe, Harrison E., 2675
Howe, Dan D., 1466
Howe, Frederic C., 2886
Howe, Henry M., 2676
Howe, Mark A. De Wolfe, 278, 1069, 2568, 2616
Howell, Edgar M., 2486
Howells, W. C., 1397
Howenstine, E. Jay, Jr., 1943, 2838
Howland, Charles R., 44
Howland, Harry S., 262
Hoyt, Charles B., 1318, 1390
Hoyt, Homer, 2887
Hubbard, Samuel T., 358
Hudson, James J., 287, 609
Huidekoper, Frederic L., 1385
Hull, George C., 1252
Hull, William I., 2181
Hungerford, Edward, 359, 785, 1889
Hunt, Edward E., 1023
Hunter, Charles H., 2733
Hunter, Francis T., 670
Hunton, Addie W., 2314
Hurley, Alfred F., 293
Hurley, Edward N., 2020
Husband, Joseph, 360, 580

Hussey, Alexander T., 1534
Hussey, Robert F., 1093
Huston, James A., 885
Hutchins, John G. B., 2021
Hyman, Harold M., 2255
Hymans, H. I., 1464

Ihlder, John, 786
Illinois. State Council of Defense, 1728
Illinois, University of, 2617
Imbrie, Robert W., 1070
Indiana. State Council of Defense, 2376
Ingalls, Walter R., 1171, 2888
Ingle, H. Larry, 1965
Iowa. State Council of Defense, 2156
Irion, Frederick C., 2080
Irvin, F. L., 1658
Irvine, Alexander, 1024
Irvine, E. S. J., 1195
Irwin, William H., 361
Isaacs, Edouard V. M., 722
Isenberg, Michael T., 2487
Ives, Chauncey, 1802
Ives, Herbert E., 2677
Ivy, Robert H., 857

Jacks, Leo V., 1263
Jackson, Orton P., 581, 787, 919
Jacobsen, A. Wilmot, 1258
Jacobson, Gerald F., 1483
Jaffe, Julian F., 2871
Jahns, Lewis E., 703
James, Bessie R., 2377
James, D. Clayton, 289
James, Henry J., 644
James, Marquis, 2846
Jamieson, J. A., 2348
Janeway, Eliot, 2889
Janis, Elsie, 808, 809
Jarrett, G. Burling, 858
Jelke, Ferdinand F., 453
Jenison, Marguerite E., 1729, 1730
Jenkins, Innis L., 254
Jenkins, John W., 557
Jenks, Chester W., 362
Jensen, Joan M., 2141
Jenson, Carol E., 1771, 2157
Jernegan, Marcus W., 268
Joel, Arthur H., 1551
Johnson, Bascom J., 2425, 2426
Johnson, Campbell C., 2349
Johnson, Clarence W., 1564

Johnson, Donald, 2102, 2142, 2161
Johnson, Douglas W., 2678, 2679
Johnson, Kathryn M., 2314
Johnson, Neil M., 2459
Johnson, Robert L., 523
Johnson, Thomas M., 524, 947, 1539
Johnson, Wesley R., 363
Johnston, Clarence D., 1174
Johnston, Edward S., 364, 525
Johnston, Winifred, 2103
Jones, Carlisle L., 1578
Jones, Dallas L., 2256
Jones, Daniel P., 2680
Jones, John, 1722
Jones, Lester M., 2315
Jones, Rufus M., 1025
Jones, Theodore K., 474
Jorgensen, Daniel P., 2460
Josephson, Harold, 2659
Joyner, Charles W., 2505
Judge, J.P., 754
Judy, William L., 454

Kahana, Yoram, 307
Kahn, Otto H., 2206
Kaletzki, Charles H., 1112
Kallen, Horace H., 2283
Kansas. Adjutant General's Office, 803
Kansas. State Council of Defense, 1748
Kaplan, Sidney, 2648
Karsner, David, 2284
Katz, Robert S., 2707
Kauffman, Alvin E., 1664
Kauffman, Reginald W., 582
Kaufman, Burton I., 2004, 2005, 2890, 2891
Kaufman, Thomas, 526
Kautz, John I., 455, 976
Keen, W. W., 859
Keller, Charles, 2041, 2042, 2047
Keller, Phyllis, 2207
Kellogg, Charles F., 2316
Kellogg, Paul U., 1026
Kellogg, Vernon, 2061
Kellor, Frances A., 741
Kelly, Harold V., 1328
Kelly, Russell A., 977
Kelly, Thomas H., 2533
Kelsey, Carl, 2081
Kenamore, Clair, 1391, 1392, 1514
Kendall, Harry, 365
Kennan, George F., 167, 686, 687, 688
Kennedy, Louise V., 17, 2317

Kennedy, Thomas C., 2660
Kennelly, A. E., 920
Kennett, Lee, 1000
Kenney, George C., 1648
Kentucky. State Council of Defense, 1752
Keough, Frederic W., 2857
Keppel, Frederick B., 87
Kernan, W. F., 1249
Kernek, Sterling J., 219, 2734
Kerr, K. Austin, 2022, 2023
Kerr, William J., 2618
Kester, Randall B., 1911
Kevles, Daniel J., 921, 2681, 2682, 2683, 2684
Keynes, John M., 2892
Kihl, Mary R., 220
Kilner, Frederick R., 1278
Kimmel, Martin L., 456
Kimmel, Stanley P., 1027
Kindall, Sylvian G., 701
Kinney, William S., 886
Kirtley, Lorin E., 1270
Klachko, Mary, 671
Klausner, Julius, 1531
Kleber, Brooks E., 1414
Kleist, Franz Rintelen von, 954
Klose, Gilbert C., 2049
Knapp, Shepherd, 366
Knappen, Theodore M., 922
Knight, Clayton, 367, 1680
Knight, K. S., 1680
Knightley, Phillip, 2482
Knoeppel, Charles E., 1894, 1895, 2378
Knoles, George H., 2649
Knox County, Illinois, 1733
Koch, Felix J., 1812
Koch, H. W., 60
Koch, Louis P., 788
Koistinen, Paul A. C., 1935, 1936
Kolbe, Parke R., 2619
Kolko, Gabriel, 2024
Komora, Paul O., 835
Koons, Jack, 1398
Koppes, Clayton R., 2285
Kramer, Harold M., 1028
Kreidberg, Marvin A., 730
Krehbiel, Edward, 742
Krey, August C., 2109
Krivy, Leonard P., 2257
Krulewitch, M. L., 527
Kuehl, Warren F., 2805
Kuhn, Walter R., 1605
Kurtz, Leonard P., 368

Kuykendall, Ralph S., 1725
Kuznets, Simon S., 2077
Kyle, Homer L., 1579

La Branche, Ernest E., 1246
La Follette, Belle C., 2721
La Follette, Fola, 2721
Lafore, Laurence, 61
Lage, William P., 2906
Lahm, Frank P., 294, 457
Laird, John A., 1158
Lakeman, Curtis E., 2858
Lancaster, James L., 2819
Land, Gary, 2461
Landau, Henry, 955
Landrum, Charles H., 1768, 1769
Lane, Anna W., 131
Lane, Franklin K., 131
Lane, W. D., 2427
Langer, William L., 1330, 1331
Langille, Leslie, 1279
Lanier, Henry W., 789
Lansing, Robert, 125, 2104, 2764, 2765
Lardner, Ring W., 2586
Larson, Cedric, 829, 830, 2105, 2108
Larson, Edgar J. O., 1426
Lasch, Christopher, 689, 690, 2650
Lasswell, Harold D., 2082
Lathrop, Julia C., 2391, 2403
Lauck, William Jett, 1989
Lavine, Abraham L., 923
Law, Hugo B., 1666
Lawrence, Andrea, 1387
Layman, Martha E., 744
Lazo, Hector T., 2534
Leach, Jack F., 762
Leach, George E., 1285
Leach, William J., 458
Leader, John, 1818
Leahy, Francis T., 2569
Leake, James M., 1853
Leary, William M., 13
Lee, Benjamin, 459
Lee, Charles H., 1170
Lee, Dwight E., 62
Lee, Jay M., 1268
Lee, Joseph, 810
Lee, Mary, 2535
Lee, Ulysses G., 2350
Lehn, John P., 1823
Leigh, Robert D., 2859
Leighton, John L., 558
Lejeune, John A., 369

Leland, Claude G., **1484**
Leland, Waldo G., **28**
Leonard, Thomas C., **259a**
Leopold, Richard W., **134**
Lettau, Joseph L., **1569**
Leuchtenburg, William E., **74, 2913**
Levell, Robert O., **370**
Levin, N. Gordon, Jr., **2766**
Levine, Isaac Don, **295**
Levine, Lawrence W., **90**
Levinger, Lee J., **2462**
Lewis, Guy, **2453**
Li, T'ien-i, **168**
Liddell Hart, B. H., **45, 46**
Liggett, Hunter, **371, 372**
Lighter, Jonathan, **834**
Linberger, C. W., **1348**
Lincoln, Leopold L., **1157**
Lindbergh, Charles A., **1966**
Lindley, John M., **827**
Lindner, Clarence R., **460**
Lindquist, John H., **2286**
Lindsay, Samuel M., **2404**
Lindstrom, Gustaf A., **1647**
Link, Arthur S., **13, 75, 105, 106, 107,**
  108, 109, 110, 111, 112, 221, 2836
Lippincott, Isaac, **2864**
Lippmann, Walter, **169, 2767**
Lipsett, Charles H., **888**
Litman, Simon, **1990**
Little, Arthur W., **1590**
Little, John G., **1424**
Livermore, Seward W., **2722, 2723**
Livingston, St. Clair, **1029**
Livingstone, J. B., **2561**
Lloyd, Nelson, **76**
Lloyd George, David, **2768**
Lochner, Louis P., **2182**
Lockmiller, David A., **283**
Lockwood, Louisa C., **1804**
Lodge, Henry Cabot, **2820**
Logan, Rayford W., **170, 2769**
Lonergan, Thomas C., **672**
Long, Howard H., **2351**
Loomis, Ernest L., **1097**
Lord, Clifford L., **618**
Lord, Russell, **1260**
Louser, Herman W., **1663**
Love, Albert G., **851, 860, 861**
Love, Thomas B., **2405**
Lovejoy, Clarence E., **1453**
Lovejoy, Esther P., **1030**
Lovejoy, Owen R., **2230**

Lovin, Hugh T., **2158**
Lower, Richard C., **2821**
Lowitt, Richard, **222, 1782**
Lowry, Bullitt, **655**
Lubove, Roy, **2440**
Luebke, Frederick C., **2208, 2209**
Lueker, Erwin L., **1778**
Lukens, Edward C., **373**
Lundeberg, Philip K., **223**
Lutter, Martin H., **1817**
Lutz, Earle, **1487**
Lutz, Ralph H., **1, 567**
Lyddon, William R., **673**
Lyle, H. H. M., **862**
Lyman, George H., **1760**
Lynch, Charles, **863, 864**
Lynch, Frederick H., **2463**
Lynn, John D., **763**

Mabry, Gregory, **1462**
McAdoo, William G., **126**
McAfee, Loy, **864**
MacArthur, Charles, **1280**
MacArthur, Douglas, **374**
McCain, George N., **2062**
McCarthy, Robert J., **1603**
McCarthy, Timothy F., **375, 790**
McCarthy, William E., **1298**
McClary, Eula, **583**
McClellan, Edwin N., **492, 528, 529, 530,**
  531, 702, 978
McClinton, H. L., **1136**
McCollum, Lee C., **1532, 1535**
McConnell, James R., **1681**
McCormick, Robert R., **493**
McCoy, Patrick T., **979**
McCrossen, Bernard J., **1449**
McDiarmid, Alice M., **224**
McDonald, Timothy G., **225, 226**
McDougall, Grace, **2379**
McElroy, John L., **1302**
McEvoy, A. L., **1099**
McGinnis, William, **1245**
McGovern, James R., **2380**
McGrath, John F., **1577**
Mack, Arthur J., **980**
Mack, Charles E., **2536**
McKenna, Frederick A., **1250**
McKeogh, Arthur, **1407, 1408**
Mackey, Frank J., **268**
McLaughlin, Andrew C., **2106**
McLaughlin, Patrick D., **532**
McLean, Ross H., **889**

McLean, William P., 1269
MacLeish, Kenneth, 461
McLeod, G. Duncan, 1726
McMahan, Russel R., 2464
Macmahon, Arthur W., 2708
McMaster, John B., 77
MacMullin, Robert B., 1331
McMurtrie, Douglas, C., 2860
McNutt, William S., 791
Macomber, Alexander, 1178
MacQuarrie, Hector, 792
MacVeagh, Ewen C., 533
Macy, V. Everit, 2258, 2259
Maddox, Robert J., 534, 691, 702a, 1536
Maerker-Branden, A. Paul, 1004
Maher, Augustin F., 1472
Maine. Adjutant General's Office, 1756
Majors, C. L., 2587
Malan, Nancy E., 2381
Malcolm, Gilbert, 1415
Mandel, Bernard, 2231
Manly, Claude C., 1506
Mann, Floris P., 462
Manning, Clarence A., 2210
Manning, Van H., 924
Mansfield, J. Carroll, 1258
March, Peyton C., 376
March, William. See Campbell, William E. M.
Marchand, C. Roland, 2183
Marcosson, Isaac F., 890, 2893
Markle, Clifford M., 723
Marshall, Conrad H., 1581
Marshall, George C., 377
Marshall L. C., 2260
Marshall, S. L. A., 47
Martin, Edward, 1373
Martin, Franklin H., 1884, 1912
Martin, Laurence W., 2770, 2771
Martin, Paul A., 1208
Marwick, Arthur, 1702, 1703
Maryland. State Council of Defense, 1758
Maryland. War Records Commission, 1759
Mason, Herbert M., Jr., 1682
Mason, Monroe, 1439
Mason, William H., 1835
Massachusetts Agricultural College, 2620
Masseck, C. J., 1427
Matheson, Martin, 1121
Mathews, Joseph J., 2483
Mathews, Shailer, 2465
Matthews, William, 378
Mattox, W. C., 2025
Maurer, Maurer, 631, 632, 1637, 2428

Maurice, Sir Frederick, 674
Maxim, Hudson, 743
Maxwell, Kenneth R., 2822
May, Earl C., 1887
May, Ernest R., 135, 185, 656, 2735, 2772
May, Henry F., 2449, 2651
May, Mark A., 2184
Mayer, Arno J., 2773, 2774
Mayer, S. L., 48
Mayo, Katherine, 1031, 2847
Mayo, Margaret, 811
Mead, Frederick S., 2621
Mead, Harry H., 703
Meaney, N. K., 2823
Mechem, Kirke, 1512
Meehan, Thomas F., 1412
Melville, Phillips, 633
Mendelssohn-Bartholdy, Albrecht, 1704
Mendenhall, John R., 1598
Meredith, Ellis, 379
Mereness, Newton D., 28, 2661
Merrill, James M., 645
Merrill, Wainwright, 982
Merritt, Albert M., 2063
Merritt, Richard L., 2724
Mervin, David, 2824
Meyer, Ernest L., 2185
Meyer, Eugene, Jr., 2000
Michael, W. H., 494
Miles, L. Wardlaw, 1538
Miles, Wyndham D., 904
Milham, Chester R., 2143
Millard, Shirley, 463
Millen, De Witt C., 1071
Miller, A. C., 1967
Miller, Carroll L., 2318
Miller, David Hunter, 2775, 2806
Miller, Henry, 1998
Miller, Henry R., 1337
Miller, Kelly, 2319
Miller, Sally M., 2287
Miller, Warren H., 312, 2537
Millett, Allan R., 281
Millikan, Robert A., 2685, 2686, 2687
Millis, Walter, 186
Millholland, Ray, 584
Mills, Quincy Sharpe, 464
Milner, Lucille, 2088
Minder, Charles F., 465, 1615
Miner, Margaret M., 292
Minnesota. Comission of Public Safety, 1772
Minturn, Joseph A., 380
Missouri. State Council of Defense, 1779

Mitchell, Franklin D., 1780
Mitchell, Harry T., 1481
Mitchell, Wesley C., 1991, 1992
Mitchell, William, 381, 610, 611
Mitrany, David, 1705
Mizener, Arthur, 2506
Mock, Harry E., 2709
Mock, James R., 2105, 2107, 2108, 2144, 2839
Moellering, Ralph L., 2466
Mohr, Harold O., 1325
Molnor, T. T., 1944
Mooney, Chase C., 744
Moore, Charles H., 1634
Moore, Douglas S., 2571
Moore, Geoffrey T., 1854
Moore, Joel R., 703
Moore, Samuel T., 78
Moore, Wallace H., 2211
Moore, William E., 269, 273, 2186
Moorhead, Robert L., 1273
Moorland, Jesse E., 2352
Morehouse, George P., 1749
Morgan, David T., 2467
Morgan, George R., 1547
Morgan, Joy E., 812
Morison, Elting E., 306
Morlan, Robert L., 2725
Morris, Otho A., 1628
Morrison, Joseph L., 92
Morrow, George L., 1465
Morse, Daniel P., Jr., 1643
Morse, Edwin W., 983
Morse, Katherine D., 1032
Morse, Lewis K., 1993
Mortimer, Maud, 1033
Moseley, George C., 466
Moss, James A., 262, 270
Moton, Robert R., 2320
Moulton, Harold G., 2877
Mowry, William J., 535
Mozley, George, 1247
Mudd, Thomas B. R., 495
Mullendore, William C., 2064
Muller, E. Lester, 1549
Muller, W. G., 1356
Munger, Donna B., 1111
Munro, Charles E., 2688
Munro, Dana G., 171, 2109
Murchie, Guy, Jr., 946
Murdick, George P., 2202
Murdock, Frank R., 1821
Murdock, Lawrence B., 559

Murnane, Mark R., 382
Murphy, Elmer A., 1378
Murphy, Paul L., 2145
Murray, Robert K., 2825, 2872
Murrin, James A., 1494
Muzik, Edward J., 2873

Nash, Gerald D., 2914, 2915, 2916
Nason, Leonard, 2538
National Board for Historical Service, 2662
National Bureau of Economic Research, 2894
National Hostess House Committee, 813
National Housing Association, 2441
National Industrial Conference Board, 1994, 2232, 2233, 2234, 2235, 2895
National Jewish Welfare Board, 2406
Naval Aviation War Book Committee, 634
Nearing, Scott, 2288, 2289
Nelles, Walter, 2087
Nelson, Arthur M., 1773
Nelson, Clifford L., 2212
Nelson, Daniel, 2896
Nelson, Keith L., 715, 2776
Nelson, Otto L., 657
Nenninger, Timothy K., 925
Ness, Gary, 94
Nettleton, George H., 2622
Nevins, Allan, 1881, 2777
Newby, Idus A., 2726
New Hampshire. Committee on Public Safety, 1783
New Jersey Cavalry. 102d Regiment, 1127
New York (City). Mayor's Committee on National Defense, 1800
New York Life Insurance Company, 383
New York Public Library, 34
Nicholas, Wayne A., 2110
Nicholas, William E., III, 2652, 2653
Nicolson, Harold, 2778
Nida, William L., 79
Niles, John J., 1676, 2570, 2571
Nims, Marion R., 14
Ninth Coast Artillery Corps., 1128
Nock, Albert J., 2779
Noer, Thomas J., 2736
Nohl, Frederick, 2213
Nolan, James B., 1608
Nordhoff, Charles B., 793, 1678, 2539
Norman, Aaron, 612
Norris, George W., 149
North, Arthur W., 1803
Norton, Nile B., 675

Norton, Thomas F., **1662**
Notestein, Wallace, **2111**
Notter, Harley, **172**
Noyes, Alexander D., **1968**
Noyes, Arthur A., **926**
Nutting, William W., **927**

O'Brian, Alice Lord, **467**
O'Brian, John Lord, **956, 2146**
O'Brien, Dennis J., **2044**
O'Brien, Howard V., **468**
O'Brien, Pat, **724**
O'Connor, Richard, **299, 2214**
Odell, Joseph H., **794**
Ohio. State Council of Defense, **1810, 1811**
Ohl, John K., **764, 1913, 1914**
Olson, Zenas A., **1584**
O'Malley, Frank W., **1719**
Oneal, James, **2290**
O'Neil, R. E., **1600**
O'Neill, William L., **2291**
Oppenheim, E. Phillips, **2540**
Orcutt, Philip D., **1072**
Orr, Harry D., **2710**
O'Ryan, John F., **1368**
Osgood, Robert E., **173**
O'Shaughnessy, Edith L., **1034**
Osofsky, Gilbert, **2321**
O'Sullivan, Mrs. Denis, **969**
Otis, Charles, **1885**
Otto, Ernst, **1001, 1002**
Ottosen, Peter H., **1636**
Oukrop, Carol, **2112**
Ovitt, Spaulding W., **1104**
Owen, Richard W., **928**

Pack, Charles L., **2065**
Page, Arthur W., **497**
Paine, Jocelyn, **2711**
Paine, Ralph D., **585, 586, 587, 635**
Pallen, Condé B., **1799**
Palmer, Dewey H., **2322**
Palmer, Don, **1398**
Palmer, Frederick, **88, 280, 300, 384, 385, 498, 536**
Palmer, Jean M., **2623**
Palmer, John M., **113**
Pappas, George S., **15**
Parish, John C., **948**
Parmalee, Julius H., **2015, 2026**
Parrini, Carl P., **2006**
Parsons, Edward B., **2736a**
Parsons, Edwin C., **1683**

Parsons, G. C., **1206**
Parsons, William B., **1145**
Patmore, Arthur C., **1797**
Patrick, Mason M., **613**
Patten, Anna B., **1720**
Patten, Simon N., **1969, 1970, 1995**
Patterson, David S., **227**
Patterson, E. M., **1971**
Patton, John S., **2624**
Pattullo, George, **471**
Paul, Elliot, **2541**
Paxson, Frederic L., **80, 2113, 2727, 2840**
Pearson, LeRoy, **286, 1382**
Pease, Marguerite J., **1731**
Peaslee, Amos J., **953**
Peck, Josiah C., **1559**
Peixotto, Ernest C., **386**
Pennell, Joseph, **2114, 2492**
Penner, Carl, **1264**
Pennsylvania. State Council of Defense, **1819**
Penrose, Laura E., **2407**
Peoples, John M., **1915**
Perkins, Dexter, **2826**
Perry, J. C., **2712**
Perry, Lawrence, **560, 561**
Perry, Ralph B., **745, 2654, 2655**
Perry, Redding F., **1126**
Pershing, John J., **387, 499**
Persons, W. Frank, **2408**
Peterson, Horace C., **228, 2147**
Peterson, Ira L., **1508**
Peterson, Wilber, **388**
Peterson, William J., **1523**
Peterson, William L., **1177**
Philadelphia. War History Committee, **1820**
Piatt, Andrew A., **1073**
Pickell, James R., **389, 891**
Pickett, Calder M., **831**
Pierson, Edward E., **1734**
Piesbergen, Clarence F., **1645**
Pilcher, Lewis S., **2713**
Pinchot, Gifford, **2066**
Piper, Paul F., **2468**
Pitt, Barrie, **500**
Pitts, Edmund M., **1114**
Pixley, Rutherford, **1839**
Platt, Rutherford H., Jr., **1307**
Pliska, Stanley R., **984**
Poague, Walter S., **470**
Pogue, Forrest C., **291**
Pohl, James W., **658**
Poling, Daniel A., **1035**

Polishook, Sheila S., 2215
Pollard, James E., 1460
Pollock, Ivan L., 2067
Porter, William T., 865
Post, Louis F., 2104
Poteat, George, 692
Pottle, Frederick A., 1213
Powe, Marc B., 949
Powell, Edward A., 892
Powell, G. Harold, 2897
Pownall, Dorothy A., 795
Pratt, Fletcher, 1539
Pratt, Joseph H., 1187
Prentice, Sartell, 1036
Preston, Antony, 929
Preston, William, Jr., 2148
Price, Theodore H., 284
Price, William G., 1217
Prince, Norman, 1684
Princeton University, 2625, 2626
Prinz, Friedrich, 2780
Procko, Bohdan P., 2469
Proctor, Henry G., 1371
Prosser, Charles A., 2861
Pugh, Irving E., 537
Pugh, W. S., 822
Pursell, Carroll W., Jr., 2689
Putnam, Elizabeth C., 1037

Quinton, A. B., 1855

Radosh, Ronald, 2261
Rae, John B., 2027
Raemaekers, Louis, 271
Rainsford, Walter K., 1530
Randall, James G., 114
Randall, Roy O., 272
Rankin, Edward P., 1190
Rappaport, Armin, 229, 1896
Rappaport, Joseph, 2216
Raquet, Edward C., 588
Rarey, G. H., 538, 539
Read, James M., 2083
Ready, Milton R., 1723
Reagan, Michael D., 1945
Reeves, Earl, 485
Reeves, George W., 1796
Reichmann, W. D., 930
Reid, Bill G., 2848, 2849
Reid, E. Emmett, 931
Reilly, Henry J., 1403
Reilly, John E., 1162
Reitman, Ben L., 2292

Remak, Joachim, 63
Remele, Larry, 2728
Rendinell, Joseph E., 471
Renouvin, Pierre, 64
Renshaw, Patrick, 2293
Reppy, Alison, 1520
Réquin, Edouard J., 2737
Resek, Carl, 2637
Reynolds, Frederick C., 1495
Reynolds, M. T., 746
Reynolds, Quentin J., 614
Rhodes, Benjamin D., 2898
Ricci, Lewis A. da C. (Bartimeus, pseud.), 568
Rice, Grantland, 2573
Rice, Philip S., 1074
Richards, G. H., 1293
Richards, George B., 472
Richards, John F., 472
Richardson, Chalmer O., 1572
Richardson, Ernest C., 16
Rickards, Maurice, 2115
Rickenbacker, Edward V., 636, 1650
Rider, Edward C., 1793
Riggs, Arthur S., 390
Riggs, McDonald H., 1307
Rinehart, Mary (R.), 765
Ripley, G. Peter, 230, 1721
Risch, Erna, 893
Robb, Winfred E., 1524
Roberts, E. M., 391, 985
Roberts, Harold C., 866
Robins, Thomas, 1897
Robinson, Corinne, 2572
Robinson, Victor, 2450
Robinson, William J., 986
Rockwell, Paul A., 987, 988, 1685
Rodman, Burton, 950
Rodman, Henry, 589
Rodman, Hugh, 392
Roff, Willis H., 2159
Rogers, Lindsay, 2446
Rogge, Robert E., 1657
Romeo, Giuseppe, 1585
Roosevelt, Franklin D., 562, 766
Roosevelt, Kermit, 473, 1226
Roosevelt, Quentin, 473
Roosevelt, Theodore, Jr., 393, 2573
Root, Esther S., 1039
Roots, Peter C., 917
Rose, Harold W., 590
Rosenberg, James N., 1946
Ross, Frank A., 17

Ross, James H., 1580
Ross, Warner A., 1588
Ross, William O., 1317
Roth, Jack J., 49
Roth, Joseph P., 1201
Roth, William E., 867
Rothbard, Murray N., 1856
Rounds, Ona M., 394
Rouzer, E. McClure, 285
Rucher, Colby G., 591
Ruckman, John H., 2627
Rudin, Harry R., 2781
Rudwick, Elliott M., 2324
Rugh, Charles E., 2470
Ruhl, Robert K., 308
Ruml, Beardsley, 2899
Rupp, Roland L., 1335
Russel, William Muir, 989, 1653
Russell, Charles E., 828, 951
Russell, Frederick F., 868, 869
Russell, James C., 269, 273
Russell, Richard M., 1222
Ruth, Harry S., 1840
Ryan, Paul B., 194, 231
Ryley, Thomas W., 232

Sadler, Edwin J., 1194
Safford, Jeffrey J., 2007, 2028, 2728a
St. Lawrence University, 2628
Salter, James A., 2029
Samond, Frederic, 1264
Samson, Henry T., 1249, 1252
Sanborn, Joseph B., 1509
Sanborn, Philip N., 1184
Sanders, Cameron H., 1272
Sanger, William C., 2574
Sargent, Herbert H., 676
Sassé, Fred A., 796
Sausser, Malcolm G., 1114
Scanlon, William, 2542
Schaffer, Ronald, 1947, 2084, 2382
Schauble, Peter L., 1633
Schauffler, Edward R., 797
Scheiber, Harry N., 2008, 2149, 2150, 2325
Scheiber, Jane L., 2325
Scheidt, David L., 2471
Scheiner, Seth M., 2326
Scherer, James A. B., 1710
Schiff, Mortimer L., 1972
Schlissel, Lillian, 2638
Schmeckebier, Laurence F., 2851
Schmidt, Hubert G., 1785
Schmidt, Paul W., 1505

Schmitt, Bernadotte E., 65, 187
Schmitz, John J., 1087
Schuler, Edgar A., 2353
Schurman, Jacob G., Jr., 1540
Schwabe, Klaus, 2807
Schwensen, Kai, 1620
Scott, Albert L., 894
Scott, Charles M., 1316
Scott, Emmett J., 2327, 2328, 2329
Scott, George W., 2116
Scott, Hugh L., 395
Scott, Lloyd N., 1898
Seager, Henry R., 2254
Seal, Enoch, Jr., 693
Seal, Henry F., 1261, 1499
Sears, Herbert M., 1040
Seeger, Alan, 990
Selby, Herbert E., 1328
Seligman, Edwin R. A., 1973
Sellery, George C., 2109
Senior, James K., 932
Seymour, Charles, 130, 188, 2738, 2763, 2782, 2783, 2784
Seymour, Gertrude, 2429, 2714
Shaffer, Walter J., 1686
Shainwald, Richard H., 475
Shambaugh, Bertha M., 1745
Shanks, David C., 895
Shannon, David, 2294
Shapiro, Stanley, 2236, 2392
Shapiro, Sumner, 704
Sharfman, I. L., 1871
Sharp, John E., 396
Sharp, William G., 2739
Sharpe, Henry G., 896
Shaw, Albert, 2841
Shaw, Arthur F., 1556
Shaw, Oliver, 540
Sheahan, Henry B., 592, 991
Shem, Carl, 1306
Shepherd, William G., 593, 2484
Shepperson, Wilbur S., 2295
Sherburne, John H., 1761
Sherman, Stuart P., 2117
Sherrill, Stephen H., 541
Sherwood, Elmer W., 1282, 1283, 1402
Shideler, James H., 2900
Shields, Mark A., 1193
Shimmin, J. E., 1328
Shine, William F., 1471
Shipley, Arthur M., 1214
Shively, George J., 1075
Shoemaker, Floyd C., 1781
Shortall, Katherine, 1041

Shotwell, James T., 1697, 2785
Showalter, W. J., 798
Shryer, Davis M., 1327
Shuford, George A., 1501
Shulimson, Jack, 501
Shumate, Thomas D., Jr., 677
Sibley, Frank P., 1363
Siebert, Wilbur H., 2629
Siler, Joseph F., 870
Silverstone, Paul, 933
Silverthorn, M. H., 542
Simkhovitch, Mary K., 2409
Simmons, Perez, 1166
Simms, L. Moody, Jr., 2656
Simonds, Frank H., 50
Simons, Algie M., 2865
Simpson, Albert F., 457
Sims, William S., 563, 594
Sinclair, Andrew, 2447
Sinclair, Upton, 2543
Siney, Marion C., 233, 234
Sirois, Edward D., 1245
Sixteenth Engineers Veterans Association, 1163
Skeyhill, Thomas, 310, 481
Skillman, Willis R., 502
Slaughter, Duke L., 1317
Sloan, James J., 1642
Slonaker, John, 18
Slosser, Gaius J., 1196
Slosson, Preston W., 81
Slusser, Thomas H., 1042
Small, James L., 2842
Smith, Alexander W., 2901
Smith, Annie S., 2383
Smith, Chellis V., 313
Smith, Daniel M., 82, 136, 150, 174, 2827
Smith, Darrell H., 2030
Smith, Fred B., 1043
Smith, Gaddis, 235, 236, 2786
Smith, Gene, 115
Smith, George O., 2045
Smith, George W., 2068
Smith, Henry W., 1614
Smith, John S., 2237, 2262
Smith, Joseph M., 1635
Smith, Joseph R., 2031
Smith, Joseph S., 397, 992
Smith, Myron J., 19, 19a
Smylie, Adolphe E., 2575
Smythe, Donald, 251, 252, 301, 302, 543, 2430
Snell, John L., 2118, 2740
Snider, Van A., 1815

Snow, William F., 2431
Snow, William J., 398
Snyder, Phil L., 2663
Social Science Research Council. Committee on Public Administration, 20
Society of the First Division, 1338
Soderbergh, Peter A., 2488
Souder, Harry J., 1787
Soule, George, 660, 1857
South Carolina. State Council of Defense, 1825
South Hadley, Massachusetts, 1767
Spaeth, John D., 823
Sparks, George M., 1566
Spaulding, Oliver L., 1342
Speakman, Harold, 399
Spear, Allan H., 2330
Spector, Ronald, 661
Spencer, Samuel R., Jr., 237
Sperry, E. E., 2119
Spingarn, Arthur, 2331
Sprague, Lloyd D., 2151
Sprenger, James A., 814
Spring, Joel H., 2690
Springs, Elliott White, 400, 401, 448
Sprout, Harold, 255, 256
Sprout, Margaret, 255, 256
Squires, J. D., 238
Stallings, Laurence, 274, 503, 504, 544, 2544
Stamas, Christ K., 402
Stanley, Frederic L., 799
Starlight, Alexander, 1366
The Stars and Stripes, 2545, 2576, 2577
Startt, James D., 2787, 2788, 2808
Stearns, Gustav, 1384, 2472
Stearns, Harold E., 2393
Steen-Hansen, Ingebord, 1029
Stein, Herbert, 1996
Stephens, D. Owen, 2473
Stephenson, George M., 2217
Stephenson, Gilbert T., 1974
Sterling, Adaline W., 1784
Stern, Sheldon M., 2828
Sterne, Elaine, 403
Steuben, John, 2238
Stevens, James, 2546
Stevens, Neil E., 2691
Stevens, Raymond B., 2032
Stevenson, Charles S., 705, 1207
Stevenson, Kenyon, 1237, 1351
Stevenson, William Y., 404, 1076, 1077
Stewart, George J., 2474
Stewart, Lawrence O., 1525

Stidger, William L., 1044
Stieglitz, Julius, 934
Stillman, Richard, 2347
Stimson, Henry L., 127
Stimson, Julia C., 871, 872
Stockbridge, Frank P., 800, 935
Stokes, Anson P., 824
Stokes, Will, 2578
Stoll, Elmer E., 2111
Stone, Arthur F., 1830
Stone, Ernest, 405
Stone, Ralph A., 2829, 2830, 2831, 2832
Strakhovsky, L. I., 706
Straub, Elmer F., 1281
Streeter, Edward, 2588, 2589, 2590, 2591
Strickland, Daniel W., 1474
Stringfellow, John S., 406, 1563
Strother, French, 957
Strott, George G., 873
Stucky, Gregory J., 2187
Studley, George M., 1173
Sullivan, J. W., 2239
Sullivan, Mark, 1698, 2033
Sullivan, Willard P., 1188
Summerbell, Carlyle, 2475
Summers, Florence E., 2592
Summerscales, William, 2630
Sumrall, Robert F., 936
Surface, Frank M., 2069, 2071, 2072
Suskind, Richard, 545, 546
Sutliffe, Robert S., 1478
Sutton, Walter A., 239, 240, 747
Swan, John M., 1110
Sweeney, Daniel J., 1791
Sweeney, W. Allison, 2332
Sweeney, Walter C., 952
Sweetser, Arthur, 615
Swindler, Henry O., 1537
Swisher, Carl B., 2152
Switzer, J. S., Jr., 547
Syrett, Harold C., 241

Taber, John H., 1523, 1526
Taft, Philip, 2296, 2297
Talbot, Henry P., 2692, 2693
Tannenbaum, Frank, 2451
Tansill, Charles C., 189
Tarbot, Jerry, 407
Tatlock, John S. P., 2120
Taussig, Frank W., 1997
Taussig, Joseph K., 596
Taylor, A. J. P., 51

Taylor, Alonzo E., 2073
Taylor, Emerson G., 1364
Taylor, Graham, 2218
Taylor, J. N., 2452
Taylor, W. P., 1658
Tead, Ordway, 2240
Teichroew, Allan, 2188
Temperley, Harold W. V., 2789
Terraine, John, 548, 1003
Thayer, George B., 1045
Thayer, John A., 1706
Thayer, William F., 537
Thelen, Max, 2034
Thenault, Georges, 1687
Therese, Josephine, 408
Thomas, Lowell, 282, 309, 646
Thomas, Norman, 2189, 2190
Thomas, Robert S., 1378
Thomas, Shipley, 505
Thomason, John W., Jr., 409, 506
Thompson, Charles T., 2790
Thompson, Dora E., 874
Thompson, J. A., 89, 2394
Thompson, John M., 2791
Thompson, Joseph J., 2476
Thompson, Terry B., 410
Thomson, Harry C., 917
Thorn, Henry C., Jr., 1550
Thornburn, Neil, 2395
Thorne, Clifford, 2035
306th Field Artillery History Staff, 1291
306th Infantry Association, 1529
Thurber, Evangeline, 2839
Thurston, William N., 2036
Thwing, Charles F., 2631
Ticknor, Caroline, 314
Tiebout, Frank B., 1528
Tierney, Dudley R., 1238
Tillman, Seth P., 2792
Timberlake, J. H., 2448
Tinsley, William, 748
Tippett, Edwin J., Jr., 411
Tips, Walter, 616
Tobey, James A., 2715
Tobey, Ronald C., 2694
Tobin, Harold J., 1858
Todd, Lewis P., 2632
Toland, Edward D., 1046
Toliver, R. F., 315
Tolley, Kemp, 707
Tomkins, Raymond S., 1401
Tomlin, Robert K., 1146

Toomey, Joseph M., 1724
Tooze, Lamar, 1587
Toulmin, Harry A., Jr., 617
Tousley, Clyde E. T., 1612
Trachtenberg, Alexander, 2298
Train, Arthur, 2547
Trani, Eugene P., 694
Trask, David F., 175, 643, 678, 679, 680, 1708
Trattner, Walter I., 2396
Trotter, Agnes A., 137
Trounce, Harry D., 412
Trowbridge, Augustus, 937, 938
Troyes, F. G., 725
Trueblood, Edward A., 413
Trumbo, Dalton, 2548
Tryon, Warren S., 767
Tucker, H. S., 1188
Tucker, William J., 1527, 2549
Tuchman, Barbara W., 66, 242
Tumulty, Joseph P., 116
Turnbull, Andrew, 2507
Turnbull, Archibald D., 618
Turnbull, Laura S., 21
Turner, George E., 1688
Turner, John K., 2910
Tuttle, William M., Jr., 2333, 2334
Tydings, Millard E., 1609
Tyler, John C., 1639
Tyler, Robert L., 2263
Tyson, James L., 1916

Underhill, Edwin H., 1098
Unterberger, Betty M., 695, 708, 709
Upson, William H., 1234
Urofsky, Melvin I., 1948, 1949, 1984
U.S. Adjutant General's Office, 729, 825, 1081
U.S. American National Red Cross. War Council, 1047
U.S. Army. A.E.F., 639, 826
U.S. Army. A.E.F. Air Service, 619
U.S. Army. A.E.F. Base Hospital No. 4, 1105
U.S. Army. A.E.F. Base Hospital No. 10, 1108
U.S. Army. A.E.F. Engineer Department, 939, 1147
U.S. Army. A.E.F. General Staff, G–2. Library, 35
U.S. Army. A.E.F. General Staff College, 662

U.S. Army. First Army, 1101
U.S. Army. 101st Engineers, 1183
U.S. Army. 113th Engineers, 1191
U.S. Army. 2d Engineers, 1151
U.S. Army. 6th Field Artillery, 1224
U.S. Army. 308th Engineers, 1205
U.S. Army. 301st Engineers, 1199
U.S. Army. 304th Engineers. 1202
U.S. Army. 214th Engineers, 1198
U.S. Army War College, 2355
U.S. Army War College. Historical Section, 1083, 1102
U.S. Bureau of Labor Statistics, 2264
U.S. Commission on Training Camp Activities (War Department), 815, 816, 2432, 2433
U.S. Committee on Public Information, 2121, 2122, 2123, 2124, 2125, 2126, 2127, 2128, 2129, 2130
U.S. Congress. House. Committee on Military Affairs, 768
U.S. Congress. House. Committee on Naval Affairs, 1930
U.S. Congress. House. Select Committee on Expenditures in the War Department, 1859, 1931
U.S. Congress. Senate. Committee on Commerce, 2037
U.S. Congress. Senate. Committee on Education and Labor, 2862
U.S. Congress. Senate. Committee on Manufactures, 2046
U.S. Congress. Senate. Committee on Military Affairs, 749, 769, 770, 1860
U.S. Congress. Senate. Committee on Naval Affairs, 597
U.S. Congress. Senate. Special Committee to Investigate the Munitions Industry, 243, 244, 1917, 1918
U.S. Council of National Defense, 1919, 1920
U.S. Council of National Defense. Advisory Commission, 1921
U.S. Council of National Defense. General Munitions Board, 1922
U.S. Department of the Army. Office of Military History, 507, 730
U.S. Department of the Interior. Bureau of Education, 2219
U.S. Department of Labor. Division of Negro Economics, 2335, 2336
U.S. Department of State, 138, 2356

U.S. Engineer Department, 2047
U.S. Federal Board for Vocational Education, 2863
U.S. Federal Trade Commission, 1998, 2001, 2002
U.S. Fuel Administration, 2048
U.S. General Staff, 640
U.S. General Staff. War Plans Division. Historical Branch, 897, 1141, 1344, 1861
U.S. Infantry School. Fort Benning, Georgia, 549
U.S. Library of Congress. Division of Bibliography, 22
U.S. Military Academy. Department of Military Art and Engineering, 38
U.S. National Archives, 32
U.S. Navy Department, 1082
U.S. Navy Department. Bureau of Engineering, 898
U.S. Office of Naval Records and Library, 598, 599, 647, 663
U.S. Provost Marshal General, 771
U.S. War Department, 250, 550, 2131, 2192, 2265
U.S. War Department. Purchase, Storage and Traffic Division, 899
U.S. War Industries Board, 1923, 1924, 1925
U.S. War Policies Commission, 1862
U.S. Women's Bureau, 2385
United States Housing Corporation, 2442, 2443
United States Spruce Production Corporation, 2266
Utah. State Council of Defense, 1829

Vadney, Thomas E., 2874
Vagts, Alfred, 176
Vail, Glenn H., 1443
Van Alstyne, Richard W., 67, 245, 246
Vanderlip, Frank A., 1975, 2902
Van Deusen, G. L., 1356
Vandiver, Frank G., 303
Van Dorn, Harold A., 1863
Van Dyke, Henry, 415, 2579
Van Every, Dale, 508
Van Hise, Charles R., 1999, 2633
Van Kleeck, Mary, 2386
Van Rensselaer, Mrs. Coffin, 2387
Van Schaick, John, 1048
Van Wyen, Adrian O., 620
Vauclain, Samuel M., 1887
Vaughn, Victor C., 2716

Veiller, Lawrence, 2444
Viereck, George S., 117, 247, 1004
Villard, Oswald G., 2485
Viner, Jacob, 1976
Vinson, J. Chalmers, 2833
Vogel, Virgil J., 416

Wahl, George D., 1233
Wait, Clara H., 2388
Walcott, Frederic C., 2132
Walcott, Stuart, 477
Waldenrath, Alexander, 2220
Waldman, Seymour, 1864
Waldner, Jakob, 2193
Waldo, Fullerton L., 417, 509
Waldron, William H., 270
Walker, George, 2434
Walker, John O., 1502
Wall, John P., 1786
Wall, Louise H., 131
Waller, L. W. T., Jr., 1693
Waller, Samuel G., 1498
Wallgren, Abian A., 275, 2571
Wallrich, William J., 2580
Walsh, Joseph, 2717
Walter, Henriette R., 1903
Walters, Everett, 2913
Walton, Robert C., 1005
Walworth, Arthur C., 118, 2741
Warburg, Paul M., 2903
War Camp Community Service, 23, 817, 818, 2357
Ward, Robert D., 750
Ward, Stephen R., 2850
Waring, George J., 2477
Warmer, L. E., 1159
Warren, Benjamin S., 2718
Warren, Harold L., 1049
Warrington, W. E., 2009
Washburn, Slater, 1242
Washington (State). State Council of Defense, 1834
Waters, Thomas F., 1765
Watkins, Gordon S., 2267
Watson, Richard L., Jr., 119
Watson, Samuel N., 419
Watts, Phyllis A., 2410
Weaver, Frederic N., 1184
Webb, William J., 2038
Weber, Gustavus A., 2851
Weber, Walter W., 1611
Wector, Dixon, 378, 2852
Weed, Frank W., 845, 863, 864, 875

Wehle, Louis B., **1888, 2268, 2269**
Weinert, Richard P., **551**
Weinstein, Edwin A., **120, 121**
Weinstein, James, 1872, **2299, 2300**
Weiss, Nancy J., **2337**
Weld, L. D. H., **2074**
Weller, Charles F., **820**
Wellman, William A., **1689**
Wells, R., **1638**
Wentsel, Claude E., **1774**
Werner, Morris R., **420**
Werstein, Irving, **83**
West, Clarence J., **914, 940**
West, William B., **1050**
West, Willis M., **2119**
Westall, Virginia C., **710**
Westbrook, Stillman F., **1476**
Westlake, Thomas H., **1562**
Westover, Wendell, **1596**
West Virginia. Department of Military Census and Enrollment, **772**
Wharton, Edith, **2550, 2551**
Wheeler, Curtis, **478**
Wheeler, R. L., **1201**
Wheeler, William J., **421**
Whitaker, Charles H., **2445**
Whitaker, Herman, **600, 601, 602, 637**
White, Bruce, **2221**
White, John A., **711**
White, John P., **773**
Whitehair, Charles W., **1051, 1052**
Whitehead, Lawrence E., **1463**
Whitehouse, Arch, **316, 638, 1690**
Whitehouse, Mrs. Vira (B.), **963**
Whitfield, Stephen J., **2301**
Whiting, John D., **2552**
Whitlock, Brand, **152**
Whitney, Parkhurst L., **1357**
Whitney, Stanton, **1604**
Wicks, Perry S., **1795**
Wideman, Ernest G., **1306**
Wiebe, Robert H., **1873, 1874**
Wilcox, Francis M., **2478**
Wilder, Amos N., **2581**
Wilder, Fred C., **422**
Wildman, Edwin, **1880, 2866**
Wiley, Hugh, **1164**
Wilgus, William J., **901**
Wilkes, James D., **2664**
Wilkins, Oliver, **1161**
Wilkins, Robert P., **151**
Willert, Arthur, **2742**
Williams, Ashby, **423, 1561**

Williams, Charles H., **2338, 2358**
Williams, Cleon L., **1454**
Williams, Frankwood E., **835**
Williams, H., **664**
Williams, John, **1707**
Williams, Oscar, **2582**
Williams, Paul B., **1078**
Williams, William A., **177, 712**
Williams College (Williamstown, Massachusetts), **2634**
Williamson, Harold F., **2049**
Williamson, W. B., **1231**
Willis, Edward F., **2793**
Willis, James F., **2194**
Willoughby, Charles A., **510**
Willoughby, William F., **1865**
Willoughby, Woodbury, **1978**
Wilmot, Mrs. Frank, **469**
Wilson, Bryant, **1587**
Wilson, Ellis E., **479**
Wilson, Henry B., **603**
Wilson, John E., **1751**
Wilson, Robert F., **880, 902, 1846, 1928, 2837**
Wilson, William B., **2241**
Wimer, Kurt, **2730, 2809, 2834**
Winant, Cornelius, **424, 726**
Winslow, Carroll D., **993**
Winterich, John T., **2508, 2545**
Winterrle, John, **2657**
Winters, Donald L., **2075**
Wisconsin, University of, **2635**
Wisconsin War History Commission, **1380**
Wise, Frederic M., **425**
Wise, James E., Jr., **277**
Wise, Jennings C., **552**
Witt, Fred R., **1271**
Wittkamp, Frank F., **1192**
Wittke, Carl F., **2222**
Witwer, Harry C., **2553**
Woehlke, Walter V., **2242**
Wolf, Walter B., **1404**
Wolfe, E. P., **876**
Wolfe, Samuel Herbert, **426, 2411**
Wolkerstorfer, Marianne K., **2223**
Woll, Matthew, **2843**
Wolle, Francis, **2509**
Wollman, Solomon, **427**
Wood, Eric F., **428, 958**
Wood, Lambert A., **1442**
Wood, Leonard, **752, 774**
Woodcock, Amos W. W., **1496**
Woodward, David R., **248**

Wooldridge, Jesse W., 1455, 1457
Woollcott, Alexander, 832, 1006
Worth, Robert D., 696
Wrentmore, Ernest L., 1467
Wright, Chester W., 1866, 1899
Wright, George, 801
Wright, Helen, 2695
Wright, Henry B., 1422
Wright, Jack M., 480
Wright, John W., 1342
Wycoff, Minnie E., 1741
Wyeth, John A. B., 2583
Wythe, George, 1431

Yale Review, 2584
Yale University Divinity School, 2479
Yardley, Herbert O., 959
Yarwood, Bertram H., 1667
Yates, Louis A. R., 2794
Yates, Stanley, 1319
Yerkes, Robert M., 868, 869, 920, 926, 937, 940, 2061, 2666, 2676, 2677,

2678, 2679, 2686, 2687, 2688, 2696 2697, 2698, 2699, 2705, 2716
Yoakum, Clarence S., 2699
Yonkers, New York, 1806
York, Dorothea, 1571
Young, Ernest W., 84
Young, Hugh H., 877
Young, Rush S., 1418, 1558
Young Men's Christian Associations. Bureau of Libraries and Periodicals, 2585
Young Men's Christian Associations. National War Work Council, 1053

Zack, Charles, 1764
Zimmer, George F., 960
Zimmerman, Henry W., 1732
Zimmerman, Leander M., 429
Zinsser, William H., 2435
Zivojinović, Dragan R., 2795, 2796
Zody, Harry, 430
Zoller, J. F., 1979
Zook, George F., 2133

The United States in World War I was compiled by Ronald Schaffer; copy editing by Paulette Wamego, proofing for the publisher by Jean Holzinger and Paul Behrens. Cover art is by Dick Palmer, typography by Shelly Lowenkopf, composition by Lienett Company, Inc., Los Alamitos, Calif., offset printing and binding by the Crawfordsville Book Division of R. R. Donnelley and Sons Co., Inc., Crawfordsville, Ind.